དད་པ་དགུ་ལྡན

DEVOTION
Following Tibetan Masters

SHERRY MARSHALL

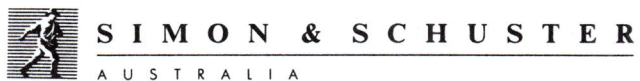
SIMON & SCHUSTER
AUSTRALIA

Calligraphy on half title by Sogyal Rinpoche

First published in Australia in 1999 by
Simon & Schuster (Australia) Pty Limited
20 Barcoo Street,
East Roseville NSW 2069

A Viacom Company
Sydney New York London Toronto Tokyo Singapore

Copyright © Sherry Marshall 1999

All rights reserved. No part of this publication may be reproduced,
stored in a retrieval system, or transmitted, in any form or by any
means, electronic, mechanical, photocopying, recording or otherwise,
without the prior permission of the publisher in writing.

National Library of Australia
Cataloguing-in-Publication Data

    Marshall, Sherry.
    Devotion: following Tibetan Masters

    ISBN 0 7318 0767 7.

    1. Buddhism — China — Tibet. 2. Buddhism — Doctrines.
    3. Buddhist converts — Conduct of life. I. Title.

294.3923

Set in Stone Serif 8.5/11.5
Cover photograph: His Holiness the 14th Dalai Lama by Hiroki
Fujita. Courtesy Office of Tibet, Tokyo, Japan
Edited by Kerry Davies
Cover, internal design and typesetting by Vivien Valk
Printed by Australian Print Group

I would like to dedicate and offer this book to all my
spiritual teachers, especially Dzongsar Khyentse Rinpoche,
His Holiness the Gyalwang Drukpa and Sogyal Rinpoche.
They know that anything is possible and through their
limitless love, compassion and wisdom have made this possible.
May their teachings continue to spread in all directions
to inspire and bless all sentient beings.

No matter what I think, my thoughts are of my teacher.
No matter what I see, I see my teacher.
No matter what I hear, I hear my teacher.
No matter what I feel, I feel my teacher within.
No matter whom I touch, I touch my teacher.
No matter whom I meet, I meet my teacher.
No matter what I dream, I dream of my teacher.
No matter where I am, where I go or where I stay,
    I am with my teacher.
Always, everywhere, beyond time and place
    I remember my teacher.
May we all have the lama in our heart.

Sherry Marshall

ACKNOWLEDGMENTS

This book is not only about devotion but also about the relationships that we all have with each other. It manifested through many people and would not have been written without their great generosity, love and support. My appreciation goes to all those who agreed to participate, and I hope their stories deeply touch, inspire and motivate all those who read them.

I would also like to thank everyone (too numerous to mention but they know who they are) who offered help and support in many different ways, both practical and emotional. My special thanks to Lisa Ogden and Noelle-Lyndon Way for tackling the main part of the transcribing, as well as for their ongoing friendship, and Chris Patch for rescuing me from ongoing computer nightmares. Also, much love to Deborah Stevenson, Jen Fox, Dr Julie Diamond, Dr Max Schuepbach and Ross MacKay, who have all encouraged, supported and challenged me throughout the years. Thanks to Julie Stanton from Simon and Schuster for having a particular interest in this book, and to Kerry Davies for patiently doing a thorough and meticulous final edit. Elisabeth Weiss deserves a particular mention, as she freely offered her time, advice and expertise throughout the whole process. I am most grateful to everyone who has taken care of Mr Zev, the dalmatian dog over the years, especially Mabelle Mellor and the Fowler family. Their loving care has enabled me to attend retreats, receive teachings and spend time with my teachers. I hope they receive all the happiness I have been blessed with. My mother Val Marshall and the Dee family, of course, deserve a special mention. May they always be happy.

It almost goes without saying that my teachers have brought about a great transformation in me, in ways that I could never have imagined. I always think that, if it can happen to me, it can happen to anyone. Words cannot express the gratitude I feel towards them and yet I also know that I am only just starting.

Author's note

The four-line prayers, written by me and appearing at the conclusion of each chapter, were inspired by Patrul Rinpoche's prayers in *The Words of My Perfect Teacher* and 'Songs of Milarepa' in *The Jewel in the Lotus*. Many of the contributors have referred to books that have inspired and assisted them in their own journeys, and a full bibliography of texts mentioned, as well as a glossary of terms and biographical notes on the three main teachers referred to throughout the book, is included at the back. There is also a list of contacts for Buddhist organisations.

CONTENTS

Foreword.. viii
Introduction... x
Leaving Nothing Unattended, Ross Mackay............................ 1
Sparking the Flame, Christine Longaker........................... 12
Breaking Preconceptions, Mal Watson.............................. 24
Deepening, Dominique Side....................................... 33
Coming Home, Rod Lee... 41
Sublime Trust, Pamela Croci..................................... 51
Just Try, Mauro de March.. 56
It's Not About Me, Julie Henderson............................... 65
The Fundamental State, Michael Kern............................. 76
The Placebo Effect, Regina Weilhart............................. 86
Nothing to Prove, Patrick Jacquelin............................. 96
Parallels, Harry Lee.. 105
Ordinary Magic, Albert-Paravi Wongchirachai..................... 114
One Continuous Mistake, Ian Maxwell............................. 126
Conclusion.. 136
Glossary.. 142
Biographies... 148
Bibliography.. 150
Buddhist Organisations...................................... 152

FOREWORD

One of the most essential verses on devotion is found in the Kagyu lineage prayer:

Devotion is the head of meditation, it is taught;
To the guru who opens the door to the treasury of pith instructions —
Bless this meditator who continuously supplicates,
So that unfabricated devotion may be born.

Mögü gomgyi gowo sungpa zhin —
Men ngag tergo chepey lama la
Gyündu solwa debpey gomchen la —
Chömin mögü kyewar jingyi lob.[1]

Devotion is the foundation that holds our practice together. With it, we gain fundamental daringness, to face all the unexpected surprises on our path. Without it, we lose the very determination and steadfastness to carry our practice to enlightenment.

Devotion brings certain transcendental vulnerabilities, so that we can be our naked selves, no longer hiding our neuroses skilfully. Without devotion you will feel afraid of being vulnerable and be a victim of your own pride, with less courage to expose yourself.

Devotion combats the doubt which arises at the beginning of our path, and which fades away only with time and practice. As long as we are on the path, devotion is the precious string that binds us to our view, meditation and action. Fully realised, it transforms into great compassion.

H. E. Dzongsar Jamyang Khyentse
17 May 1999
Cannes, France

A student asked Nyoshul Khen Rinpoche,
'What is the key to devotion?'
Rinpoche replied,
'Open your heart to me.'

Sogyal Rinpoche
London, April 1999

The best spiritual friend is the one
who attacks your hidden faults.

Atisha
From Patrul Rinpoche, The Words of My Perfect Teacher,
HarperCollins, New Dehli, 1997, p. xxxi

The purpose of meeting a teacher
is to receive the Dharma teachings.
The only purpose of receiving spiritual teachings
is to put them into practice.
The purpose of spiritual practice
is to realise the ultimate nature of things.
The purpose of realisation
is to actualise perfect freedom, inner peace and enlightenment.

Tibetan saying
From Surya Das, The Snow Lion's Turquoise Mane: Wisdom Tales from Tibet,
HarperCollins, San Francisco, 1992, p. 255

INTRODUCTION

It is amazing that one of the world's most complex and vast philosophies can be encapsulated by a clear and simple one-liner, which has captured the imagination of a generation of Western people. His Holiness the Dalai Lama, the spiritual head of Tibetan Buddhism, says, 'My religion is simple, my religion is kindness.'

This book is a collection of personal stories from ordinary people who happened to meet a Tibetan Buddhist teacher and decided to learn how to put the essential advice they received into practice. They have integrated their relationship with their guru and Buddhism into their daily lives, staying rooted in their own culture. They talk openly and honestly about their hopes and fears, difficulties and achievements, having a normal life, working and raising families and yet, at the same time, being fully engaged with the secret and sacred practices of Tantric Buddhism.

Somehow they make it sound easy and simple, yet it's hard to be kind all the time, not only in what we do and say, but also what we think. Try it for a day and see. Not that most of us intend to be cruel, judgmental or unthinking; it's just that we are not really aware of what is happening in our actions, speech and thoughts. We work, eat, talk, study, make love and live our whole lives but (as one of my teachers, Sogyal Rinpoche, who wrote *The Tibetan Book of Living and Dying*, says) most of the time, there's no one at home. We are mainly unaware and unconscious, with our minds far away from what is actually happening in the moment.

To be enlightened means to be 'awake'. Most of us think we are awake because we are not asleep in bed. In this tradition, as in many other spiritual paths, it is observed that, in fact, we spend our whole lives asleep. Our life is like a dream. Sometimes we have a nightmare and sometimes a rather enjoyable dream, but when we wake up we realise it was only a dream. If only we could wake up from our ordinary reality, like we do from our night-time dreams, we might live our lives in a completely different way. As it is traditionally taught, we need to realise that this life is but a dream, or a magic show. Then we would not be fooled by the illusion and therefore would be free. When we watch a movie, for example, we may still laugh and cry but because we know it's only a movie we don't get so caught up. We don't take it that seriously.

Attaining enlightenment

The process of waking up is what we might call our spiritual journey. We can wake up in a moment and realise that we have been dreaming or it may take many lifetimes. We may get glimpses through our meditation practice, but then we have to stabilise our mind in that state of realisation.

Tibetan Buddhism is a topic on which many books have been written. However, it is useful to understand the basic history and philosphy when discussing this ancient wisdom. The historical story of the Buddha began with an Indian prince called Siddhartha who was born in the fifth century BC. After leading a sheltered life of luxury, he became aware of sickness, old age and death and left the palace to search for a way to end suffering. He discovered that both extremes of denial and indulgence did not lead to happiness but, by following a middle path, he became a fully enlightened, awakened being, a Buddha.

Buddhism was introduced to Tibet from India in the seventh century AD. It thrived as the country's religion (replacing Bon, which consisted of animistic and shamanistic beliefs) due to the strong support of the early kings of Tibet such as Songtsen Gampo and Trisong Detsen. There are four schools, or lineages, within Tibetan Buddhism, Nyingma, Kagyu, Sakya and Gelug. Although these schools diverge in their emphasis, they all encompass the basic teachings of the Buddha. In its essence, Buddhism outlines the stages on the path to enlightenment.

The teachings, known as the Dharma, encompass 84,000 different methods for working with the mind and attaining everlasting happiness. These fit within three categories or vehicles. The first is Hinayana, focusing on contemplation of the Four Noble Truths and emphasising renunciation and moral discipline for individual liberation. The second is Mahayana, path of the bodhisattvas who focus on compassion and wisdom to obtain their own and others' enlightenment. The third is Vajrayana, relying on the more direct methods of visualisation, mantra and meditation, and stressing seeing everything purely. Enlightenment is realised for oneself and others. Guru Rinpoche, a precious master from the eighth century, said that Vajrayana would be especially powerful for people living at a time when emotions were very strong, and therefore this path is thought of as particularly appropriate for Westerners. Lama Yeshe, in *Introduction to Tantra*, says that Tantra, the root texts of the Vajrayana teachings, is particularly well suited to the Western mentality, which wants instant results, because it is the quickest of all paths. The principle of transformation is also well understood.

> **Tantra teaches us to break free from all conditioning that limits our understanding of who we are and what we can become.**[1]

This is also written in the introduction of *The Words of My Perfect Teacher*:

> **The Vajrayana is particularly flexible and adaptable to the sorts of situations in which modern people find themselves and, without losing its traditional form, has now been taught to a wide range of people all over the world.**[2]

The challenge presented to the first generation of Western Tibetan Buddhists (many of whom grew up in the sixties, when the constraints of accepted societal values fell away) is not to harm (the Hinayana path); to manifest wisdom, loving kindness and compassion towards all beings (the basic tenet of Mahayana Buddhism); and to develop pure perception (the basis of Vajrayana Buddhism). Realising that everything is inherently pure doesn't mean that we whitewash everything and think that all is perfect. It is obvious to most of us that the amount of suffering, inhumanity and pain that we manage to inflict upon one another is horrendous. As Sogyal Rinpoche said:

> **Pure perception means to see things as they are ... not to project. It is perception that is unstained, seeing things in their original, primordial nature, in the true way, untainted by the colours of emotions or duality.**[3]

Concepts about what it means to be a good person and help others are confronted by ideas that move us from what is often an idealised projection to a more real and grounded motivation and action. One of the main threads that weaves its way through Buddhism is to have the motivation to help others, not only in philosophy but also in real life. Goodness is actually the ability to have no self-interest and the opportunity to practise limitless love and compassion. His Holiness the Dalai Lama knows how hard that is for most of us, so it is useful to adopt his wisdom of being 'wisely selfish'. In other words, most of us find it impossible to be altruistic all the time. There is always somewhere, however unconscious, an element of self-interest that creeps in. Pema Chodron (a well-known American-born nun) says it is always wise to 'start where we are', rather than allowing our selfish motivation to paralyse us. We simply realise that by helping others we also help ourselves.

Yet, as humanity races on to the next thousand years, it seems that we have not yet been able to respond to His Holiness's wake-up call to come together as a human race. Somehow, if we really examine ourselves, most of us think that life is just a game and we either discount or ignore the consequences of what we do. It's not really real. Other people are somehow not as real as us. All our experiences are viewed as if through a fog. We continue to destroy ourselves and our planet, yet we don't change. We act on automatic functioning and live in a myth that 'bad' things are not meant to happen to us. They only happen to others, so they don't really matter, unless, or until, they somehow directly impact on us. Most of us don't really know that we are going to die, or that car accidents, disease, suicide, war or famine, economic ruin or psychological breakdown are going to touch us. When they do, we are often unprepared and ill-equipped to deal with them. Somehow we feel life has treated us unfairly and we become angry, resentful or depressed.

To become a 'spiritual warrior' and decide to 'wake up', through the skilful and inseparable means of mindfulness, awareness, compassion, pure perception and devotion, allows us to rest in spacious and vast mind, not just for moments, weeks or months at a time, but to always stay in that state of unlimited awareness. If we allow ourselves to realise that others too wish for what we wish for, have similar hopes and dreams, and also seek happiness, meaning and freedom, we begin to relate to all beings from an entirely different place.

Stories to tell

One of the main ways that Buddhism was originally taught was by storytelling. This is still the case to this day, with traditional tales being repeated over and over until they are remembered and become like second nature to the listeners. Stories in general are one of the ways that we make meaning out of what happens to us. Stories that are in our minds or stories that are told to us about our family, community or country give us a context about who we are, where we are and where we are going. Myth and traditions are often bound up with storytelling. It is a form of transmission that passes down through the generations. We not only love being told stories as children but, as we grow, we read and hear stories all the time. It is a simple, direct and spellbinding way of learning about different places, people and times. Stories are told over and over, and there are always old and new stories to be told, or the same story told in a new way.

We constantly create our reality by telling our stories over time so that we and our world are revisited and revised. Everyone has a story to tell. It may move us to tears or make us laugh, deeply inspire us, remind us of our own heritage, heal us, spark a half-forgotten memory, help us recognise our interconnectedness, show us wisdom, tell us about different places and times, and help us relate to one another. Stories reveal our varied lives in all different shapes and colours, textures and flavours.

Taking time to stop and listen to our own and others' stories reconnects us to the reality of our lives, to the truth of our innermost being and to our heart essence. They remind us what is really important in life and cut through all the superficiality and falsity. Every story needs to be told, even if it is only half-finished or there are only glimpses or fragments. Our stories are always in process and are always changing and are not even completed when we die. They continue in some form or other, spoken by those who knew us, and sometimes by those who didn't.

They are not fixed states, but fluid and moving like our lives. We think that things are permanent, we try to make them stable and secure, but our lives, like our stories, are impermanent. As the story is told over and over, the overall themes and elements may stay the same but, depending on the teller and the listeners, and the particular circumstances in which the story is told, it will have different atmospheres and meanings for people. The most secret and sacred stories were always told and heard rather than written down and read, and were passed from 'ear to ear'. Tibetan traditional tales are often funny or confronting, and always make a point.

This book offers traditional stories that clearly illustrate a pertinent point of the experiences of the early Western students, reflecting the coming of Buddhism to the West, just as it was transplanted long ago from India to Tibet. They tell of some of the initial seeds being sown so the teachings can blossom and grow in a vastly different environment from where they originated.

Childhood dreaming

There has been much discussed and written about the connections between spiritual traditions in the East and therapy in the West. It is fascinating that Sogyal Rinpoche, in particular, has attracted so many therapists to him and engaged in deeply examining how Dharma and therapy interact with each other. It is clear that therapy is not Dharma, even though it may begin to have some influence on how to work with the neuroses of the Western mind. As Jung discovered, when we are children, dreaming processes can shape our whole lives. According to Process-Oriented Psychology, our childhood dreams lead to our central life myth. This means that, if we know how to decode our childhood dreams and experiences, the blueprint of our adult lives will be revealed. Conscious dreams and visions have been utilised by shamans of all traditions. To know what our childhood dreams mean can provide a shortcut to giving purpose and meaning to our lives as adults.

In my case, as for many of us looking back, it now seems obvious how my childhood dreams influenced the journey I took in my life, yet it took me over thirty-five years to make sense of it. Ever since I can remember, until I was eighteen and left home to attend university, I had the same dream almost every night. I dreamt that I was taken a long way across the sea to a community of people. They were dressed in long red robes and were undergoing some sort of training. There were other people there and we were all given a particular teacher who took care of us and trained us. The training was quite hard, physically and mentally and, though the discipline was quite strict, it was always kind.

Sometimes my teacher would go away for long periods of time and I always wanted to go with him, but had to learn more before I could accompany him. Sometimes I felt that he had gone back into the world from where I had come, and I always felt a connection with him even when he was away. Sometimes, though, I felt him go far, far away, almost not in this space–time dimension anymore, and then it was harder to stay in touch with him energetically. I always felt that he was doing great work.

I remember attending great gatherings in the dream, where people understood each other without speaking and evenings were spent in magnificent rituals of swirling lights, colour and chanting. Rainbows would magically appear and strange beings with many heads and arms and legs would appear and disappear. I was never frightened, but more overawed with the nightly magical display. This built to a crescendo of energetic experiences that surpassed my understanding, although I always knew that somehow these rituals were helping people in the world.

My night-time dream became a part of my waking reality, so much so, that I took for granted that the next dream would just continue the sequence, every night. I never really thought about it or questioned it. I never mentioned or worked on my childhood dream in all my years as a therapist, until I was in my thirties and entered into Tibetan Buddhism. It had always felt special, secret and sacred and I didn't want to open it to others' interpretation or meaning. Now, when I think about it, I am amazed that I could have dreamt a similar dream for so many years and then completely ignored it. Yet, in a strange way, my childhood dream has probably molded my life, in a way that I surely could never have imagined.

Directly working with mind

Alongside my dream, as a child, I always wanted to help people. This led me to my job as a social worker, then family therapist and psychotherapist. Yet, in reality, in common with many others I imagine, my life has not turned out as I originally thought. I have not followed the more traditional path of family and children, and have chosen to live on the other side of the world from where I was born. In spite of seemingly making key decisions and having many choices, the most life-changing aspects that have influenced me have been unplanned, spontaneous and mainly outside my control.

Despite many years of working and delving into the unconscious, I also have to conclude that, to date, I am almost as mystified by my and others' motivation and behaviour as I was nearly thirty years ago. As human beings, we seem trapped into repeating our patterns, for better or worse. Psychotherapy seems to give us the skills and ability to respond differently to what is happening to us, but does not seem to prevent the original and set patterns of mind, which lead to behaviour, from arising. 'Therapy works with the stories that arise in the mind, but meditation works directly with the mind, even beyond the mind.' When I first started working with meditation, I discovered that, despite having trained and practised therapy for over fifteen years, it had merely touched the tip of the iceberg. Meditation began to peel back the layers of my mind deeper and deeper, exposing layer upon layer of unknown material until the true and natural state was revealed.

Look up into the sky,
And practise meditation free from the fringe and centre.
Look up at the sun and moon,
And practise meditation free from bright and dim.
Look over at the mountains,
And practise meditation free from departing and changing.
Look down at the lake,
And practise meditation free from waves.
Look here at your mind,
And practise meditation free from discursive thought.[4]

The highest pinnacle

As in the traditional Tibetan tales of students like Milarepa, Naropa and Marpa, who suffered through numerous hardships and adventures with their teacher to reach the highest pinnacle of enlightenment, becoming excellent and supreme teachers themselves, these Westerners also tell of their journeys of difficulty, devotion, love and struggles on the spiritual path. I have always loved hearing and reading about stories of adventure and spirituality combined. Maybe it is a way I could experience it all without the physical hardships of having to trek for days through haunted valleys or over frozen mountain tops, eating unknown food and meeting with wild animals and bandits. In my imagination, I too could roam the wild places of Tibet and Bhutan meeting strangely dressed Rinpoches, speaking foreign languages and experiencing magic, mystery and sacred secrets only conferred on the courageous or lucky few, while safely tucked up in bed with blankets wrapped around me, my electric heater blazing, warm as toast.

To suddenly meet those unknown Rinpoches in the relative safety and comfort of my home cities of London and Sydney was a way that my reading and dreaming was suddenly and unexpectedly brought alive. Little did I know that it would lead me, not yet to Tibet, but to places that normally I would never have considered visiting, like India, Sikkim, Nepal, the west and south of France, and the far west of Ireland. My childhood dream slowly became reality in far-flung places in different communities, as each day, for eighteen hours, I joined in rituals with red-robed monks chanting, beating drums, clashing symbols and blowing horns, with thousands of butter lamps burning in smoky, dim windswept monasteries. Golden-braided tangkas [scroll paintings] of deities and wrathful protectors would swim in and out of my vision from their mountings on the wall, as they would appear to come alive in certain sections of the practices. The fog would creep through the doors and windows, the wind would howl around the monastery walls and glimpses could be had of the snowy mountain, peeping through the rain as the young monks brought butter tea and soup.

I will always remember the kindness of these strangers, who had themselves suffered tremendous hardships, escaping the Chinese invaders by walking over the Himalayan mountains, some only in sandshoes and the clothes they had on their backs. They showed such care and concern for my wellbeing, when I arrived in relative comfort, with an overloaded rucksack and a sceptical mind. Their attitude follows that of His Holiness the Dalai Lama. No one is a stranger and everyone you think you don't know is merely an old friend you haven't met for a while. For moments, though, I would stop and wonder at how a middle-class, university-educated English woman found herself in the middle of this rather strange and unfamiliar setting, not as an outside observer, but as a willing participant. Maybe some would say karma, but my answer has always been, 'because of my teachers'.

They alone had directly shown me the possibility and potential of my mind, and everyone else's. Every other experience and achievement in my life paled into insignificance. Nothing could compare. The experience of knowing the limitlessness of mind and the truth that anything is possible literally blew my ordinary mind away and changed my direction in life forever.

Embodying love and compassion

I first met my teachers in 1988 in Sydney. It is traditionally said that, 'When you are ready, the teacher will appear to you.' I certainly was not, in any way, looking for a teacher and I certainly wasn't ready, on a conscious level anyway, for the direction that my life then took. From my point of view, I innocently stumbled across three teachers in the space of three months and it changed my life forever. It occurred as easily as a friend asking me if I wanted to come over for dinner one night to meet a Tibetan lama she had staying for a few days and then another friend inviting me to a talk. I have been asked many times why I became involved and I always give the same answer. When I met His Holiness the Gyalwang Drukpa, Sogyal Rinpoche and Dzongsar Khyentse Rinpoche, I experienced such a sense of love and compassion emanating from them I realised that they completely embodied what they were teaching. They were purity and goodness personified, not just for a minute or an hour, but always, in all the time I spent with them in all situations, with all different people. They were unwavering and unchanging in their total embodiment of love and compassion.

They were not 'good' in the slightly immature way that I had fantasised earlier in my life, but in the sense of being totally mindful and present, dynamic and alive, and spontaneously appropriate and unafraid. I had never met anyone, in my whole life, who so embodied these qualities. They were not just highly skilful; they lived it. There was no duality, no split between who they were and what they taught.

Most of us who are interested, in one way or another, in spirituality often have a fantasy of what the path involves. Whatever we imagine, though, is seldom what we find. From the simplest level, maybe we think we will become happier and more peaceful, meet like-minded people, even a partner, or that we may be picked out as being someone special or even recognised as an incarnated Rinpoche. We may even hope to marry a lama, or at least want to help others. Our motivations are as varied as our dreams when we begin.

Buddhism teaches that, when we realise that we are ignorant of the true nature of existence and therefore the true nature of our mind, we then want to find a path that provides us with the tools to achieve freedom and everlasting happiness. The teachings give us a clear and concise map that, if we choose to follow, can release us, once and for all, into the vast and spacious view of enlightenment.

Most of us discover that, although we like the idea of being 'awake', we don't actually like the reality of what we need to do to 'wake up'. It truly can be a wonderful journey that we undertake, but it also has its difficulties and obstacles that we may stumble over and through. It is at these times, where we are not particularly enjoying ourselves or, in fact, it is downright painful, inconvenient and not at all what we were expecting, we find a million reasons why we cannot or, indeed, should not continue.

It's not a game

However, once having committed to the teacher and this path, the realisation dawns that it is not a game. Even though we may consider ourselves to be quite adult, holding down a job and bringing up a family, we are, admittedly after a long period of time, suddenly faced with knowing that we cannot turn back from what we chose to commit to. It is not a matter of saying, 'Well, I don't like or agree with this anymore,' and leaving. We suddenly have to grow up and face certain consequences of our actions. Although we are 'big people', often inside we feel quite little, and it sometimes takes us many years before we can honestly face ourselves.

There are very few commitments that we ever make in the West that we cannot leave. We have become so individualistic and attached to what we think freedom is, without knowing the real meaning, that we leave our jobs, our marriage partners, even our children. We are constantly searching to be free but do not know how to have inner freedom, how to be free of ourselves. The spiritual path is just another thing we think we can abandon when it doesn't suit us anymore. We make vows and break them like children who promise, 'Yes, I'll be your friend forever,' and the next day, after a fight, say 'I hate you, I'm leaving.' I sometimes wonder if we have moved much from these positions even though we have grown older and bigger.

Often an image of the teachers is similar to kindly grandparents watching over the toddlers playing in the sandpit, making sure we are safe and don't hurt ourselves or each other too much. The difference between their wisdom mind and our ordinary mind sometimes seems like the toddler and the wise elder. Small children are unaware of their own limitations and, though recognising that adults can help, often feel capable of doing everything themselves, even when it is obvious that they cannot manage and just make a mess. They want to be independent and can become quite insistent that they want to do it on their own. This is also how they learn. The difference is that as 'big toddlers' we have the tools to wreak much more destruction with our neurotic games, than the 'small toddler' safely contained in the sandpit, not only on ourselves, but all other species.

'Cooking' in the devotional relationship

The opportunity to enter into a relationship that totally mirrors who we are in an open, naked, appropriate and immediate way is unusual. The closest we would normally have access to that is with a partner or a mentor or therapist. However, even in those relationships, the other person sometimes has their own projections, agendas and self-interest. To be with someone over a long period of time who is only interested in reflecting us back to ourselves, with the intention of helping us, with no self-interest at all, is almost beyond our imagining.

> This most intimate relationship between disciple and master becomes a mirror, a living analogy for the disciple's relationship to life and the world in general. The master becomes the pivotal figure in a sustained practice of 'pure vision', which culminates when the disciple sees,

directly and beyond any doubt, the master as the living Buddha, his or her every word as Buddha speech, his or her mind the wisdom mind of all the Buddhas ... They begin to see naturally that they, the universe and all beings without exception are spontaneously pure and perfect. They are looking at last at reality with its own eyes. The master, then, *is* the path, the magical touchstone for a total transformation of the disciple's every perception.[5]

In this tradition, the whole relationship with the teacher can be encompassed within devotion. Sogyal Rinpoche says,

So then, it is essential to know what real devotion is. It is not mindless adoration; it is not abdication of your responsibility to yourself, nor undiscriminating following of another's personality or whim. Real devotion is an unbroken receptivity to the truth. Real devotion is rooted in an awed and reverent gratitude, but one that is lucid, grounded, and intelligent.[6]

This is the vehicle that can be utilised to uncover the fundamental goodness that we all already have. We may have glimpses of our goodness, but it is mainly hidden from ourselves and others by all our habits. Devotion combines deep and intimate love, trust, yearning, power, relationship, friendship, spirituality; in fact everything that most of us have totally unresolved issues about. It is a dynamic and dynamite mixture. Love, relationships, sex, money, power, abuse and religion are topics that frequently obsess us in the West, individually and culturally. We have little understanding, time or stability to deeply realise what is possible. We are curious and impatient, wanting quick, easy answers that fit with our own projections and judgments on how things are, or how we would like them to be.

The process of transformation can be a life-long journey, yet, if we are truly ready, it can happen in an instant. The alchemical relationship between teacher and student can certainly accelerate the process. The ancient art of alchemy, of turning base metal into gold, also used by the Taoists for discovering the formula of everlasting life, was full of mystery and secrecy. It has been used by many as a metaphor for change and transformation. The alchemists were never sure what they would produce. Would they get the gold or a more poisonous and deadly mixture? Occasionally, when chasing the elixir of immortality, testing their brew by swallowing it, they would die in the attempt.

The Taoists believed that the spiritual was rooted in the physical ... the body was the practitioner's base for transcendence, and it had to be made into a sound spiritual vehicle.[7]

As in the process of devotion, 'cooking' in the relationship with your teacher over a long period of time is one of the ways to have all your impurities burnt out of you so that you finally end up being the gold. Traditionally it is said that if you come too close to the teacher you will get burnt, but if you stay too far away you won't feel the warmth of the fire. Nothing will get cooked and you will stay the same, with all your habits and patterns, ignorance, judgments and misperceptions. We have to learn how to walk the fine line and stay just at the right closeness and distance to benefit the most from the teacher's presence. A few people have a natural instinct for how to do that, but for some of us, it can be a painful and scorching journey.

The warmth of the teacher's wisdom and compassion will melt the ore of our being to release the gold of the Buddha nature within.[8]

The alchemists believed that the starting point, the process of transformation and the goal are, in fact, the same. It needs nothing outside or extra to be added. This is similar to the recognition that every being has Buddha nature and that what we experience within the process of devotion does not introduce us to anything new. We already are enlightened, but we don't know it and neither do we manifest it. So the teacher does not give us anything that is not already ours. We contain all that is needed inside us to be enlightened. The outer manifestation merely reflects our own inner teacher.

A living lineage

What the teacher does is to continuously remind us, by his or her own example, teachings, mirror-like wisdom and blessings, what we can achieve and, more importantly, give us the tools to do that. These teachings are alive in the sense that they have been passed down since the time of the Buddha, 2500 years ago. The time-honoured tradition of passing them from teacher to student, who then becomes the teacher, who in turn passes to the student, continues to this day. This is a living lineage.

The work of transforming base metal into gold, through the alchemical stages, provides a metaphor and a symbolic language for the development within the devotional relationship. Becoming the gold gives a picture of the work that needs to be undertaken, with all its dangers, difficulties and rewards. The reconciliation of opposites occurs, duality no longer exists and enlightenment is attained. Yet the paradox is that there is nothing to be attained; as the philosopher's stone, the *prima materia*, was seen by the alchemists as the starting point of the whole process, the agent or means, and the goal.

Though there is nothing to be attained and there is no goal to be reached 'out there', we embark upon the journey of enlightenment, because even though we are all Buddhas, we do not realise it or manifest it. The teachings say, 'There is one ground, two paths. The Buddhas went one way, we went another.' We all come onto the path through different ways and with different motivations. Some people have always been searching, others are drawn or pulled through crises or death of loved ones, some of us casually go along to a talk with friends, some become interested by reading a book.

Truly precious

Here are the tales of the joys and inspirations, struggles and difficulties that people are experiencing in a contemporary Western setting, juggling work, family and community commitments. Tales of realised masters inspire us but are not our experience, yet, within our time and culture. How do we manage to experience devotion, with our busy lives and consumer, materialistic, 'get it fast and move on to the next new thing' attitudes? How can we be devoted without going on retreat in a cave for many years, wonderful though that may seem to some? How are we devoted without being the wife or attendant of the lama or going to live in India? How are we devoted when we are still full of ego and pride? Can we really follow in the footsteps of our teachers when we wander perpetually in samsara, the cycle of life and death, which our habitual patterns trap us in? Samsara calls out to us at every turn and there are endless distractions to lose ourselves in. Can we really uncover our true nature, which is confident, pure and loving, and dedicate ourselves to benefit others twenty-four hours a day for our whole life?

Can we really realise what is truly precious, when we have so little sense of what is truly of value. In a society of the twenty-second sound bite and an attitude of 'fix it quick', how can we learn to appreciate something of immense value, if we can't stay around long enough to even get a glimpse? If someone gives us uncut gems and diamonds, we may just think they're dirty old rocks. Unless we are trained to see what is beneath the disguise, we will throw away, what is, in fact, beyond price.

We call a man a Rinpoche, which means diamond, when he has achieved perfection ... when he has transformed every evil in himself into wisdom, every dark energy into an energy of light, every movement of hatred or impatience into a blessing ... A man who no longer wants to be anything becomes everything; a man who is free of desire and self-consciousness enters with love into all things and all people ... They have given me faith ... in the powers I have hidden within myself, that we have all hidden within ourselves, and must uncover and realise.[9]

These stories, then, are the result of wanting to share the gifts that I and others have been blessed with. These people are really no different from anyone else, apart from deciding to undertake a certain voyage and stick with it. They have, through some amazing, sometimes seemingly random act of fate, bumped into a Tibetan Buddhist teacher, and stayed around and studied and practised meditation. Some people have the karma to meet the teacher, but following the teacher is another story. This book is about those who did both.

LEAVING NOTHING UNATTENDED

THE TRAVELLERS

A young man attended the teachings by the Buddha for many years in a city in the north of India, but never put them into practice. One night he asked the Buddha a question about a doubt he was having. He told the Buddha that he had observed for a long time that many people attended and that some had been liberated and some had changed. However, there were still a large number, including himself, who were left untouched and perhaps had even become worse. He wondered why that was and why the Buddha, with all his power and compassion, hadn't liberated them all.

The Buddha replied by asking the young man where he lived and where he had been born. The man answered that he travelled many times from his city of birth to where he now lived. The Buddha then asked him if friends requested the correct directions to go from one city to the other. The man explained that he could give clear and precise explanations on how to undertake the journey. He agreed that if his friends followed his instructions precisely and followed them through to the end, there was no doubt that they would travel safely and quickly from one place to the other.

The Buddha then responded to the original question that people came to him because he had followed the path from samsara to nirvana and knew it perfectly well. Therefore this is what he taught to anyone who asked. However, if people only listened and agreed but decided not to step onto and stick with the path until the end, then they would not reach the final accomplishment. He said that no one can carry anyone else and everyone had to walk the path themselves. All one can do with love and compassion is keep pointing out what the path is, saying, 'I have walked on it and, if you step on and walk, you will also reach enlightenment.'[1]

ROSS MACKAY

Ross Mackay has been a student of Sogyal Rinpoche since 1981 and is the Coordinator of the Rigpa Fellowship in Australia. I talked with Ross one evening in Sydney, after both of us had been at work all day. The mood quickly changed from normal, busy everyday life to a cosy precious atmosphere. Having known Ross for ten years and had many discussions with him, it was surprising to hear what he said. He is an intellectual, busy, organised and practical person with a 'let's get on with it' attitude and seemingly quite uncomfortable with emotions. Yet now he was showing another side of himself, talking about feelings and having dreams and visions, and tapping into an intuitive, almost mystical side of himself. His story is how, through his contact with the teachers, he came to open his heart and to be moved, in a profound and compassionate way. Yet he also possesses a great calmness and equanimity, and the ability to handle any situation, no matter how stressful or chaotic. This combination of qualities that flow through him makes his story like a Zen koan.

As he talked on in a flowing, almost unceasing monologue, it was reminiscent of how his teacher, Sogyal Rinpoche, teaches in an unbroken, endless flow of words that has no interruption and involves just a deep listening. It was uncanny the way Ross 'became' his teacher in that time. He was refreshingly honest, and the reason he has experienced so little difficulty is that he sees things just as they are, neither good nor bad. His ability not to 'make a mountain out of a molehill' demonstrates putting the teachings into practice. A way to notice how we cause our own suffering is to see how many of our problems are based on misunderstandings and blowing things out of proportion.

Sogyal Rinpoche tells a story, which he first heard as a child, that aptly demonstrates this. It is a tale of one of the Buddha's previous lives, when he had been born as a lion.

One day all the animals in the forest started to stampede in great terror. The lion roared and asked them what they were running from. They replied that the end of the world was coming. 'How do you know?' questioned the lion. 'The elephants told us,' they said. But then the elephants said it was the lions, who said it was the tigers, and so they each kept naming all the other animals. Finally it was decided that the rumour was started by a little rabbit. The lion asked, 'Tell me exactly what

happened,' and the rabbit replied, 'I was sitting under a tree wondering what would happen to me if the world came to an end and suddenly there was a big noise.' The rabbit took the lion and showed him where the earth had cracked apart, but the rabbit was too scared to look and see the end of the world. The lion then showed all the animals that it was merely the fruit falling from the tree into some noisy autumn leaves. The rest had been the rabbit's vivid imagination.[2]

So, realising that things are often not nearly as serious as we think they are, and investigating and acting calmly, demonstrates a grounded practice.

The title of Ross's chapter has great meaning for him. He has really taken that phrase as his way of life and become, himself, a role model for 'leaving nothing unattended'. In the early days of the Rigpa Fellowship in Australia in the late 1980s, Ross performed all the tasks to enable Rinpoche's teachings to be given, which are now delegated to many people. One year, when he was organising a retreat in Australia, he had been incredibly busy, working eighteen hours a day. Late one night he picked up a vacuum cleaner and started cleaning the floor of the shrine room. He just saw that it needed to be done and did it. He didn't want to leave anything undone. It is sometimes easy for people in positions of responsibility to occasionally make a 'show' of doing the more 'mundane' tasks of cleaning up and doing the washing up! From fairly continuous observation of Ross over the years it is clear that there is no 'show'. He is mindfulness in action, efficiently and quietly, whether it's cleaning the floor, making a speech, driving a teacher or teaching students himself. It's all the same to him; as long as it's attended to, that's what counts.

> The best scholar is one who has realised the meaning of no-self.
> The best monk is the one who has tamed his own mind.
> The best quality is a great desire to benefit others.
> The best instruction is always to watch the mind.
> The best remedy is to know that nothing has any inherent reality.
> The best way of life is one that does not fit with worldly ways.
> The best accomplishment is a steady lessening of negative emotions.
> The best sign is a steady decrease of desires.[3]

Ross's story

I met Sogyal Rinpoche in January 1981 at a house in Princess Road in Kilburn when I was working in a dental practice in London. I can't really say it was a preordained meeting or fate. I was already very interested in Buddhism. One of the reasons I had left Australia for Britain was to explore Buddhism. A lot of the books I had read had been published by the London Buddhist Society in Eccleston Square. So when I got to London I looked up the Society and started to go to meetings there on Saturday afternoons for group discussions and a little meditation.

Though there were some people at the Society who were quite interested in Tibetan Buddhism, I was more interested in Zen Buddhism and had read a massive amount about it and been to a monastery in Malaysia in 1980. I quite liked the very plain and distinct style of Zen. Its clarity appealed to me. There was sitting, there was calm and there were these beautiful instructions on the understanding of the nature of mind. When I was seventeen and still at school, I had read a book called *Buddhist Scriptures*, writings of different traditions and masters of meditation, including a particular Zen master whose words really touched my heart. So I suppose it was that book that started me. It was shorn of all religiosity, if I can call it that. Initially, one of the things that I didn't like about Tibetan Buddhism was all these gods and deities and teachers. At the time I thought, 'It's not for me.' In fact, I can actually remember having a very vivid dream about Tibetan Buddhism. It was almost prophetic in a way. I went to Tibet (in my dream) and saw that all these religious things had fallen apart.

Anyway, I liked Zen Buddhism very strongly. I used to read all the Suzuki books — *Essays in Zen Buddhism* and *Zen Doctrine of No Mind*. Zen is very straightforward and disciplined. It seemed to have a real heart. The heart wasn't actually in the writings but the feeling of the writings. So I had quite a strong heart connection with it. Then I met two Zen missionaries in Sydney in 1974. They used to talk about Buddhism and the understanding of mind from a Zen point of view. So very clear, very strong and without any flowery extras. Through their kindness and their teaching and a little bit of meditation, I started off.

I came into Buddhism not through any pain, suffering, loss or grief, not anything obvious like the loss of a relative or abuse in childhood or difficult periods. I came from a very good home, a very easy life actually. It just sort of all made sense to me on a very deep level. I can even remember being involved with a Gurdjieff group for a while.[4] They said to me, 'Well, you need to make up your mind rather quickly whether you are going to become a Gurdjieff person or a Buddhist person.' To me there was not even a question. I said, 'Well, if that's the case then I think I should resign from this group and become a Buddhist person.' So it's always been within me. If I look back, I see there is a very strong karmic connection to it. In lay terms, karmic connection would mean, very simply, that I have had some connection with the Buddhist teachings in a previous life. In this life it accumulated very quickly by reading the writings of great teachers and masters.

Discovering Tibetan Buddhism

The group in London talked to me about Tibetan Buddhism and gave me some books to read. It appealed to me, but because they were particularly interested in approaching the spiritual path by themselves, and not really understanding it myself, I thought I might need a group to help me. So I looked up the societies affiliated with the London Buddhist Society and under 'T' for Tibetan. The closest one to where I lived happened to be Sogyal Rinpoche's group. I didn't know it was Sogyal Rinpoche's group as it was called Dzogchen Orgyen Choling at the time. When I visited for the first time, Patrick Gaffney, Rinpoche's closest student, opened the door. In my brash young Australian way at the time, I said that I was interested in Tibetan Buddhism and that I hoped this was the Tibetan Buddhist place and asked what they did.

Patrick cordially invited me in, showed me a few pamphlets and brochures and said that there were meetings happening and I was welcome to attend. So I went along to one or two practices and a few weeks later Rinpoche was coming to teach on the Nine Yanas, which are the way the Nyingma School of Tibetan Buddhism sees the whole Buddhist path.

Making the heart connection

I can still remember going armed with pen and paper to listen to Sogyal Rinpoche, and taking copious notes. I think there were probably forty of us in the front room. Rinpoche taught all weekend and it really solidified my understanding of Buddhism and everything started to make a bit more sense. I don't remember much of what I thought about Rinpoche but I do remember being very grateful that I had gone. It really helped me to understand. Then at the end of it all everyone had an interview. We went upstairs to meet him and I remember being a little bit shy. I didn't think I had a lot to say to him and I thought, 'No, no I won't go up,' but the older students insisted and I really did have numerous questions to ask him. Having read much about meditation and about signs and colours and light, my mind was really all jumbled up and my understanding had no basis in reality or any great teaching. I introduced myself to Rinpoche and said, 'Well, I do have some questions. I've got to the point in my meditation practice where this colour and light comes ...' Rinpoche was very, very kind to listen to me. In retrospect, I was obviously way off the track.

He just replied, 'That's all fine. It's very good, it's fine. Just settle first in your meditation,' which is what he always says to people, even now. 'Really settle, just practise, let your mind settle.' Up to that point absolutely nothing was special, but somehow it was fantastic to be there.

He came up to me just as I was going. We stood up and I thanked him and was about to go. He just touched me on the arm, just between the shoulder and elbow, and squeezed me there, saying, 'Ross, I think you belong here.' From that time on I have never had a doubt. Something connected me very, very closely with him at that time. I still feel his hand touching my arm. That was a really strong heart connection. That was created there on that day. From then on I have stayed, through thick and thin.

It was, in fact, the very ordinariness of the situation that made it very profound. Anyone could have said that to me. The feeling, though, that was transmitted through the words and through touching me was something that I had never really experienced before. The feeling was more a deep instinctive knowing that was there, like an incredible confidence. There was no doubt. It was just amazing because there was no particular reason to have felt like that. I didn't feel particularly awe-inspired by Rinpoche. I mean, I was grateful to him for doing a lovely weekend's talk, but I had certainly been to hear a lot of other people talk also. It was that ordinariness of the situation, of the touch and the words, the very deep profound confidence in that feeling, that was absolutely correct at that time. It didn't bring a big passion, a big emotion, a big feeling.

The development of devotion for me has actually been fantastic and has been over a period of episodes, with peaks in the devotion, such as meeting great masters like His Holiness the Dalai Lama and Dilgo Khyentse Rinpoche. Devotion is my connection to the Dharma. Devotion is a heart connection, which develops from a very close understanding and relationship with your teacher. I think, initially, part of devotion is feeling thankful for the wisdom to help tie together all the thoughts and threads. The other part is very much the heart connection, that profound knowledge of confidence that came when he touched me.

Meeting the masters

We older students were so lucky to have been exposed to teachers such as His Holiness the Dalai Lama, His Holiness Karmapa, Dudjom Rinpoche and Dilgo Khyentse Rinpoche through Sogyal Rinpoche. I think devotion towards my teacher became even stronger because of who he introduced me to. He not only exposed me to himself but he wanted his students to meet the really great masters of that time.

Dilgo Khyentse Rinpoche came to London in 1982. He was a profound teacher. He lived in Tibet, spent most of his life as a monk and then was recognised as an incarnation, a great master who has continued through many existences. He spent many years in solitary retreat. He was one of the few masters who escaped from Tibet when China took over the country and it was due to his profound knowledge, love and wisdom that a lot of the Dharma survived and has come to the West. There are so many great younger teachers now for whom he was their focus and inspiration.

In 1982 Dilgo Khyentse Rinpoche was invited to the Rigpa Centre in London, where he gave many empowerments. We each had an interview with him. I remember Sogyal Rinpoche coming round and saying, 'Now, remember, please ask sensible and important questions and not about your relationships'. That was fine with me. I walked into the interview and there was the translator, who was also a teacher, on my right and there was Dilgo Khyentse almost straight ahead, and I got a little bit overawed.

When you come into the presence of great teachers it sort of affects you, almost like walking into a particular energy field. It touches your heart. Of course I was pretty much an Australian male, not really much in touch with heart and feelings and it was a bit strange for me. The ground started to feel a bit uncomfortable under my feet. What put me off balance even more was that the translator said, 'Are you Ross the dentist?' I replied, 'Yes, I'm Ross the dentist.' He said, 'I really want to thank you very much for helping my student to be able to come to France.' I had helped one of the students to get time off work to come to the retreat. I said, 'Oh, that's fine Rinpoche.' Then I talked to Dilgo Khyentse. I asked him questions about the difficulties I was having with my practice and he gave me very simple replies. He said, 'You just keep at it, keep doing it. That's very good.'

Having spoken to Dilgo Khyentse I was really getting a bit shaky you know. I didn't understand what was going on. My heart was getting a bit racy and I was getting a little bit teary-eyed. Then the translator started thanking me again for helping his student. It was all so strange. Here we were in the presence of this great master and his translator, whom I also had great respect for, and he was thanking me. This just really blew me apart. I said, 'Well, thank you very much,' and left quickly, straight down the stairs. I went outside and just burst into tears. I was quite inconsolable. I just quietly sat under a tree and cried for at least a couple of hours, which is quite unlike me. And I thought, 'What the hell was that? What happened to me?'

Again it was nothing he said. It was so ordinary and nothing greatly profound in the language. It was a bit like when Rinpoche touched me on the arm — 'I think you belong here.' Dilgo Khyentse just said, 'Practise a bit more. Of course it's going to work.' It was like peeling back layers and allowing me to open up. It was that openness of heart that allowed the emotion to come. It was an emotional outpouring from something very deep within me.

Devotion isn't something then, that is contrived. You can't really contrive devotion. It is something that comes from your heart when you connect with a great teacher or someone else you have a connection with. It can actually be other students. At that stage Sogyal Rinpoche, through his great humility, compassion and wisdom, edged us towards a teacher who he knew would be able to open our hearts. Now I'm a bit of a tough nut to crack anyway, so I am grateful that he pushed me up the stairs and got me in there.

Strengthening devotion

My father died in 1981. Not long after I met Rinpoche, and had teachings on death and dying from him, I had to return to Australia quickly because my father was very ill. I can still remember reading the teachings on death and dying on the way home. All that helped me in a very simple way to be with my father. It helped me understand and probably come to terms with loving him very strongly at the end. The intellectual aspect opened my heart because I could see how it helped me in my life. You could say the feeling with Dilgo Khyentse Rinpoche might be a little bit airy fairy and sort of teary-eyed stuff, even though it really wasn't, but people could see it that way. When you get profound help from the intellectual concepts and you see how it does work, especially when someone is dying, then I think your devotion, your thankfulness for the teachings, increases.

In 1983 we were on retreat with Rinpoche in France. We stayed in this great old Christian monastery. Rinpoche was talking about devotion and his masters, particularly Jamyang Khyentse Chökyi Lodro, who was said to be one of the greatest masters of this century. He passed away in 1959. He brought Rinpoche up for many years of his early life. He nurtured and looked after him like a father. Rinpoche changed the whole atmosphere as he started to talk about his teacher. He kept talking and talking and, in the end, he started to cry. He talked about Khyentse and his life, how Khyentse cared for him as a child and what a great teacher he was. I can still remember the final thing he said was, 'You must realise that your master leaves nothing unattended.' And I was in tears again, except this time the words were very profound. What it was saying was that your master would never give up on you. He would always be there. He would always look after you. That increased my devotional aspect because I started to see then, in my own teacher, that no matter how much he had been wronged by people, he would always welcome them back and look after them.

I also realised that he's always looked after me. In war, when men fighting have been shot and are about to die, many will call out for their mother. I really feel that, if ever I was in that situation, the person I would call for, to help me, would be Rinpoche. Not that I don't love my mother. She has always been a very good mother to me. But that's the level of profound feeling and love that I have for this man. It's a tough one to explain. I suppose it is because of what he has very subtly done for me. He has shown me lots of things about myself, a lot of them incredibly confronting. But in essence he has shown me that there is a way to get out of the cycle of suffering. There is really a way to do it. It's not only written down but is also passed on through the teachers. They have some understanding of death, the process of death and what goes on afterwards in rebirth.

In 1994, at Lerab Ling, the retreat centre in the south of France, the older students and national directors were asked to come together to do some training. We did an exercise where I ended up talking about appreciating Rinpoche and what he had done. I said that I appreciated Rinpoche for helping me along and opening my heart and I just really wanted to thank him. I suppose I had never really had much of a chance to say that. Whenever I got a chance to talk to him, it was all organisational details or thanking him formally for coming to Australia and it always sounded so hollow to me.

It was strange because, although I was glad that I had that chance to do it, it was also a real physical thing for me. I had this real pain in my heart, a very strong pain, while I was saying this, and felt very emotional about it. I felt like something had broken through, like it was a physical manifestation of an opening. In a way it was something that happened devotionally but the feeling afterwards was of an open heart almost to the point of pain. It made the devotion in me even stronger.

It's just so nice being around 'the boss'. I call Rinpoche the boss. When you are close to a great teacher like Rinpoche and you connect with him intellectually and emotionally, you begin to almost feel what he is feeling. I remember once a woman asked him about her son dying. I could feel in my heart a really strong sense of Rinpoche's great compassion towards this woman. He drew out her question to make sure that he could help and had done his best for her. Little things like that happen quite a lot to me now with my connection to the teacher. It's good for me too, because I lead quite a busy life, with my family and my work. I think it's quite easy to lose the connection to the teacher and the teachings. So I think I'm lucky to have such a connection to a living teacher who can just rekindle the devotion that holds you to the Buddhist path by just being around him.

It's not so bad

I've never really had much difficulty with devotion because it slowly developed for me. I didn't have great devotion from the beginning, but it grew slowly and profoundly over time. I thought initially Rinpoche was a good teacher and I helped out and enjoyed being around him. He's never asked anything of me that I've considered to be too much or out of line or seemed to be very difficult for me. Sometimes when I'm tired and there's this hassle or that hassle, I just go back to the teachings.

I always remember when His Holiness the Dalai Lama was younger and there were big problems with the refugees coming out of Tibet. Many people were dying and it was very hard for them in the camps. He said that whenever he got a bit despondent he would read through the teachings and see how difficult it was for a great teacher like Milarepa, who was a Tibetan saint. Milarepa had a very difficult time and he often came close to death, but he stuck with the teachings. His Holiness would think about Milarepa and how tough it was for him, and then realise that things were not so bad for him so he should not get despondent. I take it the next step down and think, if things are tough for me, look at His Holiness the Dalai Lama looking after 100,000 refugees, and it's not so bad for me. Then I just let the difficulties go. It's really not so bad. Others have far worse problems. In a way, I just think that I've been lucky.

Understanding devotion

There is a whole linguistic, semantic misunderstanding about the term 'devotion' itself. I have found that there is also a very big cultural Christian aspect to it. Devotion is not a blind conceptual situation where you are devoid of intellect and do exactly what you are told. That is often the feeling of the teacher–disciple relationship, where devotion is the central theme. Once you experience devotion in Buddhism, you quickly realise that is a total and complete misunderstanding. The problem is on the surface; when we don't understand, it can appear that way.

Often people coming originally from a Catholic upbringing (and I have a great respect for the Catholic religion) have reported that they had difficulty with the devotional aspect of Catholicism when they were children. Talking with newer students about devotion, when, for example, they have had a Catholic background, there is often a strong resistance. It seems that devotion often has a sense of subservience. We are a fairly individualistic society that says to get out there and do the best for yourself. Being devoted often makes people think they have to give up that strong sense of self and ego, that ambition, or become subservient to someone else. Of course, again, it's definitely not that either. We have difficulty with this term because of Western religion, our intellectual misunderstanding and the cultural aspect of being a fairly macho society.

Also we see the hideous abuse of devotion that has happened, for example, in the Jim Jones mass suicide. So the devotional teachings of the East and West, if they are misunderstood or abused, can kill people. Then I become so sad as, every time that happens, people become more wary and maybe don't connect with a teacher who really, through devotion, can help them a lot.

Uncovering the answers

A few years ago the most profound thing of my life happened to me. I was a little confused in my mind about some things. I had this really burning question and I got so centred on the question that it got right out of proportion. I remember at that stage I was doing Guru Yoga practice, which is a practice where you visualise your teacher and then you visualise your mind becoming one with theirs. I really wanted to know the answer to the question on my mind. I was out jogging in Centennial Park, and this question was really affecting me, just completely overtaking me. I called out to Rinpoche asking, 'Please tell me what I should do.' I had two alternatives. He came to me in a very profound vision. It was like I was running but I wasn't there anymore. I just kept running and there was Rinpoche in front of me and there, very strongly, all around Rinpoche were other great teachers of the Tibetan lineage, with very profound light all around them. I was standing there in front of them, even though I was still running. It was just in my mind — this vision. I was really taken.

Rinpoche just looked at me, a big beaming smile on his face, and he said something that I had never heard him say before. He said, 'It's not so serious.' Something clicked. It's not so serious. The whole thing was not so serious, and he just broke it for me there in the vision. From that time on, even though it was a very difficult time in my life, I sorted it out. They say that in the most difficult times, the teachings are the greatest, and this was certainly true for me. The teachings were very profound and it was very personal because it was obviously just for me. It didn't finish there actually. I got a phone call a couple of days later from Rinpoche. 'Are you all right?' he asked. I told him I was and he said, 'I had a dream about you the other night.' And then he asked, 'Did someone phone you from me?' And I said, 'No, no one phoned.' Rinpoche had never spoken to me in this way before. He then told me the dream he had of me being in a green car going downhill and about to crash. Somehow he stopped me crashing the car. The whole episode was pretty amazing and I've never forgotten seeing all the teachers up in the sky while I was running.

It is often said in the teachings that if you ever really need the teacher, he will be there for you. When I've prayed to Rinpoche, it has certainly been proved to me strongly that it works. The teachings also take care of us in that the answers are there, the help is there. I see Rinpoche himself as the active aspect of the teachings. He's the one who can really show the teachings to me and help me understand.

Attraction, sexuality and gender

In Tibetan Buddhism teachers work in four ways: pacifying, enriching, magnetising and subjugating. The way a lama teaches and the way he presents can be very magnetising, not necessarily physically, but I have noticed women can find this attractive. After having discussions with female students, some have said they see the teacher as a father/lover figure. I have often wondered if it is easier for some men when they initially come to the teachings, as they may not have to deal with the possible complications of this physical attraction.

I see the intentions of Tibetan lamas teaching and working with people on the spiritual path as coming from a good and compassionate motivation. However, the issue of sexuality is often raised. In Tibetan Buddhism, not all lamas or Rinpoches have celibate vows. This can be confusing for Western students who think everyone in robes is a celibate priest. In some people this can bring up questions of sexuality and power, leading to confusion and obstacles on their spiritual path. It is said in the teachings that we should go beyond our concepts to realise spiritual fruition. If you create a conceptual framework you will make it difficult to experience the benefits of the teachings. If you just open up, just be a little open to the teachings, mull over and think about them and then try them out, you will see if they work for you. In essence, don't create concepts around the teachings but rather experience them.

As most Tibetan lamas are men it may appear that women are not so important, but this is not true if you really look into the teachings. There have been many great women teachers in Tibetan Buddhism; even today the wife of Sogyal Rinpoche's teacher, Khando Tsering Chodron, is recognised and respected as a great practitioner. Because of the feminist movement, I feel as Buddhism comes to the West there will be a much greater recognition of the feminine aspect and many more great women teachers.

Meeting the spiritual longing

It would be nice for people to have the opportunity to meet any great teacher, because I think within every one of us is a great spiritual longing. There is a part of us that cannot ever be satisfied with the usual way we live this life. There is a longing that is beyond the material world, beyond the family world, beyond a lot of things. I think that appears in people often in a very negative way, in a sense of loss and lack. We lack spirituality in the West. We have that spiritual longing in the sense that we all feel that there is something more to life than just the material level. It is important to know there are great teachers out there who can show you a way, not even necessarily Buddhist. So, if you feel in your heart that you want more out of life, explore that by reading and talking to people and listening to teachers when they give talks. Just give yourself a chance to feel that longing and bridge an abyss that may be there in your heart, and to connect to your essential spiritual self.

The Buddha talks about how you should see the phenomenal world and existence around you. He says, 'Know all things to be like this, just as a magician creates illusion, horses, ox and cart and other things, nothing is as it appears.' That's always been very profound for me, nothing is as it appears. If nothing is as it appears, then we shouldn't take things too seriously.

Sticking with the path

The one thing I would say to people, and maybe I have a little bit of insight now, having been on this path for seventeen years, the one heaviness in my heart is that I feel that people sometimes don't stick with it. However difficult it may seem at the beginning or even how great it is and then maybe it gets a bit hard, when you stick with it, that is when the benefits come. If you really stick with a path that you've chosen, that you have a heart connection with and that intellectually makes sense to you, then go with it. Then you see what devotion really is. Things begin to happen and experiences come and it confirms what you're doing is right and it's helping you. Then devotion comes automatically. You don't have to worry then whether the path is right. Once you are there, you can continue with it. I think sometimes there is a lack of consistency in us and in our society. We have a great desire to get something quickly, to be successful, see quick results and then move onto something new. That often drags us away from the thing of real benefit. Getting things quickly doesn't work so well with the spiritual path. It requires diligence and consistency through thick and thin, through good and bad times. People really need to see that, to start on the path and to stick with it to get there.

As a rainbow glistens in shimmering light,
I cannot see things just as they are.
I long for pure vision, clarity and spacious mind,
but I solidify and conceptualise.
Teach and transform me and all those like me
who struggle with illusory appearances,
So we may rest in vast peace in the nature of mind.

SPARKING THE FLAME

Be helpless and dumbfounded,
unable to say yes or no.

Then a stretcher will come
from grace to gather us up.

We are too dulleyed to see the beauty.
If we say *Yes we can*, we'll be lying.

If we say *No, we don't see it*,
the *No* will behead us
and shut tight our window into spirit.

So let us not be sure of anything,
beside ourselves, and only that, so
miraculous beings come running to help.

Crazed, lying in a zero-circle, mute,
we will be saying finally,
with tremendous eloquence, *Lead us.*

When we've totally surrendered to that beauty,
we'll become a mighty kindness.[1]

Christine Longaker has been a student of Sogyal Rinpoche (author of *The Tibetan Book of Living and Dying*) since 1980 and served for nine years as the National Director of Rigpa Fellowship in America. She became a pioneer in the hospice movement after her husband died and she now trains people on the care of the dying throughout America, Canada, Europe and Australia.

    I am sitting on the verandah of Christine's room at the top of the hill at Lerab Ling retreat centre in the south of France, looking out over clear blue sky. I am waiting for Christine, one of Sogyal Rinpoche's senior students and author of the book, *Facing Death and Finding Hope: A Guide to the Emotional and Spiritual Care of the Dying*

CHRISTINE LONGAKER

(now published in nine languages). I wait and wait, sitting on the wooden floor, avoiding the puddles from the recent rainstorm. From the room next door come sounds of children laughing and some French people playing a guitar and singing. I begin to wonder if this meeting is ever going to take place, and then Christine arrives, her gentle smiling face full of apologies for being held up. She is, in fact, in the middle of moving rooms, as well as trying to set up in her new house close to the retreat centre. She has also been ill. Finally we settle inside, where she lays a brightly coloured sarong on the bed to sit down on while I perch on a cushion on the floor surrounded by boxes.

Such warmth, gentleness, softness and caring emanate from her that I am momentarily surprised. She shows, in her nature, how her own suffering, grief and despair, which she was confronted with so many years ago when her husband died, has led her onto a path that has helped so many other people in pain and suffering themselves.

Often when we are faced with the death of a loved one, we are unable to transform our own anger, grief, depression and pain. Through meeting her teacher, Christine was able to take the very circumstance that hurt her so deeply and find a way to make it useful to thousands of others. As she has written, 'In truth, facing illness, suffering or death is a "fall into grace". When Lyttle [her husband] and I were forced to acknowledge his eventual death, we finally understood the truth that everything is impermanent.'[2]

In the middle of talking, we are interrupted by people coming to help her move. She takes time in an unhurried way to stop and talk to the Australians who have arrived. I begin to feel a little impatient, concerned that she may lose the thread of her thoughts. However, she is with them as she is with me, giving her undivided attention and interest in a focused and loving way until it is no longer needed. After a while, she thanks them and they leave and she returns effortlessly to the focus of her story. She appears unflappable and calm in each moment. My mind, as usual, is racing ahead, worrying if we will run out of time or if someone else will need her before we are finished. However, she talks on and on, like a lazy river unwinding its way to the sea, with only the occasional ripple or wave on the surface. By the end of my time with her I feel speechless, and say so. I have been blessed and inspired by her presence and her story. She gets up and gives me a big hug and I am transported back into the ordinary world again, realising that any one of us can take our deepest tragedies and turn them around into a life path to serve and help others. As she has written,

> Most of us feel that living is hopeful and that death represents the loss of hope ... To feel that we can face our death with hope, then, we must be willing to take our life seriously now, and use its rich potential for our own change and growth ... For an individual who takes the teachings to heart and cultivates a deep experience in her meditation practice, applying herself with sustained commitment to realise her highest spiritual potential, death can be an extraordinary opportunity to reach enlightenment — complete liberation — a state that is totally free of all suffering, fear and delusion.[3]

Christine's story

I was born and raised in southern California and both of my parents were from the mid-west of the United States. My religious education was a very traditional Catholic one and certain parts of that tradition were very inspiring for me, particularly the aspect of devotion, since I felt a close and personal connection with Christ. So I have a very deep appreciation of Christianity and even now I feel that it is part of my life. In the middle of my university studies I dropped out, got married and had a child. For a few years I worked and helped support and care for my family. Then, just after he had finished his professional training, my husband Lyttle was diagnosed with acute leukemia and I took care of him for a year until he died.

During that year I was able to go back to university so I took courses in sociology, psychology, philosophy, American Indian studies: all subjects that I found interesting. Lyttle and I weren't practising actively in any spiritual tradition at that time, so we didn't have anything to rely on spiritually during his illness. Throughout the year he was ill, we made mistakes and sometimes failed to understand each other, yet overall we really learned about love, deepening our communication and our relationship. He died in 1977, and my son and I moved soon after to Santa Cruz in northern California, where I felt there was a sense of community. I had a feeling of gratitude for my husband's life and his peaceful death and I wanted to give something back.

A spiritual path

In 1978, while I was finishing my university degree, I met a group of people who were interested in starting a hospice home-visiting program. Because of my own experience, I felt drawn to help others have an easier time in their dying, and so I became part of the core group that helped to found the hospice. Doing this work, and contributing to the dying and their families this way, made my life meaningful and I was happy.

Even before my husband fell ill, I was looking for a spiritual path, but I didn't know how to do that in southern California. In Santa Cruz it was easier to explore, because the area was a 'spiritual crossroads', with many centres and teachers from all different religious traditions. Over time I became clearer as to what I was looking for in a teacher and a path. In 1980 one of the hospice volunteers, Dorje Seawell, who is now a Buddhist nun, introduced me to Sogyal Rinpoche. She told me she had invited a Tibetan Lama to teach in Santa Cruz on *The Tibetan Book of the Dead* and inquired if the hospice would like to sponsor his talk. Initially I wasn't interested because our hospice was already having a hard time being accepted by the medical community. Dorje replied, 'Well, you might find it interesting for yourself personally. You should come and hear him talk because it's really about the work that we do, and it might give you new insights and skills for your work.'

Perceptions of death and bereavement

In Sogyal Rinpoche's public talk he emphasised two vital things to remember when we have a loved one who is dying: first, to give them our love fully and to let them go; second, to find a practice that they can do to help them prepare for death and for whatever ultimate potential they believe comes after, so that they are prepared to let go in the best way possible. Rinpoche then told a story about the death of his great aunt, who was a Buddhist nun. In the last part of her life, she had been practising her prayers and meditation night and day. One morning the signs came that she was very close to death and she was no longer able to speak. An old man who was the cook for the household, and also her spiritual mentor and friend, came to her room to give her his loving encouragement and say goodbye. He reminded her to rely completely on the spiritual teachings and practices she had received for the time of death, as this was the moment for which she had prepared her whole life. He encouraged her not to worry about anyone else, but to concentrate on her spiritual practice until her last breath, and then, he reassured her, she would be fine. Finally, he said, 'I am going shopping now, and perhaps when I come back, I won't see you, so goodbye.' Although she was not able to speak, the old nun understood the heart of his message, and she nodded and smiled her goodbye.

When I heard this story I was riveted to my seat, because I recognised it. About six months before my husband died, a *Psychology Today* article offered evidence about the survival of consciousness after death by recounting the then new 'near-death experiences'. The article also explained that *The Tibetan Book of the Dead* describes one's existence after death in great detail and provides essential spiritual guidance for the dying and their loved ones. Sogyal Rinpoche's advice, and his aunt's story, were offered to illustrate the essential points from the Tibetan Buddhist tradition.

On reading it, I was really struck by the potency of that message and story. I thought, if I were a close friend and spiritual mentor to someone who was dying, I would think I should stay right by his or her side and guide them at the moment of death. How much love and trust there must be in the spiritual path that this old man could say goodbye at the door and let her go. How much trust he had that she would be all right spiritually. It completely changed my perception of bereavement and death and what spiritual practice can really mean, especially at the end of life. I was quite shocked when I read this story in the spring of 1977, yet also inspired and moved. Later I thought I had forgotten all about it.

Giving love and letting go

However, six months later when my husband was in intensive care and his physical condition deteriorated to the point that he was very close to death, I wondered, 'What can I do for him now?' I felt very helpless in the intensive care unit because all his other needs were being taken care of. Then that story came back to me, along with Rinpoche's advice: 'Give your love fully and let him go.' It was important to consider

Lyttle's needs and forget myself, so that at the moment of death, I could give him the support he needed, with all my love. Just the day before, we had asked each other forgiveness for the difficulties we had had that year. We also expressed our gratitude for the precious time we shared, for all we had learned and come to trust about love, and we said our goodbyes. Now, when he was actually dying, I knew that fully letting him go with all my love was the last gift I could give him, and there was a deep peace in my heart. But I also knew, as he lay dying, that one day I was going to die. Before that happened, I decided that I wanted to have a much deeper understanding of death and clarity about how to spiritually prepare for my own death.

When Sogyal Rinpoche gave this advice again in his public talk two years later, I was immediately grateful that this teaching and teacher helped me at a very profound moment in my life. I was also convinced that he had a lot more to give that could help me in my hospice work and in entering a spiritual path. A path that could support me in going through the sufferings of life, including my bereavement, and especially at the time of death.

Lighting a flame

For me, Rinpoche was embodying what he was saying. When he was teaching about our absolute wisdom nature, he was also in that state of pure vivid wakefulness and compassion. Through the teachings, Rinpoche was awakening that state in me, almost like 'lighting a flame' inside my mind and heart. I felt that Rinpoche — and the lineage of masters, teachings and spiritual practice to which he is heir — have the means to take me all the way to enlightenment. Tibetan Buddhism, and Sogyal Rinpoche, have many of the qualities that I was looking for in a path: wisdom, clarity, spaciousness and skilful methods. A quality of profound compassion and also a sense of being very connected to life. Not denying life, or family or laughter, the path shows us how to be in the world without becoming trapped in it.

It was important to me to choose a spiritual path that wasn't too restrictive, one that I could introduce to my family. Rinpoche has a special quality of humour and groundedness. He has experienced life's sufferings and joys and he sees and encourages our ultimate potential. This really sparked a connection in me.

The universality of death and loss

My husband's death awakened me to the realisation that one day I was going to die and for this I needed a real spiritual training. There isn't anything else I really need to do in life. The pain of bereavement was beyond anything I could have imagined, and I was in the middle of it at the time I met Sogyal Rinpoche. The only hell worse than what I was feeling would be the pain of losing my child. The Buddha's teachings show that life is imbued with suffering. Even if you are not suffering now, it's still going to come sooner or later.

Going through the pain of bereavement was much harder than my husband's illness and death. I also realised that sooner or later I would lose my son — either through his death or mine. It was just a matter of time before loss or death would come again and I had nothing to help me cope. This thought was excruciating. Thus I found myself at the beginning of Krisha Gotami's story.

Krisha Gotami was a mother whose only child died as an infant. She kept begging people to bring her child back to life, and someone finally sent her to the Buddha. The Buddha said, 'I can help you — but first bring me a mustard seed from a household where no one has known death.' After going from house to house, Krisha started to see the universality of death, bereavement and loss, and realised she was part of the human condition. Understanding that her intensive pain was also part of the inevitable suffering of life, Krisha Gotami became determined to get out of the cycle of unending, painful attachment and loss. She went to the Buddha and said, 'Please show me the path to be free.' The Buddha's compassionate offer to help didn't mean he could make her immediate grief disappear, but that he could help her to see the truth, and show her the path to liberation. Krisha Gotami's painful grief led her to follow the Buddha's teachings, and it is said that before she died she finally attained enlightenment.

No greater gift

My first experience of devotion was one of immense gratitude to Sogyal Rinpoche and the teachings for how they had helped me. I didn't feel I was 'worshipping' someone outside of me; devotion was a feeling of close connectedness and wonderful interdependence. Every time Rinpoche taught, he was reawakening a connection to this inner wisdom, or buddha nature, as though he were relighting a light inside of me. My devotion is a profound appreciation of that potential, that spark, that interdependence. I felt he kept giving me a gift. Yet he wasn't giving me something new, he was helping me glimpse and recognise what had always been there. With this recognition, it was clear that on the level of our true nature, the teacher, student and all beings, are the same.

Hearing Rinpoche teach, I also felt an appreciation that this path could help me heal my bereavement and, if I chose, it could enable me to use my life well in preparation for death. It's impossible to repay this, for there is no greater gift than the ultimate hope of knowing who we truly are, of discovering this deathless nature that is always there. I reflected as well on everyone else who was caring for a dying friend, all those who might be feeling suicidal, or going through bereavement and feeling despair or helplessness. The hope offered in this deeper spiritual perspective could help many people relieve and heal their suffering, and I appreciated that these teachings and practices could also help me serve others more effectively and compassionately in my hospice work.

When I met Rinpoche I was president of the board of directors for the hospice. I invited him to come back to America again and again over the years to give teachings and retreats. Over time, the teachings and the practice began to unfold for me. I was able to understand my own condition, my suffering and patterns, and, I hope, able to develop a little more compassion for others — keeping in mind that, although we all have suffering, we also all share the same ultimate potential. Even though I was very busy as the work increased over the years, and had less time for formal meditation practice, there was always a blessing when I was able to really open my heart in Rinpoche's presence: my mind would become more and more clear, more spacious and free. Make no mistake, my mind does not stay that way all the time! But these glimpses showed me what the teachings say: when you have devotion, the blessings are spontaneously present. In the presence of the sun, the clouds just melt away.

Devotion is profound love

The word devotion is sometimes misunderstood. Devotion is not giving love to the buddhas or masters because they need it, nor the sense they are superior to us and must be 'worshipped'. I remember once seeing a quote on a poster that was a key for me: 'You've been spending so much time searching and searching for love and always getting disappointed. What you need is a love that will last forever.' For me, this is what devotion brings. It has nothing to do with conditional or temporary love, nor love based on ordinary levels of relationship, which are subject to impermanence and death.

Devotion is the highest, most profound level of love, a love which radiates from our absolute nature, like the sunlight. When I open my heart, I don't experience it as a dualistic love that's going from me to someone else. Devotion seems to simply radiate from my heart, while at the same time it rekindles my mind and heart, fulfilling me. With conditional love, we give something away with attachment or fear, and then measure whether we are going to get anything back. This is how we get burned out, frustrated or hurt. On a spiritual level, devotion constantly nurtures us, because it is the doorway into who or what we really are.

Pure love has a quality of appreciation and gratitude; you find it is there almost as soon as you have opened your heart to give it. Devotion can be inspired by a deep reflection on how meaningful our life has become now that we've met a teacher and entered a spiritual path through which we can attain enlightenment. On one level, we don't need a teacher because the potential is already there. However, on the relative level, if we didn't have a teacher point it out, we could easily miss it, and always feel some lack in ourselves, some disconnection or yearning.

Devotion especially seems to help me on the path. When I am able to fully open my heart, I can really hear the profound wisdom of the teachings, and I can receive the blessings and love coming toward me from the buddhas and my masters. In the Tibetan Buddhist tradition the relationship between teacher and student is for life, not just this existence but for all lifetimes, until we attain enlightenment. Therefore, it is beyond birth and beyond death. Devotion has a quality of unconditional compassion and wisdom that is available to everyone, like rays of sunlight. I've been grateful to find that the connection doesn't go away if I make mistakes or get moody. This helps to deepen my trust, and I feel safe to open more.

In choosing a spiritual master, I realised that for my tough and stubborn ego it wouldn't help to study with a teacher who was very sweet and nice all the time, because my ego would be very comfortable and might even get stronger. Perhaps I could develop some positive qualities, but my spiritual progress would be limited by what the ego liked or didn't like. So I wanted to find a master who had the clarity and compassion to serve as a mirror to me, and a path that could help me overcome my judgmental, selfish mind.

The teacher as a mirror

Sometimes, in remarkable ways, my teacher seems to be a mirror reflecting back my true nature. I've experienced glimpses of the vastness, the freedom, the ultimate joy and the deep love and compassion that radiates from that state. As life does sometimes, the teacher can also reflect everything I don't want to face and acknowledge in myself — all of my nonsense, negativity and habitual patterns. Like having a smudge on my face: when I see it in the mirror, I am embarrassed because I have been walking around with it all my life, but now the spiritual path gives me a way to finally clean it off.

I was actually very privileged to work with Rinpoche for many years and see him in many situations. Many times I observed him doing what was appropriate for me in the moment, even though it didn't fit with my wishes or concepts. Sometimes he would correct me very strongly and I would wonder why. Yet each time it helped to clear the ego out of the way — my attachment to everything being perfect. With the teacher's skilful support, sometimes I could cut through the ego's games, dissolve my grasping and fear, and simply rest in that sky-like state of openness and peace.

Everyone has a different sense of connection with a spiritual master. In my own experience I have had a confidence about Rinpoche's compassionate motivation and his realisation since the moment I met him. That confidence was only strengthened over the years when I witnessed how the other Tibetan masters related to Rinpoche — seeing, for example, how he was treated by His Holiness Dudjom Rinpoche — which showed that he is respected and deeply appreciated as a lineage holder.

The main disciple of Padmasambhava (also known as Guru Rinpoche) was Yeshe Tsogyal, who became the heir to the lineage. Originally, the lineage was named after her. Padmasambhava taught that women should be revered because of their qualities of wisdom, openness and devotion; and, if women applied themselves to the practice, enlightenment may come easier to them. It's not been a problem for me that many of my teachers are men. In many ways on this path I've felt lucky to be a woman. In the Tibetan Buddhist tradition, devotion is described as a skilful way to help us realise our absolute nature, the union of wisdom and compassion. This is possible whether you are a man or a woman, for, as the teachings say, 'The Dharma belongs to those who practise it.' The teachings, the entire path and the blessings are equally available to all.

Unrepayable kindness

One aspect of Rinpoche's kindness that I can never repay is the fact that he took me to meet his own masters, including His Holiness Dudjom Rinpoche, Dilgo Khyentse Rinpoche and Nyoshul Khen Rinpoche. This is a very personal story, when Sogyal Rinpoche not only took us to them but taught us how to understand who they were and how to be in their presence.

It's difficult to understand, being born and growing up in the West, the impossibility of making such a connection in the way that many of us did, and the gratitude I have for that. There was a time in 1984 when we had a summer retreat in the Dordogne valley in France. We were going to receive teachings and empowerments from His Holiness Dudjom Rinpoche and His Holiness Dilgo Khyentse Rinpoche. I had heard for years about these great masters with whom Rinpoche was studying. I had met Dudjom Rinpoche a few times before, but not Dilgo Khyentse Rinpoche.

Sogyal Rinpoche told us that many Tibetans used to say, 'If the Buddha was alive today, he would probably look just like Dilgo Khyentse Rinpoche.' Rinpoche would talk about his special qualities and I yearned so much to see him once in my life. It was on the birthday of Guru Rinpoche and we had received an empowerment of Guru Rinpoche from these great masters, sitting together in a large converted barn in the French countryside. Afterward, Dilgo Khyentse Rinpoche was sitting in the shade and Sogyal Rinpoche brought his students, one by one, to receive a blessing from this great master. It was like being in heaven.

We were also brought to receive a blessing from His Holiness Dudjom Rinpoche, and this would be the last time I saw him alive. My deepest wish was to never be separate from him. Feeling so much love for him, as I put my head in his lap, I felt as though I was saying goodbye to a beloved spiritual grandfather and, from the depth of my heart, all I could say was 'Ah'.

With humility, Sogyal Rinpoche used to tell us that he himself was not a master. After years of translating for these great masters, he realised that most Western students do not know how to be with them, or how to understand what they can offer. He felt part of his work was to prepare us to meet them, so we could receive what they were capable of giving. At the same time, I feel Rinpoche himself has become heir to the compassion and wisdom his masters embodied.

Over the years, Rinpoche continues to invite great masters from the Tibetan and other Buddhist traditions to give teachings at our centres and retreats. My gratitude for being in their presence and receiving teachings and empowerments from them is a gift I could never repay. The legacy and the blessings and the transmissions they have poured into me and other students of Sogyal Rinpoche are incredible.

Perhaps it is like meeting a living saint, one who lived in a former time, like Francis of Assisi. They are coming to visit your town and you can actually meet them and receive teachings and blessings from them that could transform your whole life. Even though you cannot stay with them forever, through your spiritual practice you slowly find that the blessing of their presence never goes away, but always remains part of your heart and mind.

The potential and the pain

One thing that perhaps is the hardest part of the Buddhist path for us in the West is that, even though we are shown glimpses of this glorious potential that is within, we are also left to do the work ourselves. Nobody can magically take all my pain and suffering away, nobody can remove all my negative habits and past karma for me. Teachers and masters can inspire and help to awaken me and, through the teachings and practices they can show the way, but in the end I am left to do the work. This is the 'long-term' vision of engaging on the spiritual path, and it's not easy. I found I had to be very careful to acknowledge and let go of my high expectations of instant change, and instead be nurtured and renewed by continuing to meet the teacher again and again, through the teachings and in my practice.

The difficulty is in making peace with these two sides of my mind. One side is my conditioned habits and negativity, my grasping and fear. The other side is this sublime nature that is always there and that I can tap into again and again. When I get a glimpse of that openness, I feel free. Yet I get discouraged with all the time I waste looking for temporary happiness and going up and down with emotions and pain and disappointment.

In my early years I had become frustrated because of my unrealistic hope to serve perfectly the whole future of the teachings by trying to bring benefit to others and relieve suffering. In organising the work of Rigpa (USA), one of my main expectations was that other people would be as inspired and grateful and wanting to give time and energy to this vision. My frustration was between what I felt was possible and what was actually possible. And I feel sad when, even after joining a spiritual community, I find I am still holding on to old unconscious habits — ways of thinking or speaking that may bring misunderstanding or pain to others. My tendency was to want everything to be perfect, valuing the work more than the people. So my difficulties have been feeling split even in this 'spiritual work': serving the program in the midst of all my faults and stubbornness, and at other times tapping into this vast appreciation of the tremendous hope and light that the Buddha's teachings can bring to our troubled world.

A taste of freedom

Rinpoche used to give this example for the feeling of relief and freedom you have when you are able to bring your mind to rest in its true nature. Imagine your negative patterns and emotional suffering are like being stuck outside on a terrifically hot and muggy day, and the atmosphere is so hot and oppressive that you cannot bear to be in it. Meditation practice is like going through the glass doors of an airport and then 'Whoosh!' you are in this wonderful air-conditioned hall. You feel the cool relaxation and ease — all your cares just fall away in this vast and open space. Then suddenly you find yourself back outside again, suffering in your old stuff, and it's easy to get discouraged. The teachings remind you, when you solidify your sense of self and your suffering again, to bring your mind home through the practice of meditation. Through the practice you get another glimpse of your true nature and 'Whoosh!' you come through the airport doors and experience that spacious, open sense of relief. But why don't you stay there?

Well, I keep falling back into my old habits, even though they end up bringing me fresh suffering. It's easy to get discouraged and put myself down. Yet even that is a trick of the ego, an old habit of mine. The point is to start fresh each time, and realise it's time to practise, to come back to the teachings and find the relief and spaciousness of my true nature once again.

Rinpoche points out that this is the reason that we do the preliminary practices, called Ngöndro, so many times. Students sometimes wonder if all this is really necessary. We have to do them so many times because we're trying to break the habitual mechanism that sends us back into our patterns of suffering and negativity. The commitment we make to regular practice is so that we keep entering the airport doors until we finally break the mechanism and stay in that state of ultimate freedom and peace.

Understanding the relationship

I've had many different kinds of teachers in my life, and have learned many kinds of skills that have helped me in my development and in my work. Different teachers have their own knowledge and levels of mastery, and I continue studying with them according to what else they can offer that helps me. In relationships with all the other mentors in life, my motivation is usually based on acquiring something that will enhance me.

Those sorts of relationships are fine. However they are in the realm of what we call 'samsara', a habitual cycling in and out of suffering, based on the ego's schemes for grasping at our desires or avoiding discomfort and pain. Even though we sometimes get what we want, eventually we experience disappointment and grief because whatever we have does not completely fulfill us, and because everything changes.

I've seen two common misunderstandings that can come up in looking for a spiritual teacher. One is to approach the relationship with the motivation to make ourselves feel good, or to acquire something for our CV — better to learn computer programming, I think! The second is to transfer the view of the teacher–student relationship — its purpose, how it works and so forth — from one spiritual tradition to another. This simply doesn't work, even within one religion. For example, most Christian traditions have the role of a priest or preacher, yet not all of them define that person as one's personal spiritual teacher. There is such a role in some parts of the Russian Orthodox tradition, for example, between the 'starets' and their disciples.

The inner prayer of the heart

Reading about the Continuous Prayer of the Heart, taught in the Russian Orthodox tradition, rekindles my devotion. The devotional quality of this practice reminds me of the Tibetan Buddhist practice known as 'Lamai Naljor' or Guru Yoga [uniting with the wisdom mind of the master]. The Prayer of the Heart is described in a book called *The Way of a Pilgrim*, by an anonymous author, and it originates in the contemplative practices and writings of the early Desert Fathers. Reading about the practice lights a fire inside me, and I begin to understand the whole purpose of Guru Yoga on a deeper level. Really understanding the benefits and the power and result of doing such a continuous prayer gives me fresh inspiration and motivation for my daily practice.

In the first part of the Guru Yoga practice, we invoke the presence of a Buddha and recite thousands of mantras. The mantra strengthens our sense of the 'presence' we've invoked and is the means by which we pray and request purification and blessings from this enlightened being. After concluding the practice, we train ourselves to keep this presence always with us, and continue reciting mantras or prayers lightly under our breath, or mentally, in our heart. We are taught to do the practice as a formal meditation and to train so that it becomes our constant experience throughout the day.

Training in the Continuous Prayer of the Heart is similar. The Christian teachings say that, through prayer, we receive the grace of God. From the Orthodox perspective, this training in prayer can also bring us directly into the 'presence of God'.

One way to think of prayer is as a solemn request to God, a formula issued in praying, something expressed in words. Specifically prayer can be thought of as an act of asking God to confer some benefit, but this is an external level of inner prayer. The second definition, that comes from a Russian 'starets' of the last century, is far less exterior: 'In prayer', says Bishop Theophan the Recluse, 'the principal thing is to stand before God with the mind in the heart, and to go on standing before Him unceasingly, day and night, until the end of life.'[4]

This is the essence of devotion. Once on a video I saw a Catholic Cardinal and an atheist debating about the existence of God. After forty minutes, the atheist turned to the Catholic priest and said, 'I am becoming increasingly uncomfortable arguing about the existence of God with someone who is so clearly standing in His presence.' This is where devotion brings us — developing such a deep connection to the absolute truth, our fundamental goodness, what we might call the 'divine within', that it becomes our own presence. This presence blesses our mind and our being, and from that we can become a source of tremendous benefit and blessing to others.

Do not forget the Lama
Pray to him at all times.

Do not be carried away by thoughts
Watch the nature of mind.

Do not forget death
Persist in Dharma.

Do not forget sentient beings
With compassion, dedicate your merit to them.

His Holiness Dilgo Khyentse Rinpoche

As the seasons revolve and leaves fall to the ground,
I know my death will come.
I know I cannot cling, but am frightened to let go
because I'll lose everything.
Teach and transform me and all those like me
who turn away from movement and change,
So we may face the reality of death and
realise impermanence.

BREAKING PRECONCEPTIONS

THE MAN AND THE MELON

There was a man who wandered into the Land of Fools from his own country. Many people were running away in terror from a monster in their wheat field. When the man looked, he saw it was a watermelon. He decided the best way to show the people that there was really nothing to be afraid of was to kill the monster and eat it. So he did, chopping the melon up and eating a slice. When people saw this, they thought that he was more terrifying than the first monster and ran far away from him, screaming and shouting so that he would not attack them. Some of the local villagers summoned their courage and attacked him, thinking that he might eat them next.

The same thing happened to a second man, who had wandered to the same spot. However, this man was a little wiser than the first and took a different approach. The villagers pointed to the terrible monsters in their field and explained that the demons were preventing the harvest of the wheat and that the crop would be lost, thereby endangering the survival of the village during the winter. The man agreed with them. He too thought that the monster must be dangerous, and gained their confidence by quietly moving himself and them away from the perceived threat. He then chose to stay there and get to know them and then he taught them, not only how to lose their fear of melons, but also how to grow them.[1]

I remember first meeting Mal Watson in 1988. I didn't know, back then, that he had been on the spiritual path for a while. He had struck me as more suited to the rugby oval, with his height and broad shoulders, rather than chanting sacred texts. I expected him to be rather loud, chatting up women and generally behaving like an Australian larrikin. So my preconceptions were broken by his soft-spoken, kind, honest, gentle and shy manner.

Soon after I met Mal he left Australia to help the work of Dzongsar Khyentse Rinpoche in India. He travelled with Rinpoche around South-east Asia and spent nearly three years working on the design and construction of the Sea to Sky Retreat Centre in British Columbia, Canada. Mal returned to India, designing and constructing retreat centres and schools, and assisting Rinpoche in the overall management and accounting of many

MAL WATSON

projects including, for example, the White Lotus Project. This is a children's sponsorship program, originally started by monks at the Dzongsar Institute in India, to provide an education for children who can't attend school due to financial hardship. The Institute also runs a nine-year degree course involving 250 monks, and there is a publishing wing in Delhi that prints texts for all the monasteries. There is also a travel desk that assists tourists and Buddhist pilgrims to travel around India. Since mid-1998 Mal has devoted most of his time to producing the movie *The Cup* — Dzongzar Khyentse Rinpoche's filmmaking debut.

Talking with Mal materialised unexpectedly. He was living in India and I had not seen him for a number of years. Then at Easter in 1998 Rinpoche visited Sydney and, as I walked in to meet him, there was Mal, large as life, still looking as if he had just come off the football field, smiling and saying hello. Despite his lack of time and his shyness, he agreed to be included in the book and we finally met late one night at my house to discuss his adventures with Rinpoche. We drank some wine and he talked, openly and honestly, about his spiritual journey. He commented on how it had influenced and affected him, and how, again and again, it had broken down all the ideas he had previously held about what it meant to be spiritual.

Mal talked about the experience of enlightenment as having one's ego extracted, believing that most people have little realisation of what this means. It reminded me of the story of a student who asked a teacher if enlightenment was painful. The teacher replied that of course it was not. However, he added that sometimes the journey was painful — it hurts to pull an arrow out of a wound, yet it has to be done for the healing to take place. Similarly, for awareness to develop, the ego has to die. The teacher advised the student to be happy that he had understood enough to choose this misery and that he should always keep going and never give up, to trust even in the midst of desperation and always to keep an open heart. This is often the part of the journey that is not so openly discussed, showing Mal's courage in speaking about it.

He also mentioned trust, and testing himself in his mind. There are three different types of trust or faith, particularly connected with taking refuge, that are identified as we step more formally onto the Buddhist path. The first is vivid or inspired faith, which we may experience after meeting a great teacher. The second is eager or enthusiastic faith, when we are enthusiastic about the teachings. The third is confident faith, which is total trust in Buddha, Dharma and Sangha (the community of practitioners), and allows the blessings to enter us. It is the 'absolute unwavering trust', irreversible no matter what happens.

Often we only trust what is trustworthy. However, the price we pay for not trusting is higher than trusting and feeling betrayed and hurt a few times. Blind trust is not required, but the story that Mal shared demonstrates irreversible trust.

'Come to the edge and jump,' he said.
'No.'
'Come to the edge and jump.'
'No.'
He pushed me and I flew.

I think that Mal is flying more than he knows. He wasn't in any way looking for a teacher, but found the perfect one.

Mal's story

In 1985 I graduated from university and decided to go to India for seven months because I wanted to have an 'Indian experience' and sample cheap drugs. I met an Iranian woman called Maryam who asked me if I wanted to know about Buddhism. She said she could introduce me to a real live lama. After a couple more months of travelling, I met her in Katmandu and she introduced me to Chökyi Nyima Rinpoche. He gave me a wonderful opportunity by showing me around the monastery and answering all my questions. At the same time Maryam suggested I should read *Cutting Through Spiritual Materialism* by Chögyam Trungpa. This combination started my head spinning, though there was never any feeling of being pushed into Buddhism.

This leads me back to when I was trying to complete university, being a lousy student, because I didn't apply myself. I enrolled in architecture through a method of crossing off what I didn't want to do. However, my lecturer in Japanese and Chinese architecture took an interest in me.

He was living on the North Shore of Sydney and invited me round so he could give me access to his books. I remember every room was filled with books, not even on bookshelves, but just piles of books. He was completely imbued with the spirit. He started me reading Alan Watts and many other books on Buddhism. Books have played a significant role for me, even though they can never replace having direct experience. I found the reading interesting but it didn't really change my life. I just kept struggling through university, passing, failing, passing, failing.

I came back from India in 1986, after some time in Katmandu. I heard there was a young Rinpoche in Melbourne, so I set out to find him. At that time in Sydney, I didn't know any Buddhist centres. The concept of Australian Christians becoming Buddhists didn't exist or, if it did, I didn't know about it. So I hitchhiked down to Melbourne to find the Rinpoche and to ask him to teach me how to meditate. I thought he was going to bestow some great gift on me but all he did was say I should read books and do some meditation. I've always had some quite bad preconceptions or assumptions about the spiritual path, which have all been blown apart along the way.

The meditation worked though and I managed to experience and stabilise being calm. I had some control of my breath and not too much of a wandering mind for short periods of time. Then, by pure chance, someone told me that a Tibetan lama was in Sydney, so I went to see Dzongsar Khyentse Rinpoche teaching at the Buddhist library.

Being ready to accept

I have to say Rinpoche was rather impressive and very articulate. He seemed older than his age. He was exotic, from a strange country called Bhutan that I had never heard of before. He had a great sense of humour and could be joking one minute and yet deadly serious the next. Even back then his English was very good. He used a lot of books in his teaching. He had a small table with books strewn all over it and bookmarks in all of them, yet he could still quote from memory. If anything sums him up, from that initial outward appearance, it is his most beautiful smile, a sincere open smile. When he taught, he didn't sit on a throne in the traditional manner, but would sit on the floor with us. I remember his good humour, excellent explanations, openness and that beautiful smile.

When I think back, I was really lucky that my mind was ready to accept. It was maybe a chance in a million. I could think of so many other times that I would not have been open to him at all. It was a most fortunate occurrence. Still, at that time it was just interest. There were many things I didn't understand but I patiently hoped it would mean something in the future.

Opening the door

I was very taken by Rinpoche but I wasn't looking for a teacher. Soon after, though, Rinpoche was teaching a meditation retreat at Vajradhara Gompa [temple] in northern New South Wales and I decided to go. He taught solidly for five days on many things, including emptiness. This is the central viewpoint that sets Buddhism apart from any other philosophy or religion in the world.

That was really the catharsis for me. It's almost impossible to describe. He was talking about emptiness and I was trying so hard to get my mind around it. For two days I was listening but it was like my mind was in a fog. I even had a headache. It was like all my ideas and conceptions had been thrown into a big thick stew cooking in my brain.

I'll always remember the moment I got some inkling of understanding of what he was talking about. It was like being in a long corridor with a whole series of doors. I was standing at the beginning of the corridor and all the doors were open and there was this cool, clear, clean breeze flowing right through my mind, right down the corridor. Everything felt light and clear and I felt that I understood everything. I realise now that it's really nothing like that. What I felt was a temporary aberration of the normal dullness of my mind but, nonetheless, it instantly 'blew my socks off'.

I always considered myself a student of Rinpoche's after that. There was never anything formal. In fact I couldn't even speak to him; I was tongue-tied. He was really normal and yet I was embarrassed and had nothing to say to him. I remember the first time I spoke to him — what I said didn't really matter — but I was blushing and thinking, 'My God, what a stupid thing to say to the guy who has just blown the cobwebs out of my mind.'

Making sense

So that was the real start of it. I had wandered the earth for some thirty-odd years and I was an angry young man. Nothing was right. Society was failing and there weren't any solutions. I was very cynical. I even joined the Labor Party because I thought that was the way to change things, but even there people seemed only interested in themselves. I had gone to them full of idealism about nuclear and environmental issues, but the deals that I saw done in the support of personal power upset me.

No system made sense. Religion didn't make sense, politics didn't make sense, it all seemed terribly unfair. I could never work out why I was born with nice parents and in a part of the world that always had good food, good schooling and opportunities, whereas on television I would see people starving. When I read about Buddhism though, for the first time in my life I found a conception of society and the universe that made sense, contained in a holistic framework. It fitted all unknown, unanswered phenomena in my mind. It was a cohesive philosophy that gave me faith to try the practice. Then when I did, it gave me further faith.

I also had two very strong dreams, which I knew were significant because they were so clear. In one I was sitting round a table with Maryam and Rinpoche, full of blissful feelings. That was great. The other dream was simple but very long-lasting and powerful. Chökyi Nyima Rinpoche's face faded gradually into Dzongsar Khyentse Rinpoche's face. That morning I woke up with faith in Dzongsar Khyentse Rinpoche.

At that time, in the mid 1980s, I heard many stories about students wanting to get into the Dharma and seeking desperately to find a teacher. All I can say is that I was extremely fortunate. I wasn't looking and I found the perfect one.

Testing devotion

There are three different forms of Buddhism: Hinayana, Mahayana and Vajrayana. Rinpoche has been teaching in the West for fifteen years and now wants people to get a very firm foundation in Mahayana and Buddhist philosophy, before he teaches Vajrayana. Devotion in Mahayana has a different view of the teacher, who relates in a more academic way and explains the commentaries and the philosophies. It relies on the idea of respecting and listening to someone because they have knowledge.

Vajrayana to me, though, seems to take a step further. I describe it as the sort of 'colour and movement' form of Buddhism, in that it initially attracts people's attention. In Vajrayana, you have a deep and intense devotion to the teacher and regard him or her as a very special person. There is a story that demonstrates this kind of devotion. Imagine standing at the edge of a cliff and your teacher says, 'Jump because you can fly.' I want to have so much trust, that I would be able to jump off without fear of whether I was able to fly or not. I always fail when I think about that story as I can never imagine myself jumping. Of course, let's be clear, this is a metaphor and not to be taken literally. No teacher would ask me or anyone else to start jumping off cliffs. It's just a story I imagine to test myself.

Doubting

I have sometimes been quite naive and full of doubts, with so many preconceptions. I thought that anyone who wore robes was a monk and enlightened, and when I realised it wasn't true I was so disappointed. In Tibetan Buddhism, not all people who wear robes have taken a vow of celibacy. This has caused some problems, particularly for some women. They have assumed their teacher's celibacy, which has made them feel very safe and non-threatened, and then become offended when they have discovered otherwise. I remember once Rinpoche asked me if I thought I could give up alcohol and I said, 'Yes, but I don't think I can give up women.' He just laughed and said, 'That's all right, you're probably going to have many girlfriends.' Whether that was true or not didn't matter. It was just his way of breaking yet another assumption I had about what he might say and how I thought he should behave.

Once, when I was in retreat, going further and further into the practice of taking refuge, which is connected with trust, a lot of doubts arose about Rinpoche. I was confused about what vows he had taken, about the fact that he was a filmmaker and whether I could trust him or not. They kept growing like a festering sore in my mind. I couldn't ignore them and it caused me a lot of difficulty. I was very disturbed and angry, and I eventually confronted Rinpoche. He was fantastic and knew exactly what I was going through. His gentleness and understanding and explanations just resulted in my devotion growing even more. I realised that, despite thinking that I was dealing with all my doubts, in fact I had merely been suppressing and avoiding them. This particular practice of refuge really helped me face myself and recognise how much I actually didn't trust myself.

Removing the limits

Many people approach Dharma with a whole suitcase full of preconceptions about being good and being nice. People often say, 'Oh, aren't you a Buddhist; can you eat meat, drink alcohol, etcetera?' Actually, in Vajrayana, there is no limitation on what you can do. In fact, the limitations fall off and you can perhaps do a lot more. The point, though, is actually to be mindful. You are not following any particular habit or pattern. You start to develop some sort of responsibility for your mind and your practice. I suppose there are certain vows that we take, like not to do harm, and when I go into retreat I may take other vows for a particular duration of time.

I remember one of my vows was not to drink coffee, which had both its medical and its mind reasons. It's some sort of discipline, but it's not a prerequisite. Buddhists can drink coffee but they may choose at a particular time not to. So what lamas can or cannot do depends on what vows they have taken rather than how they dress. Some students maybe have projected their own assumptions onto the teacher, which bear no relation to the reality of what is actually happening. They then perceive the teacher as being faulty and tell other people that. It often has nothing to do with the teacher at all, only the preconceptions of the student.

The thing about devotion is that I do surrender, even though I don't hand over responsibility for myself. This is a very difficult thing to understand and can be confusing, but no one else can be responsible for my mind. I do not surrender my own personal responsibility or 'hand myself over'. In fact, I'm careful to have more personal responsibility and maintain my own judgment. I guess it depends on perception and viewpoint.

Destroying the ego

Dzongsar Khyentse often says that I have 'hired' him to destroy my ego. I wanted someone qualified to guide me on how to operate on my ego. There's no point complaining now that my ego is hurt. It's not a painless process to extract the ego.

It's like saying to the dentist, 'Please remove my tooth,' and expecting him to make it disappear without any pain.

The relationship in Vajrayana between the student and teacher is far beyond an employment contract. You want the ego extracted or you want to know how to extract the ego. You 'sign up' with a particular teacher to do exactly that. The danger of Vajrayana, in my opinion, is that most people never sign up fully, only partially, because it looks good, or they think it's fun. They assume that it's going to be a painless extraction.

One of the ways Rinpoche works with people is to tease them. This results in making all the emotions rise up. There is nothing to operate on, so long as we keep things hidden and simmering below the surface. If you have an animal you want to catch and it lives in a comfortable hole in the ground, what do you do? You have to get it to stick its head up if you want to catch it. To get the ego to come out of its hiding place, you have to tease it, and it shows itself. Then if you are stable enough in your meditation, you can 'put it to death'.

People come and ask Rinpoche to help them get rid of emotions and to destroy their ego, but they don't want to be teased, for example, on their relationship. 'I'm happy with my partner, that is an untouchable item.' That is like a partial extraction, taking the top of the tooth but leaving the root in. It's going to cause problems later on. I'm not saying that relationships have to be removed. It's an example. If we say, 'Please operate on me,' we have to give the person the full range of tools to operate with. There is a danger in the West of limiting the tools available to the teacher because of our preconceptions about sex and power. We are trying to gain freedom from suffering but we just complicate everything.

Love is one of the most beautiful emotions but, in its temporal form, it carries with it so much baggage. Love, as we know it in everyday society, is guaranteed to cause suffering, because of our attachment. We only have to break up from a relationship, even amicably, to know how attached we are. The day feels empty, the room is empty, we are unhappy. We don't want to suffer, we only want the nice side. The trouble is, if there is no suffering, there is no niceness.

Being 'cosmic'

Rinpoche often asks, 'Do we really want enlightenment?' Often I just want to be a happy person, a nice guy. I just want to be wanted, and to feel good about myself. That is fine, of course, but if I wish to become a source of never-ending energy to benefit others, things become a little more rigorous.

At first, I thought I had a lot of devotion, but now that I understand a little more about it, maybe I have less. Initially I just went where Rinpoche wanted because it was a novelty and highly rewarding. It gave me pleasure and took me to new places. It was a seductive path where I did many different and interesting things and felt a temporary sort of freedom.

That's often the initial stage that happens in meditation. It's tremendously liberating. You feel light and untroubled from the general anxiety we often carry around; anxiety about the next moment, the next day, the next relationship, the next job. It disappears and you feel that lightness. Some people start the journey, have this first experience and want to stop there and hold on to it and repeat it. They get anxious if they are not feeling that freedom all the time. They meditate and talk about meditation with friends and become a bit 'cosmic' or intellectual. Yet, after a while, they realise that the feeling they want is no longer coming. But instead of continuing with the journey, their ego has attached to this first small step along the path and they stop there. I think it is sad and actually harder to recover from than if they had never started the journey. Maybe it's better to remain just a normal 'neurotic' person, rather than think you are on the path and 'getting liberated' when you're not.

Using appearances

This is the difficulty that we all have to face as practitioners, to continue and not stay where it is comfortable all the time. Maybe the basis of my devotion is that I trust in Rinpoche's motivation. Whatever he does, I trust his bottom line, that ultimately he will benefit all sentient beings. In this age of communication, of environmental destruction, of industry, politics and commerce, if you really want to have an effect on people you have to be out there with them. No one is going to listen or even see someone who sits in a cave in the Himalayas for their whole life in retreat. Even though it may still have a good effect, generally people won't know. So Rinpoche sometimes uses appearances to deliberately make a connection with people, in their way. He might wear black jeans, black shirt, beret and cowboy boots, and hang out in coffee bars. This, of course, also challenges our belief systems, although I have also seen him behave in a very traditional manner. People are still attracted to him and make a connection with him even if they don't know he is a great teacher. Then they might find out who he is and want to know more.

I have learnt so much about myself and others. I've realised more and more about suffering and maybe developed some real faith and improved as a human being. Sometimes I seem worse — I never thought of myself as an angry or jealous person, for instance, but actually I had both emotions buried inside me. If I look back, I was extremely jealous but didn't admit it to myself. Now if I get jealous it comes out instantly; I recognise it and it only lasts a short time.

My feeling for Rinpoche has everything to do with who he is and what he does. It's not just that he is handsome, talented, a great filmmaker and I like the idea of being associated with him. I experience such an overall love and joy when I see him. Sometimes when he is away and I'm busy working, the frustration and anger can build up and my mind gets a little twisted and non-directed. Then he arrives and I feel an immense relief. The weight lifts, difficulties seem smaller and I feel a great joy. It is the most marvellous opportunity. Because he is there, though, often the work increases and there are many sleepless nights. Then after a little while I think, 'Rinpoche please go, so I can sleep or rest.' He goes, I sleep, I get on with work and everything goes along sweetly. Then the longer he is away, the frustration builds up again. Then I always feel great joy when I see him. I guess it's a bit of a pattern for me.

Being free to succeed or fail

Rinpoche has done so much for me personally. I don't think I ever had much confidence in what I did. Working for Rinpoche has helped me develop trust and encouragement and given me confidence to do things, as well as get things wrong. What used to stop me previously, I'm sure, was that I didn't want to fail. Rinpoche has given me confidence both to succeed and to fail. I regard this as a true gift as, for many of us, the fear of failure is what drives us.

In the end, I have always felt that Rinpoche was telling me something that was true. As you can only follow what confirms your innermost truth, when you meet someone who mirrors or reflects that truth, you cannot deny it. We all 'go to the edge of the cliff' in different ways and, whether we jump or not, fly or crash, are pushed or hang around and look at the view, or get bored and go home, doesn't really matter. What matters is that we realise and stay mindful in each moment.

Lightning forks through the sky to strike my delusion,
but I continue to project and misperceive.
Thunder reverberates through my ignorant thoughts,
but the storm of my desires stubbornly persists.
Teach and transform me and all those like me
who wish to roam free of obstructions,
So we may overcome illusion and cultivate
the wisdom of clear discernment.

DEEPENING

THE STREAM AND THE DESERT

High in the mountains a stream travelled from her source across many countries and landscapes. She wound her way easily downhill, gurgling and bubbling happily along and, when her way became difficult to pass, she slowly wore down the obstacle and just kept going. Finally she reached a seemingly impassable hurdle, the desert. No matter how hard the stream tried, knowing it was her fate to cross to the other side, she kept running into the sands and disappearing.

Then a secret voice spoke to the stream telling her that the wind could cross the desert and therefore so could she. The stream protested saying that she did not know how to fly. The voice informed the stream that doing things in her accustomed way would no longer work and that she must allow herself to be absorbed and changed by the wind. Then she could successfully cross to the other side. The stream, not at all trusting the strange and hidden voice, did not accept this option at all and, fearing to lose her identity, never to regain it, refused.

The voice, which seemed to come from the sands of the desert itself, continued to explain to try to calm her fears. It clearly pointed out what would happen, saying that it was the job of the wind to pick up water, carry it across the desert and let it drop as rain to then form a river again. The stream, though, was still very attached to remaining unchanged, but the voice, patient as ever, reminded the stream that this had happened to her essential part many times previously. Suddenly the stream remembered that perhaps she had been carried in the arms of the wind before. So the stream, after much deliberation, finally realised that this was the only real and obvious solution, and allowed the wind to lift her vapour and carry it to the other side, so she could then fall softly as rain upon the mountain top. The stream, because of her doubts, remembered more clearly next time and was able to learn from her experience. The sands whispered that they knew, because they saw it happen day after day and therefore could impart their knowledge and wisdom to those who had forgotten their true identity.[1]

DOMINIQUE SIDE

I met with Dominique Side in one of the rooms at the Lerab Ling retreat centre in France, overlooking green summer fields with distant and misty views of the Pyrenees mountains far off in Spain. She struck me as a very matter-of-fact person, openly and honestly announcing that she 'didn't suffer fools gladly'. She seemed very intellectual, almost scientific in her approach, with an eye for detail that probably comes with being an experienced translator and editor. She had, until recently, been editor of Rigpa's international magazine, *View*.

At first she seemed a little uncomfortable and reluctant to talk personally, in an English reserved sort of way. However, we quickly settled into a more relaxed manner with each other. She was obviously a powerful woman with a great deal of strength and determination to continue on the spiritual path, despite the difficulties she has encountered. There had evidently been times when things had not been at all easy for her. Yet these problems, instead of putting her off, had in fact encouraged her to deepen her interest and experience. She discovered why things weren't working for her and was determined to keep changing and growing. The idea of 'taking everything onto the path', whether difficulties or successes, is integral to Buddhism, and Sogyal Rinpoche often encourages his students to never give up and to use whatever happens to us as a practice. Whether good or bad circumstances, everything can be related to as a teaching, so that whatever happens in our lives becomes part of the path and the journey. Dominique's story is living testimony to this.

Often we misunderstand why a teacher points out our mistakes and hidden faults. In fact, as Dominique notes, it is said that the best teacher is the one who does point out hidden flaws. Dominique talks personally and courageously about these issues, which need to be recognised and dealt with by the student, if they are to progress along the spiritual path. It is often the 'shadow' side of ourselves that the teacher will reveal to us — the selfishness, jealousy, ambition, competitiveness and desire. These are qualities that we all have, but often only judge in others, rather than identify and see in ourselves.

Dominique discusses how she wants to always 'get things right', and do her best. However, when her mistakes are pointed out to her, despite the pain that brings, she finds the ability in herself to observe her patterns of reacting and take them to a deeper level.

She not only overcomes her obstacles but uses them to transform, by not taking things so personally and working with the teachings, particularly those of the eight samsaric Dharmas: fear of loss and hope for gain; fear of suffering and hope for happiness; fear of blame and hope for praise; and fear of insignificance and hope for fame. She goes beyond her everyday, ordinary understanding and changes her perspective to recognise that everything is a teaching. She tries to see the situation and truth as it is, rather than through a filter of emotion and conditioning. Her examples show clearly how we all want to be liked and praised and how strongly we dislike not doing everything correctly. However, when we know that it is the learning that is important, our perspective shifts and we are no longer afraid of failing.

While discussing this, questions arose on a similar theme. When everyone seemed to be doing their best, why were we asked to improve? The answer is that, if we close ourselves off to the possibility of improving, then our best always stays the same. We stagnate and stop growing and learning. Dominique shows quite clearly why and how to keep going in that process. When I left her I felt that here was a woman forged through fire, with utmost hidden passion and determination, who was not about to let anything stop her from accomplishing what she set out to do.

Dominique's story

In 1975 I was working in London as a translator and editor. One evening in early January, some friends invited me to a dinner party with Sogyal Rinpoche. He was new to London, having just moved there from Cambridge University, so the dinner had been arranged to introduce him to a few people. I immediately made a strong connection to him, though at that point it was more fuelled by curiosity than anything else. I had no idea what a lama was or anything about Buddhism. I found him intriguing because I knew there was something special about him, but I couldn't put my finger on what it was. It started as a feeling when he entered the room. He had the special quality of attracting many people to him effortlessly, and I had a strong sense that he was always at the centre of wherever he was. That was my first impression. As I am quite intuitive, I followed that feeling of wanting to know more.

Rinpoche was starting an introductory course three days later and I decided to go along. The beginning was really that simple. I went to his nine-week course, one evening a week, in Swiss Cottage. It was held in the large ground-floor flat of an Australian friend. Rinpoche would sit next to the large black shiny piano she had in her living room, and we assembled in front of him on three rows of chairs. He began with the life of Buddha and continued with a general overall view of Buddhism.

Hearing him teach this course was a turning point for two reasons. First, it was quite clear to me that what Rinpoche was saying made complete sense, and that Buddhism had such a vast view that everything in the world, and in my head, fitted somewhere. The Buddhist view was complete; I could think of nothing that was outside it. Intellectually that really attracted me, because I had been a philosophy student and this was the first time I had come across any view that was so all-embracing. Second, I had the definite sense that Rinpoche was an authentic person. That was rare. I had been to different groups and had never come across the combination of someone who knew what he was saying and who also had a personal experience of that. Basically from that time on, I've never looked back. Since then I have followed Sogyal Rinpoche.

Seeing the human side

My idea of devotion has certainly evolved over the years — to begin with I didn't have any idea of what it was at all. Learning what devotion is has been an ongoing process and, in fact, I would say it is one of the main themes on my path.

In those early days the situation was very simple, in that there was no formal Buddhist context at all and there were very few students. I remember teachings were quite informal, with no attendants, no ceremony, no shrine, no throne. After the teachings we would even go to the pub with Rinpoche for a quick drink. We had a personal relationship with him as a human being. So my devotion started by relating to his more human qualities, to his warmth and friendship and humour, and this gradually deepened as I grew to see him in a different way.

Although his qualities remained basically the same, my understanding of them changed because I slowly saw him not as another human being but as a master. This means, for example, that I found his mind to be completely different from mine. His mind is so vast and all-encompassing that he understands many things all at once. There is a sense of extraordinary wisdom and understanding of people and life.

I felt a real dimensional difference between him and myself and it's that understanding that is the basis of my trust in him. This is not simply a blind trust in whatever he does or says, it is entirely based on personal experience. It is from experience that I know that he knows. Because he is an incarnate lama, recognised as the incarnation of a previous master, he has been trained and educated so that his qualities are highly refined. We can all develop in the same way but we're just slower, much slower.

Finding the boundless dimension

Being near to a master made me realise that his living qualities are in everything he does; they do not only appear when he is teaching. There is no question about this in my mind because I experienced it every day for many years. One example is the way he really does love and care for everyone equally. People are so different — some people are really boring, while others can be prickly and difficult. All types of people would go up to him and he would treat each of them equally, which for most of us is very hard to do in practice. Another example is that I found, whatever he does or says, he always has your best interests at heart, even though you may not think so at the time.

His main quality is his extraordinary ability to relate the teachings, showing us through his example, guidance and instruction, year after year, twenty-four hours a day. He never tires of teaching the same point a hundred times over, until we understand. He has this extraordinary limitless quality of kindness, love, understanding and patience. It extends completely across the board to absolutely everyone, in every moment of the day or night, to every activity and facet of life. There is really a boundless dimension to him.

One memorable occasion that comes to mind is when Sogyal Rinpoche was translating a teaching for His Holiness Dilgo Khyentse in Paris in the early 1980s. It was so moving we were all in tears. Dilgo Khyentse literally took Rinpoche in his arms, cradled his chin, lent on him, touched him and held him with extraordinary affection. It was like a father with his only child. It was so touching to see a supreme master show his appreciation, recognition and love in the same sort of way that Rinpoche shows his love for us. The love between them filled the room. But it is not love in the way we normally think about it; it is so deep. There's no holding back, there is no edge to it at all.

If we say devotion is love, that can bring many questions in some people's minds, about unhealthy power relationships and so on. However, whenever I have seen love and devotion expressed by such masters, it has always been completely natural. They're just expressing what they feel, in mutual recognition, and there is no problem with that. It is total love, an openness of heart, a warmth and a transparency. If there is any power in such a relationship, it is simply the power of love. Seeing this has helped me to accept that it is all right to let myself feel this love, which should not be confused with ordinary love relationships. In this context, I saw and understood its deeper meaning.

Coping with life

Devotion itself is also a tremendous source of strength in coping with life. There were several times when I lived with friends who were slightly against Buddhism. This created conflict in me and made me very unhappy. I remember several times when, just as I was in the middle of a big argument, Rinpoche would ring and completely cut it. Just hearing his voice again would bring me back to feeling confident and clear. At the time I thought it was amazing, not only because he was extremely helpful but especially because it seemed so remarkably far-sighted of him to know just when to ring. Repeated experiences like these have meant that I feel in touch with him all the time. The mere fact he may not be with me physically doesn't mean he cannot help me through difficulties. It may sound a little strange to people who haven't experienced this but, after a few occasions like this, it becomes the most natural thing to accept that whenever you turn your mind to him your teacher is never far away.

The main point is really how I perceive him. If I see Rinpoche just as a human being, then I'll have problems because I'll interpret my feelings in terms of normal human relationships. This won't work because the teacher–student relationship doesn't operate in that way. The teacher is not simply a person, he's a principle, a state of being. And that state of being is not only his, but is also mine.

There have been many stages in deepening my understanding of the guru or lama principle. In a way my struggle to understand devotion as something other than a human connection is what has fuelled my need to deepen the process. If it doesn't work, then I try to go into it more deeply to find out why. That process of going backwards and forwards is continuous.

Going beyond normality

I've really had to go beyond my normal perception and thinking. That in itself is extremely difficult. Yet loving is beyond the normal conceptual mind anyway. True love means that, whatever happens, you stay in the process and find a way through, rather than just being conditional and giving up. For example, sometimes I would do something to what I thought was the best of my ability and, rather than Rinpoche saying, 'That's wonderful, you've done the best you could,' like I thought he should, he would tell me what was wrong with it in a rather wrathful way. I used to find this very upsetting and think it was really unfair. I would think he didn't appreciate me and didn't understand. I had all sorts of reactions.

In that sort of situation how can I reconcile those sorts of feelings with the love and trust I have underneath? If I'm going to reconcile the two, then it's the negative emotions that have to be transformed in the light of the love and the trust. In other words, the love and the trust are my strength. In fact they have been the fuel propelling me through this process of going deeper and deeper, beyond my ordinary limits of understanding. I have discovered some other level at which things make sense.

Part of the practice is just continually doing that, time after time. It is said that the best teacher points to your hidden flaws, so that they are dealt with, so for Rinpoche to point out my mistakes is actually the most useful thing he can do. Patting me on the back is not really going to help me much, though it may feel more comfortable.

Being deeply true

I accept the teacher's criticism because I trust there is something else behind the bald fact of being told off. The most important thing is not to disown or conveniently forget the love and blessings as soon as something unpleasant comes up. That's why stability in devotion is so important. Regardless of how the lama is, and whatever the circumstances, once you have accepted him as a teacher, you never forget that connection — you remain true to it. Not having any doubt has definitely been my strength, because devotion is actually your connection to yourself and your own nature. Devotion basically touches your deepest self and, if you're true to that, you're really being true to your own deepest experience of life. By seeing everything from that perspective, you don't get confused or muddled in the more difficult times.

I'm not true to Rinpoche just to please him, but because I know this is a way of being true to myself. Of course there have been times when I have struggled, when there were things I didn't want to do. I would start thinking, 'Oh, I don't want to do what you're telling me, I want to do something else.' That's precisely when I would realise that I had the wrong end of the stick, because I think I am supposed to follow someone else's words.

When he asks me to do something or criticises me, he's simply expressing the truth of the situation very clearly. It's not just his own personal view. If I'm really in touch with myself, I immediately recognise what's being said and actually see it as the truth myself. I immediately think, 'Aah yes, he's right.' However, if I react emotionally, then I'm in a muddle, and that's when all the resistance starts. When I've seen it for myself, then I take it on board.

This is such an important point. When I haven't been able to see the truth for myself it has been a struggle. When the student misunderstands it translates into a struggle between teacher and student. The teacher is actually voicing a truth that isn't his 'own truth' or his 'view' or his 'interest', yet that's how we often view it. So there is a struggle, you could say it is the human struggle, and I went through periods of this many times.

Sometimes it tore me apart, it was so painful. How did I come out of it? Simply by finding my way back to the love and trust that I have so strongly inside. This is my foundation and the ground I always return to. It is something that I can never deny or reject. With that as the cornerstone, every painful experience can be transformed, because slowly I come to reassess everything in that light. Everything else has to fit in with that love, rather than the other way around.

Using the practice

It took years to reach this understanding. Stability doesn't come overnight. After a while though, I began to even out. One factor that is helpful in this respect is the practice. Once I was extremely depressed, living in a terrible flat in London. Rinpoche was teaching but I was so down I just didn't want to go. I guess I was really being stubborn in wanting to remain miserable. He rang me and the care that Rinpoche showed had the effect of completely transforming me. He always finds a way to remind me of the inspiration and connection.

I remember when I first discovered how I could actually use the practice to transform my unhappy moods and emotions, I felt for the first time that I had tools in my own hands. Until then I felt quite dependent on the lama in a sense, because he knows the teaching and the practice and has the blessings and the guidance. In comparison I felt I had very little. Once I learnt how to use the practice for my own benefit, it increased my confidence a hundredfold.

This happened for the first time in Paris in 1982. I was in a relationship that was not going very well. I was miserable and crying all the time. I had been in the Dharma for years but nothing had really changed. That weekend Rinpoche taught a practice where you breathe in the blessings of the buddhas and the masters and let them fill you with bliss, and then you breathe out good thoughts and wishes to other people. As I did this, it was the first time I had ever experienced a practice transforming me. It was so nourishing to feel the blessings coming into me that I stopped crying.

It marked a crucial turning point, when I found that you can actually use the practice to help yourself, rather than just doing it mechanically like a good girl. Then I realised the blessings are not all 'out there', not even really in the teacher, but they are part of me. The teacher is like the outer manifestation of my own wisdom, my own buddha nature.

I'm now much more aware and conscious of that source within than I was at the beginning. Deepening and deepening means that I now have an understanding that devotion is an expression of my own qualities, it's an offering to the most precious person in my life, the person who shows me myself. It has a flavour that combines my understanding, insight, compassion, recognition and gratitude. It becomes deeper as I am more in touch with myself and it comes straight from my heart. Anything I do that serves to help me express my true self, I call devotion.

Finding a confident space

Some people believe that, in general, women have stronger devotion and that it comes more easily. Maybe that's how we're made. Women can have a strong and confident heart and an intuition that we have the strength to stand by. At their best, women can use that to inspire themselves and to sparkle. But at the end of the day, when you're practising Buddhism at our beginner level, it doesn't really matter if you're a man or a woman, as the practices are the same. What we're really talking about is going beyond the conceptual mind.

Recently Rinpoche mentioned that devotion not only benefits our spiritual life, but also our everyday life. He said that if you deepen your experience of devotion, so that you understand it more as an expression and anchor of your own nature, then it is really helpful in understanding your emotions and personal relationships. In other words, if you can remain true to that which is deepest, then all other thoughts and emotions settle, and then you can see them for what they are. So, in terms of human relationships, you can see a superficial attraction for what it is. You can experience anger, attraction or desire for what they are because you have this ground that can let them dissolve. You have a confident space.

Most of the emotions we talk and think and dream about are like the waves on the ocean. They come from the ordinary mind that is attracted by external objects. This is the mind that craves love, support, reassurance and desire — all those things. The trouble is that by definition, those thoughts and feelings are very transient and that's why we get so frustrated. They come one day but are gone the next. We try to get them back again but it doesn't work so we get into all kinds of muddles. When, however, there are some deeper feelings that are not so based on external circumstances, that come from deep down, from your heart, these don't go away. There is a stability to them, there is a truth to them that is timeless. I am sure many of us have had a taste of this.

This is the essence of you, which is unchanging and is not conditioned by circumstance or time, or space, or other people. You may have loved someone and that love doesn't go away. You may not even see that person for twenty years, but it's still there. You're in touch with something that is beyond your normal parameters.

So when you cultivate and deepen your devotion for a teacher, you can also use that to deepen the love you have for other people. Then it benefits not only you, but others as well. Learning and struggling and understanding all this has certainly helped me deepen and shift the entire perspective of my awareness and mind.

The cool pale moon casts a dark shadow,
like my actions that follow me wherever I go.
I want to forget the mistakes I make,
yet somehow they happen again and again.
Teach and transform me and all those like me
who are ruled by our fate,
So we may rest in the warmth of silvery destiny.

COMING HOME

SHABKAR, THE SINGING YOGI

A singing yogi, Shabkar Rinpoche, was travelling over the mountains with his two students. They met a poor old beggar woman lying immobile on the road asking for food and water. He freely gave her much food and water but, despite his generosity, she then asked for clothing and his horse, in fact everything he owned. His two disciples were somewhat reluctant; they needed these things for their own journey, but the yogi, through his great compassion, offered all and invited her to accompany them so they could take care of her.

The old woman then transformed herself from her disguise into the Queen of Great Bliss. She praised the yogi for his generosity and limitless compassion. With rainbow light pouring out of her, she danced, handed the yogi a sacred medicine bag and flew into the sky. The yogi then flew after her, leaving his amazed disciples behind.[1]

Rod Lee worked for a number of years in advertising and marketing, until he decided he didn't like big business very much. He then started a health food store and currently works as a masseur, teaches T'ai Chi and runs stress management courses. He has also developed meditation and relaxation programs for passengers of Qantas Airways.

In 1976 he met his teacher, Geshe Loden, who is part of the Gelucpa school of Buddhism. Rod met Sogyal Rinpoche in 1988 and has maintained a strong connection with him since. Often Rod appears at retreats to reconnect with Rinpoche and to give him massage, as he did for a day during the 1998 Australian retreat. That day was full of teachings, meditation and discussion, and over dinner we sat and reminisced about past experiences. Back in Sydney one night we talked in more depth about his teacher and his connection with Rigpa and Rinpoche.

I had always known Rod as a director of the Tibetan Buddhist Society, but didn't know much about his original teacher. Rod is a very straightforward, solid man who emanates a quality of caring and humour. He is not a person who promotes himself and, despite what he says, really has little or no self-interest. This is remarkably rare, and people respond to

ROD LEE

that in him by frequently asking him for guidance. He is someone who they feel safe talking to and confiding in. He has an ability to clearly see through situations, particularly those involving personalities, conflict and power, and supports all without judgment.

He talked of starting the path in an idealistic way, which many of us will identify with, and transforming an outer meditation practice into an inner, deeper and more meaningful practice. So many people who embark on a spiritual path think that they won't have any more problems. He too thought he would magically and mystically be empowered with special gifts and maybe even fly through the sky!

In regard to flying, in 1997 I was travelling on an extremely bumpy and turbulent aeroplane, feeling increasingly nervous and unsettled as the plane continued its 'dance' all over the sky. As I was not succeeding in calming my mind with the different techniques I know, I switched on the music channels. There is a saying in Buddhism that you are never separate from your teacher and, the minute you call on him, he is with you. Suddenly, as I was switching music channels, there was Rod's actual voice, calmly and reassuringly taking me through my meditation practice, thinly disguised as a colour and music visualisation meditation. It was unbelievable. It was as if my teacher had instantly appeared in the form of my friend Rod's voice, guiding me and reminding me of my practice. Instantly, I felt detached and amused, as if even the thought of falling out of the sky and dying was just a huge joke.

Yet, perhaps more miraculous than being able to fly is Rod's ability to remain true to himself and not be influenced by position or power. He calmly transforms difficulties and negativity into clear solutions and positivity. As others mention, intrinsic to Buddhism is the notion that we all want to be happy, but often spend our lives doing the very things that are going to make us unhappy. Rod discusses how our modern minds always ensure that even if we manage to be happy for a while, we make sure that it doesn't last long.

Sogyal Rinpoche points out that, even though we spend a lot of time chasing happiness, we somehow have much more capacity to be miserable. It's almost as if we cannot tolerate too much happiness, even though we think that's what we want. Also, we often don't even recognise happiness when it comes along because of our expectations or because we thought it would arrive in a different way. Even when we are happy, usually we are always thinking about or moving on to the next achievement, grasping, clinging and hoping, only to be disappointed again. This is a point particularly relevant to Rod's comments on how strange it must have been for Tibetan teachers to encounter the Western neurotic mind and to make the ancient teachings relevant to this modern world of ours.

Rod's story

I guess that from the age of about thirteen I had always had a strong interest in the East. My great-grandfather and grandfather had been involved in importing tea into Australia and they had travelled extensively in that part of the world. I was more interested in the spiritual side of things though. I was drawn to Eastern martial arts, and read a lot on Zen and started doing yoga in my teens. Interestingly enough, I had never really looked at Buddhism as a spiritual direction and had actually pushed it away a little bit — I thought that maybe it was a bit too disciplined — feeling more comfortable with Hinduism. After I read *Autobiography of a Yogi*, all I wanted to do was run off to the Himalayas and become a yogi.

When I was twenty-three, a friend of mine went to help at the Chenrezig Institute in Queensland [the first Tibetan monastery to be established in Australia]. He kept sending me letters saying that it was the most wonderful place and that I should visit. We had actually looked at many different spiritual paths together and he kept urging me to have a look at the Tibetan path. I had a very strong feeling that this was right for him, but I wasn't interested. As it turned out, I was travelling in Queensland in early 1976 and by sheer chance ended up walking through the gates to Chenrezig Institute. I immediately had this extraordinary feeling that I had come home. It was quite overwhelming.

At that time Lama Yeshe and Lama Zopa had just left the Institute and Geshe Loden and his translator Zazep Tulku Rinpoche had not yet arrived, so there were no lamas to connect with but there was still this strong sense of coming home. Later that year I heard that Geshe Loden had arrived at Chenrezig Institute. For some reason, without even meeting this lama, I felt a connection to him — connection in the sense that 'maybe this person is going to be a teacher of mine'. Again this sounds surprising but is not unusual. Yet I really had no basis to think this, it was just a feeling.

A spiritual student

I had to wait until the end of the year until Geshe Loden arrived in Sydney. I can remember the sense of awe, expectation and excitement when I was going to meet him. I thought that this teacher might also recognise me as his student. Now I realise this was extremely arrogant but I was only twenty-three. I'd been looking for a spiritual teacher and I can remember the day very clearly when Geshe Loden walked down the stairs of the house he was staying in. I pushed my way gently to the front of the crowd. When he got to the bottom, I thrust out my hand, being the first one to greet him, thinking he would recognise a spiritual student.

The most surprising thing happened. He took my hand and dropped it like a piece of rotten fruit and turned his back on me. I had this extraordinary instantaneous feeling of 'I want this person to be my teacher' because he immediately saw through the game of spiritual materialism I was playing. I guess, at the bottom of my mind, I was thinking that I was special and might get chosen as a disciple. He just seemed, in one motion, to say 'let it go'. My ego was squashed but I didn't feel at all rejected. It was a wonderful revelation and I had a really strong instant connection with him. I felt elated that he had been able to see through my egotistical grasping. I've gone over this many times since and, because of the spontaneity, it showed me the wisdom of a teacher being able to cut through and give me a teaching the instant I met him.

Becoming Buddhist

In 1978 I again went to Chenrezig Institute to do a month's course with Geshe Loden. I remember being extremely nervous and frightened because I had never done a meditation course before. I felt very exposed and tense on the first day. I was sitting in the meditation hall and I remember seeing him walk in and sit down. Very quickly an absolute sense of peace descended over me, so much so, that after about an hour I was almost dropping off to sleep. I felt so relaxed, it made me realise how stressed I'd been. I looked forward every day to attending the teachings and being in Geshe Loden's presence. I knew within a very short time, my tension would drop away. I didn't really question it, I just knew that he was a link to me being relaxed.

Yet there was still a certain fear there. In a way I did see myself as a Buddhist, though I hadn't taken refuge, which is committing oneself to the path of Buddhist practice. I had an opportunity during that course to take refuge with Geshe Loden. I remember the day before, I decided it was such an important decision, that I had to review my whole understanding of Christianity, which I had been brought up in. I went through a very big day of self-analysis and at the end concluded that Buddhism was indeed now my path.

Being dissatisfied

I had always had a slight dissatisfaction all through my life even though I had a very good upbringing. My family were very stable and my parents were very loving and connected with each other and with my older brother and myself. I looked at Christianity at the age of twelve or thirteen and I didn't see it giving me the answers I was looking for. I always had this sense of searching because of a pervading insecurity and restlessness. Whatever I did, I always had a sense of agitation and dissatisfaction. Everything seemed to hold a promise of happiness, whether it was achieving the next grade in karate or mastering a yoga posture or maybe buying a new car or progressing in business. Society kept promising me satisfaction and yet when I'd consumed the next promise, so to speak, I would think, 'Well, what's next?' It never 'fixed it'. There was momentary elation in my successes but there was no ongoing feeling of happiness. When I started to practise Buddhism, I had a sense of 'I think it's going to be OK' and the sense of dissatisfaction lessened. Over the years my sense of happiness has definitely increased. This is very much due to the Buddhist teachings and the practice and my teacher.

I think maybe it's wise to entertain the possibility that someone else might have more wisdom than yourself. A spiritual path might be able to alleviate the dissatisfaction in your life. I think my first connection with my teacher was really a momentous experience for me, even though I probably didn't realise it so much at the time. I guess the point is that I had a slightly different concept of a teacher. I thought he or she patted you on the back and said, 'Good boy, you're very clever and it's very easy to progress on the spiritual path.' What I didn't realise was that a real spiritual teacher makes you let go of things that you shouldn't be holding on to anyway.

Flying through the sky

My early concept of devotion was that you became devoted and got magic gold dust sprinkled over your head. All of a sudden you became a powerfully enlightened being who was able to fly through the sky and perform miracles. This came out of some of the books I'd read in my teenage years. I really thought teachers did that; you show them some kind of faith and they give you presents. I was always interested in the mystical side of things, mystical in the sense of inner wisdom or understanding the way things are, how the universe works and whether there is a God or not. I had a feeling that a spiritual teacher could tell you all that, but also that they would bless you so that the journey would be very comfortable and very easy.

I remember reading one of the chapters of Geshe Loden's book *Path to Enlightenment*, where he talks about when difficulties arise. This stopped me in my tracks. I realised I had an underlying belief system that when you enter a spiritual path, everything is fine from then on. You don't have to worry about anything because you're saved. Here were these words 'when difficulties arise', not if. It goes on to say, 'When difficulties arise, one handles them in a way that doesn't cause the mind to be completely ruffled, agitated or negative.'

My wellbeing at heart

The practice of devotion to my teacher gave me a plan of how to deal with situations. When a situation arises there is a particular way of thinking about it. The key question is, 'What is my underlying motivation?' My teacher gave me a very clear definition that my motivation should be great love and compassion. I say the word 'should' because I'm human and certainly not an enlightened being. However, at least I know the direction I'm trying to head in.

As it's changed over the years, I've realised that devotion to my teacher can show me the way out of my muddled thinking. I have certainly consulted Geshe Loden on, not only things of a spiritual nature, but also emotional and business issues. I'm amazed and comforted by the fact that every single time over the twenty years that I've been with him, he has given me absolutely clear advice. It has worked every single time, if I've been clever enough to take it. So devotion is respecting and honouring the guide and knowing that he has my truest wellbeing at heart. Even though his answers have sometimes been surprising, he has always given them with a sense of compassion.

An outward practice

Over the years he's given me some unusual advice to carry out. One example of this was when I separated from my wife in 1981. I was going through quite an emotional time, feeling angry and frustrated. I thought the marriage was going to last forever and it didn't. His wisdom was extremely clear and compassionate, not just to myself but also to my wife. He told me that life was impermanent and that all relationships were impermanent and would, at some point, end. My relationship was now ending. Again, maybe I was a little naive. I had felt that, as Buddhists, somehow we were blessed for eternity and would stay together. I didn't believe we could have differences because we were on the same spiritual path.

So here was the big hiccup. I had gone through the teachings of non-attachment and certainly thought I had non-attachment, until my wife left me. Then I knew how strongly I was actually attached. All of a sudden I realised my practice had been an outward practice. Now I had to look at the face of disaster. I felt rather inadequate and I went to Geshe Loden for inspiration and clear advice. I went through many emotions and appreciated that he was available to listen to my problems and feelings at any time of the day or night, even though he was very busy.

He always showed the greatest patience, compassion and love for me, yet he didn't try to soften things up. He still faced me with reality. It was then time for me to go back home for Christmas and naturally I was rather nervous about the whole thing. I felt the marriage was over. Geshe Loden said to me before I left, 'Look after your wife for your whole life.' I asked, 'What about divorce?' He said, 'It doesn't matter, divorce or marriage doesn't matter, just look after your wife.' I was kind of shocked. Through being with him for three months and the great kindness he had shown me, I felt I had to agree and made a pledge to carry out his request. I thought it was really unusual and didn't actually know what he meant.

However, when I returned home, things were in disarray because my wife had also gone through a traumatic time. Despite my anger and worry, I realised that I had made a promise to my lama and I could not direct anger towards my ex-wife. So I had to let it go. It put me in a very difficult position because I kept feeling angry with her. I had promised him that I would not cause harm and I would look after my wife who was leaving me.

This created an extraordinary bond between my ex-wife and myself. We didn't damage each other and we actually acted out of compassion. To this day we are very, very good friends and are able to bring up our children in a way that is appropriate. Years later, I am still quite in awe of that decision he had helped me come to.

Caring and trust

Devotion for me is having a great love and respect for my teacher. Maybe in the Christian sense it is something like loving God. I'm lucky enough to have a teacher who is in human form. So I feel even luckier than those who have a mystical teacher who is not physically available. Devotion is the sense of being cared for, being looked after, but that doesn't mean abdication of responsibility. If anything, it often means more responsibility. As Director of the Tibetan Buddhist Society in Sydney, part of my outward practice of devotion is helping to run the centre. I think one of the best things we can do is to help others, so I try to do that. If one has a spiritual path, it helps develop some inner strength to be able to deal with difficulties.

When I was young I thought you grew up and had a nice life. Then when I came across divorce, death, dissatisfaction, losing my job, not getting what I wanted, getting what I didn't want, all these things were very confusing. Taking refuge gives a sense of protection, shelter and trust. It's not protection from these things happening, but the teachings give a method of working with them so that they don't damage you. You don't become hardened, angry, bitter or disappointed and depressed. Not that those fluctuations don't happen, but they're not an ongoing theme.

My teacher represents the pinnacle of Buddhist practice for me and he displays the qualities that I would like to have — purity, wisdom, compassion, clarity. The lineage in Tibetan Buddhism is particularly special because it means that my teacher had a wonderful teacher who had a wonderful teacher, and so on. Each teacher is answerable to a teacher. This keeps the lineage pure and clear and not so many misunderstandings or abuse of the teachings arise. In some other spiritual disciplines, you will find 'New Age gurus', so to speak, popping up and proclaiming themselves as gurus. I'm not denouncing them or patting them on the back, but sometimes you will find that some of their teachings are not in the best interests of their students. When that happens I have to ask, 'What are they doing it for, maybe for wealth, power or fame?'

Devotion is not naive, blind faith. You don't suddenly meet a teacher, give everything away and abdicate your responsibility. The best kind of faith is one that is coupled with wisdom. In other words, you have to digest the teachings and find out if they actually work on a practical level. Even though I had an instantaneous connection with Geshe Loden, it really developed over the next ten years until I saw him as my absolute refuge, or absolute guru. I was given lots of time to check on him constantly, so, in a sense, my devotion was based on my experience. Never at any time have I come across a lama who says, 'You have to join Buddhism.' You are given the opportunity to make your own choices and I think that's the wonderful freedom you have in this tradition.

Another common misunderstanding is to think that, when you become spiritual, you throw everything away, you no longer need money, clothing or whatever. However, we have to be part of the society we grow up in and therefore we do need money to survive. Having a hippy mentality of 'It'll be fine,' and letting the government provide for you is not part of the teachings. Geshe Loden insists we all remain members of the community and work.

Our neurotic mind

In the early days of Tibetan Buddhism in Australia, everyone decided they had to go slightly or completely Tibetan to become Buddhists. Meanwhile the lamas were saying, 'No, don't take up the Tibetan culture, you have Western culture.' Over the years I think that the Buddha Dharma in Australia has matured. It's the way we act as human beings, not the cultural background, that is important. Down the track being a Tibetophile is not necessarily being a Buddhist. Bringing Buddhism to the West is a way of helping our modern neurotic mind. I think probably the Tibetan lamas were surprised that the modern mind was so up and down. For a lot of us, one minute we're happy, then we're sad or depressed, and then maybe we want a new television set because the old one isn't good enough, or maybe we need a new car or a new relationship. Nothing really makes us happy for long.

I still see this dissatisfaction within many people and Buddhism is saying, 'Let go of all this grasping.' That doesn't mean get rid of everything; it's to do with your attitude to the material object. It's not to do with whether you have a big or little house, and I'm sure you can be sitting in a cave and be just as attached to your stone seat. Or you can be living in a mansion and not be attached to the things around you. Buddhism is about changing your attitude, your perspective, so it not only makes your life happier but also benefits others.

If we are less agitated and become more peaceful, we are naturally going to benefit others around us. A simple, everyday example of this happened to me recently, when I was driving on a freeway. Someone decided to change lanes and I was in his blind spot. We were going quite fast and I saw him and blew my horn and he wobbled back into his lane. I guess my normal reaction is to be annoyed and angry that this guy was trying to run me off the road. However, I decided right at that moment, that the man didn't really want to die or even kill me. He just made a mistake. Then I thought about how many mistakes I had made on the road and got away with. Instead of driving up beside him and shaking my fist angrily at him, I let the situation go. A kilometre further on, we pulled up alongside each other at some lights. I just looked across and he turned his head and waved his hand and said thank you. I realised that from my one act of non-aggression came an act of connection with another human being. Shantideva, a great Buddhist scholar, said:

> Why be unhappy about something
> if it can be remedied?
> And what is the use of being unhappy about something
> if it cannot be remedied?[2]

Tireless openness

One of the things that has always impressed me about all the lamas I've met is this inexhaustible quality of giving. I was involved with the visit of His Holiness the Dalai Lama to Australia in 1996 as the Security Coordinator for Sydney. I had a team of eighty people working twenty-four hours a day in eight-hour shifts. I observed that His Holiness and the monks around him didn't go on shifts. They seemed to be working all the time, though they did go for some sleep in the night. I was sometimes there at 5 a.m. and they would arrive completely fresh and happy, greeting everyone, with no early morning grumpiness. There was this tireless openness that went on all day and into the evening.

Then I heard that people were getting worn out and couldn't keep up with the Dalai Lama, yet we were all young and His Holiness was in his sixties. He was happy to give interviews, talk to everyone and always seemed to have time. The load on him was just extraordinary, but he never wavered. Everyone was in awe of it, this endless energy and happiness all the time.

Undeniable perseverance and energy is an inspiration to all the students. I feel very much that lamas teach and lead by example. We are inspired to work even harder. However, it's not like being a workaholic. The motivation is completely different. It's not about getting the job finished, or getting over the next hurdle or working to make ourselves feel better. No one's told people in the West that it's a circular track. The grasping at getting the job done, over and over, is for me a fabrication of Western greed. The perseverance of practising a spiritual discipline is different in that it's working towards a happy, peaceful, generous, loving and compassionate life for everyone.

Finding the time

I think you actually develop from having problems and recognising difficulties in your own mind. You develop an ability to let go and not worry. I've had a long connection with my teacher and, from the beginning, there has never been any pressure to become 'the devoted disciple'. There has always been complete openness in my choice and so the relationship has deepened between us over the years. Through that deepening there has come a greater acceptance of teachings that he's given me.

Sometimes at the Society, I have to do something that requires greater effort from me than I originally realised. Now I don't see it as a difficulty and, if someone asks me to do something and I don't have the time, then I just make the time.

I remember years ago when Geshe Loden first asked me to teach once a week, I thought, 'Oh, I work every evening, where am I going to find the time?' Then what immediately popped into my head was, 'If my teacher is asking me, then the time will appear.' And it did, and I didn't lose any income and I started spending more time at the Society. Through some of those experiences, I've realised that letting go of your perceived resistance to things is the best solution. The nature of having a teacher means that you have to work through some of your resistances. The attitude that I have is one of ultimate trust, rather than a developing trust that I had closer to the beginning.

Sometimes ordinary life somehow seems more attractive to me, in that there's a television to switch on or a movie to go to. In a sense, that's always been a struggle for me. So one of my joys is to go on retreat where I'm not so distracted. I live a busy life and sometimes that overtakes my meditation. It doesn't mean I can't go to a movie or enjoy these things, but there are times when I need to focus more on meditation. The temporal benefits are that when I do, my mind feels calmer, I feel more centred and I'm actually happier. I don't necessarily get that from a movie.

The quest

There is a saying, 'You don't choose a teacher, the teacher chooses you,' and I think you just have to relax into that. You have to diligently search for your spiritual path if that's what you want to do, and you should check all religions. Go and visit teachers of all denominations and faiths and lineages that you are drawn to, follow the direction that feels right and then listen to teachings and see if a connection is developing. Then wait for a number of years and gradually see how that develops. It may not develop in the way that you want it to, so therefore you have to be open to looking at things a bit differently.

I know in Tibetan Buddhism that some people have started off with one teacher who they greatly respect, but have actually found their true guru in somebody else. I think one needs time and patience, but one also needs to search. By saying that a teacher chooses you, you can't just sit there and do nothing. You have to start walking in a direction towards teachings and see what comes out of that and have faith that your teacher will appear.

Very early in my spiritual quest I did have a feeling that there was someone there for me. It wasn't terribly conscious but my quest was to find a teacher. Finally I came across one and it wasn't one I expected. For me, that was the end of that particular spiritual quest but the start of another journey of being on the path. The most amazing thing that has happened to me, I guess, was becoming a Buddhist because I finally felt that my spiritual quest had finished. In fact, it had only just begun. Just looking for the teacher or at the path isn't actually walking on it. Meeting my teacher and becoming a Buddhist has been the basis of my life and it has allowed me to experience many things that I don't think I would have done in an 'ordinary' life. It has been unexpected and extraordinary and, in a way, my early notion of flying in the sky could be one description of walking on the path.

*A shooting star falls in the night sky,
reminding me of past hopes and dreams.
Undistracted I wish for solitude,
but the world calls to me in all its guises.
Teach and transform me and all those like me
who are mesmerised by mystery and magic,
So we may believe in the truth of the teachings
with unfailing conviction.*

SUBLIME TRUST

BEN OF KONGPO

Ben of Kongpo had tremendous childlike faith and total trust. On visiting a beautiful and holy statue of Jowo Rinpoche, the young Buddha, in Lhasa, he treated the statue as if it were, in fact, a person. He ate the cakes dipped in butter, which were, of course, offerings that were not to be touched. He thought these were the cakes that Jowo Rinpoche ate and he should do as Jowo Rinpoche did. He talked to the statue, asking the Buddha to look after his boots, as it is traditional to remove your shoes on entering a temple. He then invited him back to his house and the statue agreed to come and visit. The statue also stopped the furious caretaker from removing Ben's dirty boots from the altar.

The next year Ben's wife told him that she had seen something in the river. Ben, seeing the statue floating down the river, thought that Jowo Rinpoche was drowning and leapt into the water to carry him out. Returning to Ben's house, Jowo Rinpoche said, 'I cannot come into the house,' and dissolved into the rock. The form of the Buddha can still be seen in that rock and the river to this day, and both are places of healing.[1]

Pam Croci was born in New Zealand in 1951 and has two sons, Alexander who is nineteen and Cielo who is three. She lives in the Blue Mountains just outside of Sydney, with her partner Hugo, whom she met ten years ago through the Dharma. Having Cielo, which means 'sky' in Spanish, has been a major life-changing event for her in the last few years. Pam comments on how having a child again has shifted her whole perspective. Being with a child has helped her to steady and focus her mind, to stay more open and in the present moment. The child becomes the meditation, is the meditation. It is no accident that her son is called Sky, as this image is prevalent in talking about the ultimate state of mind that a practitioner can reach, 'the sky like nature of mind', to represent spaciousness, clarity, purity and wisdom.

Her varied career has included medical work, ceramics and interior design. She is, in fact, a highly talented interior decorator, though her modesty keeps her out of the limelight. She presents as a very down-to-earth mother, an unpretentious person who has always worked at 'whatever comes up'. 'My life could consist of one day working at a canteen and serving sandwiches to five hundred students and then leaving at midday to

PAMELA CROCI

buy some interior detail for one of the wealthiest pop stars in the world,' she says. 'I experience all this the same — the same level of enjoyment, same level of frustration. I have never had that sense, which I'm sure some people have, of being born to do something, a career. My mother always said I was born to be a lady and not required, meaning that I am happy to take it easy. The ego, though, doesn't always allow this.'

I have known Pam for many years and have experienced her caring and almost motherly ways within the community, long before Cielo was born. Often the sitting meditation practice would be held at her and Hugo's flat in Sydney and they would always create a warm and welcoming place for people to come and meditate after a hard day's work. I spoke with Pam just before Christmas and the atmosphere was peaceful, loving and cosy. After dinner, Hugo read a storybook of Tibetan tales to Cielo so we could talk undisturbed, but occasionally the young boy would wander in, looking sleepy and alert all at the same time, and bury his head in her lap for a while. It felt like being transported back to childhood, full of anticipation and excitement, but hardly able to stay awake. I felt, just by being there, I was being given a gift of experiencing the joy of family life with them in a simple and caring way. There was none of the fuss, tension or arguing that often surrounds families. Just a calm, peaceful and loving feeling.

Pam admitted that, since being asked to tell her story, it had set in motion quite a process for her, as she had deeply examined her relationship with her teacher and what it meant to her. She makes it very clear that it is important not to get caught up with the teacher, but to follow the teachings. Sometimes we have unresolved issues with power, authority figures, ambitions, hopes for love, and fear of rejection. All this 'baggage' that we carry around with us, often unconsciously, makes us project onto the teacher. We expect so much that we completely miss the point. However, if we listen and learn, and test out and use what we hear, then we see the results very quickly, rather than getting bogged down in our own neuroses.

In fact, the Buddha himself advised not to get caught up, in what is known as 'The Four Reliances':

**Rely on the message of the teacher, not on his personality;
Rely on the meaning, not just on the words;
Rely on the real meaning, not on the provisional one.
Rely on your wisdom mind, not on your ordinary judgmental mind.**

Pam also realised that she has developed incredible trust not only in Rinpoche but in herself. Of course, it is impossible to deeply trust others if we don't have that in ourselves. However, it clearly illustrates the point that the relationship with the teacher is actually about the relationship with ourselves. That relationship helps us become more authentic, more of who we really are. The external teacher merely mirrors or reflects what is there. Sogyal Rinpoche often uses this example. We know what our face looks like when we look in the mirror, but we have never actually seen it directly. The teacher introduces us directly to who we really are. So the outer teacher is the reflection of our inner teacher. The teacher embodies the teaching.

> **Our buddha nature, then, has an active aspect, which is our 'inner teacher' ...The inner teacher, who has been with us always, manifests in the form of the 'outer teacher', whom almost as if by magic, we actually encounter... At the deepest and highest level, the master and the disciple are not and cannot ever be in any way separate; ...The outer teacher introduces you directly to the truth of your inner teacher. The more it is revealed through his or her inspiration, the more you begin to realise that outer and inner teacher are indivisible.** [2]

Pam spent many weeks contemplating her contribution to the book, not rushing but being ready in her own time. She always says Rinpoche never gives people more than they can handle, even if things appear difficult. This is part of her total trust. Her story is told precisely and exactly, with no extraneous words. It is like she has pared herself down to the bare essentials with, as she says, little fabrication.

Pam is a person who demonstrates the possibility of how to combine the demands of bringing up a small child, working in a creative, dynamic way and incorporating the Dharma into day-to-day life, staying grounded, sensible and caring. The trust that she has in her teacher is merely a reflection of the trust and confidence that she has developed over time in herself.

Pamela's story

One of the most joyful events in my life was the arrival of our son Cielo. Taking care of him has been a deep and enriching experience and a most transforming practice. To be with a child is indeed a form of practice, a mind training. You have to remain focused and open as this little being develops, with all the moment-to-moment changes. The impermanent nature brings with it the opportunity to keep an ever-flexible attitude. Any expectation is a waste of time and energy. Of course I am no angel. At times, I am not as patient as I would like to be but then I've learnt not to give myself a hard time. Best just to recognise where my mind is and try to do something about it. There is balance between keeping everything organic and also keeping an awareness of the outcome of my actions, the interdependence and the responsibility.

Through the blessing of my teachers and the practice of meditation, I am developing an unshakable confidence and trust in my path. Directly connected to this is that my link with the teachings and my teacher has deepened. Slowly I am allowing myself to let go and just let things be. One day may the responsibility that I mentioned occur unfabricated and my mind become more and more flexible. This is paramount to the process of caring for children and anyone else for that matter. I don't think I would have experienced motherhood to the degree I have if Dzongsar Khyentse Rinpoche had not advised me to concentrate on Cielo and to dedicate this to the benefit of all. However, I must admit that my first reaction to this instruction was of all my old unworthy thoughts rising up, thinking, 'Oh hell, he is turning me away.' However, the reverse has been the outcome and it has been great.

An expression of freedom

I see Dzongsar Khyentse Rinpoche as my present teacher. However, in the past I have had the good fortune of meeting and receiving teachings from other great lamas. To me the most precious is His Holiness the Gyalwang Drukpa. I first met His Holiness in Ladakh at Chemry Monastery, sitting with about three hundred Ladakhis and two other Westerners chanting 'Om mani padme hung' for several days — a Mani prayer [the mantra of compassion]. It was quite an introduction, especially as it had only been a month or so earlier that an old friend and student of His Holiness had given me my first Dharma book to read, *Magic Dance* by Thinley Norbu Rinpoche. I was also given teachings such as 'Heart Advice in a Nutshell' by Jamyang Khyentse Chökyi Lodro and 'Oral Instructions for Mountain Retreat' by Dudjom Rinpoche.

There I was, sitting in the dirt, chanting the mantra, thinking, 'How did I get here?' and at the same time trusting the situation implicitly. You don't ever forget that initial ripening time — so unique — it has a secret quality. I took refuge at the time and I know that the Dharma name that His Holiness gave me has guided me to where I am now — such kindness; so precious. The strength of trust that I have had from the very beginning, I guess, comes from my previous mind connection with certain teachings. I do know that the transformation that I experienced when I met His Holiness meant that I felt the validity of the method he transmitted immediately. The connection with His Holiness turned me away from a fairly hedonistic lifestyle. At the time I met him, I was endeavouring to set up a pottery factory in the Philippines. My motivation was questionable. Needless to say that was a financial disaster. Some of us need a good kick to get us started.

When I left Ladakh I travelled overland to Delhi. I remember walking through the streets of India and everyone's eyes sparkled like diamonds and I felt such joy. Previously I had often felt so separate because my judgmental mind was always present. I don't think I was even aware of how much I labelled and criticised. Thank goodness for impermanence. I began to realise that everything is connected to my own state of mind and that every moment could be an expression of freedom.

The hook of compassion

I first met Dzongsar Khyentse Rinpoche in 1989 at Vajradhara Gompa. Hugo said, 'Come and meet Rinpoche,' and I thought, 'Oh well, here we go.' I can still remember clearly the feeling, that of a wind rising, like a warrior going into battle. There was nothing earth moving about the first meeting, but then somewhere between that meeting and Rinpoche leaving Australia I knew I loved him. I was hooked.

I have had a teacher–student relationship with Rinpoche now for ten years and it has been through all sorts of manifestations. Believe me, not always very elegant from my side. However, I know that he knows me very well. I can never fool him. He gives me an undiluted experience of my neurotic mind. Once again, thank goodness for impermanence. I'm reminded of a line a dear friend once wrote to me, 'It is not all molten lava.' Gradually my mind is returning to a state of equilibrium as I endeavour to put my interpretation of the teachings into practice. I do this through meditation methods, contemplation and action. Of course I slip up, but I have learnt to just recognise it and keep going. I accept that this journey will have its unstable moments and continue to have enthusiasm for the process even when it can be very confronting. Ah, to strip away all the fabrications. Yes please.

I try to keep a freshness to each moment and within this freshness is a relationship that is developing in a very organic way. Again, within this is an openness. There is a trust, a sublime trust, and this to me is devotion.

Postscript

It is several months since I gave this interview and, while essentially I am what I said, something has deepened. It is an intense awareness of the preciousness of the teachings and guidance I have received from Rinpoche and the need to preserve and honour the lineage of all teachings. The rest is silence.

The wind ruffles the surface of the lake,
like thoughts agitating the peace in my mind.
Authenticity is the path to genuineness,
but the current of naturalness lays deep below.
Teach and transform me and all those like me
to become childlike in our being,
So we may be present and celebrate in the uncontrived
ease of each moment.

JUST TRY

THE TENT MAKER

A girl went on a journey with her merchant father, hoping to find a husband, and was shipwrecked. Her father was dead and she was found by a family of clothmakers who adopted her and taught her their trade. She overcame her sadness and settled into her new life. Then, one day, slave traders kidnapped her and she was sold to a man who built masts for boats. Once again overcoming her misfortune, she worked so hard that he freed her and sent her on business. Again she was shipwrecked. Now she cried bitterly, thinking, 'Whatever I do, nothing works out in the way I expect it. Why am I so unfortunate and have to suffer so?'. She received no answer and no one came to help her, so she started to walk towards the town.

In this land there was a legend that a stranger would arrive and be able to make a tent for the emperor, as no one in that country had the skills to do so. When she arrived, she couldn't understand the language, but people told her through an interpreter that she had to see the emperor. She realised that, through her life experiences as a spinner, clothmaker and mast builder, and remembering all the different tents she had seen on her journey, she had all the skills to make him a tent, and proceeded to do so. She was richly rewarded and lived happily ever after, with everything she desired. She realised that what appeared to be such difficulties at the time had, in fact, contributed to ensuring her ultimate happiness.[1]

Mauro de March was born in Italy and has lived and worked in India since 1989. After a number of years running a small business (which he says he's still waiting to become successful), he became Sogyal Rinpoche's and Rigpa's representative there. He also developed a strong connection with Dzogchen Rinpoche, who is the joint director of Rigpa and Dzogchen Monastery in the south of India.

I first met Mauro in 1997 when I was on retreat at Lerab Ling in France. Actually I didn't really meet him, in fact I didn't speak to him at all. I was very aware of him though, as he was often helping Rinpoche. So were other people, but there was something about Mauro that caught me. He seemed so sweet, like flowing nectar, and I felt a strong immediate connection to him.

MAURO DE MARCH

Mauro's name came up a number of times the following year and in 1999 he came to Australia for the January retreat, where I interviewed him. There was this incredible feeling about him, like I had known him forever. He also couldn't believe that we hadn't met before or even spoken. One afternoon, after he had had a massage and acupuncture treatment and before he was due to cook dinner for Dzogchen Rinpoche, we sat crosslegged on the bed in a hot little cabin at Myall Lakes, on the north coast of New South Wales. Cars raced past on the road and there were the occasional bursts of loud rock music blaring out from holidaymakers. I realised then that I, in fact, didn't know this person at all. Yet my initial feeling of his sweetness persisted, and his simple and uncomplicated way of speaking about his devotion to Rinpoche and the teachings opened my heart more and more.

As his story unfolded, my admiration grew. He seemed not so much to dismiss or downplay the difficulties he had encountered, but was really quite unaware, in a way, that they were difficulties. He talked about having gone to live in England, attending the teachings for a few years without understanding any English and working incredibly hard for days and nights to set up shrines, only to dismantle them. Then he went to live in India, with no money, living in really basic conditions, sleeping on a straw bed, with no electricity or water. Throughout all this, his trust in Rinpoche was unshakable and, as he himself says, he never doubted, not for a moment.

When he talked about his regret at not meeting Dudjom Rinpoche while he was alive, it brought a sharp memory to me, of having a similar regret at never meeting His Holiness Dilgo Khyentse. Like Mauro had with Dudjom Rinpoche, I had sat with His Holiness's body in Nepal, also deeply sad that I had not had the good connection to realise who he was and make an effort to meet him while he was still alive. We do sometimes realise a little too late. Can we really change or are we just destined to repeat the same patterns?

Sogyal Rinpoche says that we can attend teachings and meditate for years, but it often doesn't touch or change our basic being. The whole point of meditating is that it can change our fundamental attitude and that we should not keep our meditation and our daily lives separate. It can change who we are, so that we do realise before it is too late, before we or others die. We seem to stubbornly persist in our habitual patterns, despite intending to change. After a while we can also become what he calls 'Dharma stubborn' or

'Dharma immune'. We think that we have heard the teachings before and don't let anything in. We have to complete all the teachings, rather like taking a course of antibiotics, finishing the whole cycle. Otherwise we build up a resistance. Because we think we know better and don't have the humility to know our own ignorance, we close ourselves off and the ego becomes even stronger. We become frightened to be open and vulnerable, and to take risks to trust and learn new ways of being.

At all stages, Rinpoche reminds us how we have been conditioned by samsara for years and years, and therefore how easy it is to forget the teachings. He says, over and over, 'Remember to remember.' We have a tendency to forget, just at the very time we need to be remembering. The way Mauro talked about his experience made me want to cry, because it brought home to me how much we forget. Only when we lose someone, through death for example, do we realise what we missed. We often don't recognise what we have until it has gone.

When Mauro talks about daring to let go and be a fool for a while and simply have the experience of doing what Rinpoche asks, even just once, he touches on one of the key points of resistance and fear that we have as Westerners. We are so afraid to just give in, even once, and do what the guru asks of us. We think that it means that we have fallen under this person's control and that we will somehow lose our freedom and independence, our free will and therefore our money, partners and family and become part of a cult. It's amazing how our minds will conjure up the worst possible scenarios, even if Rinpoche is just asking us to undertake a simple task in a particular way. However, Mauro shows that the paradox is that, in letting go of our own fixed and rigid ideas, opinions and belief systems of a reality that many of us don't really question, but which has been indoctrinated into us by societal norms, we find the real freedom. We find the space and ease and comfort of becoming who we really are, not a mindless vegetable following the dictates of a demanding and rigid teacher, but becoming more and more authentic, real and present in the moment to deal with whatever is happening.

As well as his sweetness and softness, like his teacher, Mauro also demonstrates that he can be extremely powerful when the occasion calls for it. His experience of working closely with Rinpoche and other lamas over the years has honed his awareness and skills so that he can help other students effectively. He explains clearly the usefulness of Rinpoche teaching in a wrathful manner, cutting through directly to the heart of the matter, and he also embodies that quality himself. His ability to let go of himself and encourage all of us to take a risk and just make the attempt to try, is his gift to us.

Mauro's story

I was born in Italy in a small village called Borsai in the Dolomite Mountains and I grew up in a poor family living a simple life. Ever since I was young I wanted to be useful to others. I grew up as a Christian and went to church regularly and used to teach catechism and served at mass until I was about fourteen or fifteen. After compulsory army service in Italy, I felt dissatisfied with my life and, in fact, had always had an inner searching. So I travelled for a couple of years in the East when I was twenty-one, hitchhiking from Italy to Pakistan to Nepal and India.

I was on a search but I didn't really know what I was looking for. I used to blame my family, the government, politics, the church, and always thought that my unhappiness was caused by these external factors. Something incredible happened on that first trip that really showed me something. I travelled for a while with a friend and when we had problems I used to blame him. Then I travelled on my own and noticed I still had problems, and I had no one to blame any more. I thought that everything was fine with me, but was unhappy because of others. I slowly had to realise that it was to do with me. I wasn't in Italy or with my family or my friend. It was quite painful, but somehow the finger turned from pointing to the outside to inside. That was a great discovery, shifting to realise that what we have to work with is not so much what is out there, but is very much within ourselves.

Treasuring life

After a second trip to India, in my hippy days, I returned to Italy very sick and was diagnosed with bad hepatitis. I had a long month's journey by bus from Katmandu to Venice and was taken to hospital. The doctor was very worried because my liver was in very bad condition. I had actually always been very interested in medicinal plants and was quite health conscious. I started to study about liver disease and how it could develop into sclerosis. The liver either becomes hard like a stone or it disintegrates and you just shit it out. When you have hepatitis, your excrement is light yellow but in my case it also had pieces of purple tissue in it. I thought, 'Oh, this is the end, I'm going to die.' I really went through a lot of fear and bargaining and 'Why me?' and 'If it doesn't happen, I will be good.' I'm sure everyone facing death goes through all this.

The curious thing is that after a few days I came to terms with it. I realised that being young or old doesn't really mean anything. If it's my turn, then I'll die. From then on I stopped worrying about the past and the future. I remembered everything that I was doing, like having a cup of tea and looking out at the garden, or hearing a bird sing, or someone talking. Everything became so meaningful and I was enjoying each moment. I thought, 'There is not going to be a future. I'm going to die soon and it will be finished.'

A few days after, I found out that I was not dying, not yet at least, and the purple in the middle of yellow excrement was the skin of dried plums that I used to eat every day. Looking back it's quite funny, but at the time it really changed me. (One's life can change by the peel of a plum.) I left hospital and went to live up in the mountains alone for a year. I didn't know anything about Buddhism or meditation, but I used to sit in the morning for a couple of hours, waiting for the sun to rise, the same in the evening at sunset. I lived a very simple life, with no electricity. I cooked on a wooden stove, eating only vegetables and grains. The things that I thought were so important in life were not actually so vital anymore. I treasured the fact that I was alive and realised then the preciousness of life. The winter came and the little money I had to buy food finished, so I decided to work at a ski resort for a couple of months.

I found that the equanimity and openness and clarity that I had gained in the mountains disappeared. Soon after the winter season finished, I returned to the mountains and I tried to bring back that feeling of wellbeing and freedom, the feeling of love for everything and everyone. I tried so hard but I couldn't get it back. I remember I cried so much trying to bring this feeling back. Then one day a friend visited me and said that there was a Tibetan lama who was teaching a one-week seminar not far from Venice and invited me to go. At that point I had no idea what a Tibetan lama could have been, and I was not so keen to leave the mountain. However, I decided to go for a couple of days and I met Sogyal Rinpoche. This was in 1981. Rinpoche was very slim then. Wearing a black Japanese kimono and white trousers, he played football with us. My friend left after a couple of days and I stayed for the whole week.

It was so amazing. Here was this person telling me exactly how to reconnect with all the experiences in my life up to that point, like my ambition as a child to be of help, my inner searching and my experiences on the mountain; how to bring back, through meditation, that feeling of wellbeing and openness. In the mountains during those years I used to do a lot of things, without knowing what I was doing, that gave the mind that space of meditation — sky practices [looking at the sky], enjoying the simplicity of nature, watching the sun rise and set. Then I naturally entered the state of 'meditation'.

Later, when I began to receive Dzogchen teachings, I realised what it was. I had lost that sense of wellbeing, and was trying to get it back, but couldn't. In the mountains I wasn't trying but it just happened. So Rinpoche was showing me a path, a technique, a teaching that I could follow and develop to contact that basic nature, that Buddha nature.

It reminds me of the story of the Buddha meditating in the forest. The monkeys imitated the Buddha and, just by imitating, they obtained enlightenment. So, I thought to myself, 'Wow, this is it,' and even then I knew that I was going to go to England. Going to live in a big city was something that I would previously never have considered, as I love the mountains and nature. My father died during this period and this was an even bigger teaching for me, as it brought back even stronger the reality and truth of death. The longing to follow the path of the Buddhas grew and grew.

In those days I couldn't speak a word of English and we would have a translator during the retreats. I told Rinpoche, 'I'm going to come to London,' and he said, 'you know, it's a big tough city and it won't be easy for you.' However, my mind was made up, as the questions that I had asked for so many years were being answered by Rinpoche. I hadn't been aware before this that there was a path, but now he was guiding me, showing me a way, I wasn't going to let it go.

I was penniless and spent a few months earning some money. In that period I received teachings from Lama Zopa and Namkhai Norbu [another Tibetan Rinpoche], who taught in Italian. He is a wonderful teacher, so I couldn't understand why I wanted to go to Sogyal Rinpoche. Of course, I understand now, but it's something that is hard to explain. It would have been much easier to follow a teacher who could speak your own language and who was renowned and knowledgable. Still, I had this longing to follow Sogyal Rinpoche. There was a very strong bond with him from the first time I met him, or I guess I would call it karma. Namkhai Norbu was teaching the highest Dzogchen teachings, yet still I couldn't be persuaded to stay.

Just being there

In early spring, Sogyal Rinpoche came to Italy and taught in a place near Lake Como. Then I left Italy, still with long hair and long beard, with my rucksack half full of medicinal herbs that I picked up in the mountains, and went to my first Easter retreat in a place called Winehall in England. So I received teachings for the next few years, usually without understanding a word of English, sitting there with trust and faith and love, but not understanding anything. For a while it didn't matter because I had such strong personal, inner experiences, just sitting in the same room with Rinpoche.

He has such a presence. It is not out there, but within yourself, you have to work with. This being has the lineage of holding these incredible teachings and, by following, you can slowly receive the wisdom and bring yourself out of all the suffering. So it didn't matter much if, for a while, I couldn't understand the words. Just sitting there, watching my own mind, the thinking mind fell away and I found this incredible space. Just being with him I experienced an openness, relaxation and wellbeing.

I did a lot of prostrations, Ngöndro practice, and earned my living by working in an Italian restaurant. After three years or so, though, I began to realise that it was important to understand the teachings, not just be there, but my English still was not good enough and I lost heart. I began to wonder what the chanting and prostrations had to do with me. Rinpoche talked about anger, frustration, attachment and jealously, but I didn't think I had any of those things. Somehow I just fell out of the whole thing for two years. I stopped going to the Rigpa Centre and just worked, swimming deeply in samsara. Then I had all sorts of ups and downs, anger, jealousy and fear. I think though that the main difficulty was that I couldn't understand the teachings, or find the right way to integrate, and I couldn't ask questions or clarify anything. However, even then I never doubted the teachings or the teacher; it was more that I had to sort something out in myself.

Then I met Sogyal Rinpoche again, on an occasion with His Holiness the Dalai Lama teaching in London, and he was just so warm towards me. I realised that it was time for me to go back. I realised that I had a lot of anger and suffering and jealousy and I needed to find out more about that. I remember I had a little tree, made of stone and golden wire and I gave it to Rinpoche and he still keeps it on his shrine. When I saw him at the Rigpa Centre in London, he just gave me this big hug and wouldn't let go. I felt that I was at home again. Slowly I got involved, helping with Ngöndro courses and attending all the retreats.

Losing the opportunity

My biggest regret during those two years of not being involved was that His Holiness Dudjom Rinpoche passed away. I remember I travelled to the Dordogne with two other students. We went inside where His Holiness's body was and I felt so sad and so empty. I had so many prayers I wanted to do there, but when I entered the room my mind became blank. I felt that I had lost such an incredible opportunity not to have met such a being as him. I walked through the fields and I was just crying. Then something quite incredible happened. I had this huge vision of Dudjom Rinpoche in the sky and I had this feeling and certainty that I was meeting him. It didn't seem to matter any more that I hadn't met him in the flesh. With Rinpoche we used to practise 'calling the lama from afar', which is still the most inspiring practice for me. I am a lazy practitioner, if I can even call myself a practitioner. But this prayer comes to my mind so many times in a day, by itself. It doesn't matter where I am, and just by reciting this it brings the view of spaciousness back in an instant. That experience swept away all my grief and I felt I had met him.

The transforming process

I was getting closer to Sogyal Rinpoche and he was always very kind and caring to me, sometimes in a very wrathful way too, but I perceived his wrathfulness as a way for him to teach me more strongly. I started helping with the shrine and at every retreat we would transform any place into a most amazing and inspiring shrine room, once even out of a horse stable near the Pyrenees. There were three of us who would build up these shrines. We would spend days and nights without sleeping to make up these shrines and then we would take everything down. It was a practice in itself. It's like when we talk about impermanence or visualisation and dissolution. We put in so much hard work and it took so long and then in a few hours everything was gone. It was some process for the mind itself in that it gave you a taste of reality, this change, this impermanence.

It's like a little taste of life. We struggle so much to achieve something and we think it is permanent and yet we have so much fear of losing it. We always try to build something up to have and to hold. Life itself though is not like this. Impermanence — it's not a choice, it's what is. Whatever Rinpoche does I never question, in that I never doubt, I always perceive it as teachings. I've always had this incredible trust and I think this is a strength of mine. People often say, after practising even for some time, that they don't see changes. It's not true though, because there are subtle changes, which alter your life completely. If we look back a few years we know something has changed.

When I go back to my village and see my friends, I realise how fortunate I have been to have had such an incredible opportunity being with Rinpoche. They have so much suffering and questions and bitterness, especially when they encounter difficulties. For me now, even when things are painful, it doesn't matter that much. I know that after a little while, I'll be fine. It doesn't worry me so much. Discovering this incredible treasure that he's given me, of knowing I can make a choice, I just don't question. We usually question everything, but I just trust and I see that it works. There is always a reason, even if I don't know it. By Rinpoche working with me, even if he is scolding me, I realise that just having the attitude of being open and flexible, not being stiff or right, and just giving up all my resistances, changes everything.

Daring to try

I have seen through the years how Rinpoche skilfully trains people. I know that where I put the resistance is where I get stuck. When we have this strong idea of the 'I' who knows it all, Rinpoche points out where we lack. I don't become a slave, I actually become more free. I think that if we use our reasoning mind, we can't get it, because we are too clever. How are we actually reasoning? Through our ego. So we will always find reasons that we shouldn't do this or that when he asks us to do things. I would say just be a fool for a while and try. Just say, 'I'm going to give up one time and do what Rinpoche asks.' Then just by letting your attitude go it doesn't really matter. Then you will have the experience of understanding why he is asking you to do something in a particular way.

Just try. What are we always looking for? Do we want to get to the end of it? I think you have to really want to find out the truth. Do you really want it and just don't care about anything else? You just have to dare to give up and when you do there is just this incredible space. There is no defence mechanism, no 'I' that is so tight and feels pain when Rinpoche scolds you. He is teaching you something that gives an opportunity not to grasp, which we normally do. It's a pity when we can't trust and we can't try. Just be a fool and then you will find out for yourself that it is not being a fool at all. I found my ground more and more and more. The teacher will do this with you until he sees that you have given up the stubborn 'I'. It's not like this all the time. He stops when he sees you have dropped your judgmental mind.

Going beyond the hurt

Another time I met Dzongsar Khyentse and there was no difference for me between him and Jamyang Khyentse Chökyi Lodro, who Dzongsar Khyentse is the incarnation of. We had lunch together at the Kushi Fuji restaurant in Katmandu and he was asking me a few personal questions and I felt very safe to just be very straight with him. He invited me to go with him to Sechen Gompa where His Holiness Dilgo Khyentse was, and he told me to wait. So I waited and waited and he didn't come back for a long time. Then he appeared and he turned towards me and said, 'Oh, you're just like the others anyway. You can go now.' That was quite a shock to me. What I realised, though, is that if you hear a teacher's words through your ego, it can be very painful — the more you grasp the more painful it becomes. This is why we get hurt, but it is just by going through that hurt that we learn to go beyond the hurt. Then you don't really get hurt because it frees you; people can say anything to you and it doesn't really matter. If you take things too personally, they become so painful. However, if you let words bounce off you, then they have no meaning at all and don't touch you. The most important thing is to find your integrity, so that 'you know you'.

How easy it is to miss these opportunities with the teachers, because we grasp so much with the 'I'. We make ourselves so solid, and then we have a lot of pain because we take things too seriously. We need to just use what the teacher does and then just observe what happens to the attitude of our mind. It's not the nice politeness that gives us the opportunity to make that choice. The teacher puts your ego down, your hang-ups, fears and resistances.

When you look at the stories of the masters like Milarepa and Marpa, it can be very inspiring. Sometimes I think that now we receive the teachings too easily. We are in a tent and if there is a draught or it's too hot or cold or our cushion is uncomfortable, we don't realise or appreciate what we are really getting in these amazing teachings. We should just look at how few human beings receive the opportunity to hear these teachings that can actually make you free. It's not just an intellectual exercise, but we need to try to start to live the teachings. I always used to ask myself, 'What has all this to do with me?' and then I'd try and I would understand what it had to do with me. Try and you will see.

Living devotion

I remember once we went on a pilgrimage with Rinpoche to Nepal and Sikkim. What an incredible time that was. We went to the Palace Gompa and the room of Jamyang Khyentse Chökyi Lodro. I actually go back there at least once a year and I always have the same feeling when I enter that room. I just enter and I'm all right. Rinpoche introduced us to Dilgo Khyentse Rinpoche. I always felt intimidated and pierced through by him. I feel a little sad about those days because I was not so true or truthful. You know I think I pretended a lot. I always felt that with a great being like him I was holding back. I think it is a process of learning when you see what your mind does.

Khyentse Rinpoche, with his huge hands and long nails used to scratch through my hair sometimes while giving his blessing and it was so cosy. Yet I was still afraid. I wish I had been more receptive and a little bit more open then, as I am now. I have met many, many lamas and some I've had more of a bond with. Rinpoche took us up to see Tulku Orgyen and he gave this incredible pointing-out introduction to the nature of mind. I always felt like he was my grandfather, like I'd known him for so long. I would cry at times when leaving Nagi Gompa. I felt I should have spent more time with Tulku Orgyen but I didn't. But maybe that's how we learn. Now I realise that there were all these great masters and now when I look there are fewer and fewer. Then we realise that these masters are only here for a while and then they're gone. We need to treasure the opportunity when we have it.

So we can only know devotion by living it, by having total surrender, trust and love. You can then see the result. Without a student having devotion, the great masters say, especially in the Dzogchen teachings, there will be no introduction to the nature of mind. For people who doubt the value of devotion, that is maybe an answer. Do you want to try? Do you want to take the chance to try to know what devotion is?

Sometimes I look at myself and I think that I'm very dumb. I'm not an intellectual person at all. Sometimes I think it's a handicap but sometimes I think it's such an incredible fortune and blessing for me. Through my life I have seen that, just by using my heart, and not through an intellectual understanding or analysing the teachings too much, just putting it all into action, I can see the result. I see it work. If it works with me, it can work with anyone. This is where the gratitude comes. It's a pity that some people never get it. There is so much suffering in the world. Then you look at this being who gives you the chance to rediscover your own nature, who shows you your Buddha nature, and he shows you a way out.

The river in flood eddies and flows,
and likewise I am deluged by doubts and dismay.
I yearn to be flowing and fluid like the
meandering stream,
but am caught in disorder and disarray.
Teach and transform me and all those like me
to receive the lineage of the treasure teachings,
So that the minds of all beings may melt into
the space of great bliss.

IT'S NOT ABOUT ME

SEEING THE OBVIOUS

A wise teacher was asked by a student seeking the truth if he could follow and study with him. The teacher agreed, even though he knew that the student would not be patient enough to learn and would only see the obvious. However, there was one condition, that no questions would be answered until the correct time. They boarded a ferry and the teacher made a hole in the boat. The student, jumping to conclusions, declared his doubt about the teacher's actions, forgetting his promise just to learn. He was confused, as he could not imagine why his teacher would commit such an act, but asked to be forgiven and to continue.

After travelling, they entered a country where they were welcomed by the king himself and went hunting. The teacher found an opportunity to twist the ankle of the young prince, hid him in the forest and left the kingdom as fast as he could.

Again the student roundly criticised the teacher, forgetting once more his promise not to question. The teacher merely reminded him that not many people had been given the honour of the position of observer and that he was wasting it because he was so full of prejudice. They continued until they reached a city where, rather than receiving hospitality, the dogs were let loose on them. They ran to the outskirts where the teacher instructed him that they had to repair a ruined wall. For hours they toiled, until the student finally gave up and said he could go on no further.

The teacher decided it was time to clarify the meaning of his actions. He explained that the boat was not taken for a war because it was damaged, thus allowing the ferryman to continue to ply his trade. The young prince was saved from usurping his father, as had been plotted by some ministers, as only the physically strong could inherit the kingdom. He then revealed that there were two orphans in the city who, when they grew up, would find treasure concealed in the wall. This would allow them to take control and reform the whole city for the better. With explanations complete, the teacher left the student to contemplate on his judgments and continued his work.[1]

JULIE HENDERSON

I met with Julie Henderson late one afternoon, at a friend's house on one of her visits back to Australia from America, where she had returned to live in 1993. I drove up to the gate and there she was, sitting on a rocking chair on the front porch, with her hair pulled back into a bun, smiling and waving at me. In that moment and, in fact, throughout our meeting, I was flooded with memories of my contact with her over the years. I had met Julie in Sydney in the 1980s when looking for a group of therapists to connect with, after leaving dear friends and colleagues behind in England. In meeting Julie, the opportunity was given to build new contacts and friendships among peers and not to f eel so alone with my work.

She conducted weekly supervision groups at her home, with a log fire blazing in the winter months and her very large and rather smelly bloodhound dog, who used to snore so loudly we sometimes couldn't hear ourselves speak. Her cats would race through the loungeroom and jump on top of the kitchen shelves and you would never quite know what you would encounter in her cupboards. In subtropical Sydney there are always many insects, and she would rarely kill them. In addition, there were always some exotic and unfamiliar teas or food or Tibetan pills that she would pull out and offer to all who were there. It was like entering another world, unfamiliar but fascinating.

She also introduced me to my teachers and Tibetan Buddhism, for which I will always be grateful. She has also, unselfconsciously and naturally, brought many, many others into the Dharma, as a natural extension and progression of her own work and who she is. As we all grew and changed and challenged her and moved on, many of us forgot the many gifts and treasures of teaching and kindness that she gave us.

In those initial years, she really was a role model for many of us younger women. She seemed so independent, resourceful, sensual and powerful, yet loving, with a vast knowledge of therapy and Dharma. She was one of the few people who could translate the teachings into the language of therapy. She built a bridge, in those early years, between the world that we knew, of therapeutic understanding and words, and the knowledge and practice of meditation. We also saw her struggling at times as a human being, as we did, with her relationship with the teacher, and often her direct experiences helped us, when we felt lost or confused or doubtful. She had an amazing capacity to name what we were feeling. Over the years I have watched Julie work with many people and have observed, over and over, her ability to bring them to a deep awareness of body and consciousness, the ability to know and name what is happening in the moment.

Julie's use of language, in turn, used to fascinate and irritate me, and that has not changed to this day. The paradox is that she has such a wonderful access to words and naming but, at times, she also has a particular way of speaking that is partially incomprehensible. Of course, this is also what makes her so fascinating, because she really is forging a new language, which reflects a certain way of thinking and being. So, as many other pioneers before her, she is sometimes misunderstood.

As we talked, I had images especially of Bairo Rinpoche, His Holiness the Gyalwang Drukpa's father, who spent much time in her home. Bairo Rinpoche, the incarnation of the great translator Vairochana, is a great Dzogchen master and was once renowned as a great healer and teacher in Tibet. When his son, the Gyalwang Drukpa, was born and recognised, he devoted his life to him. I remember the warmth and the laughter and the practices we did together. He was, to me, like everyone's favourite grandfather and I often felt like a child with him. He used to sit and tell us story after story, none of which have been written down, let alone published. Unfortunately, in those days we didn't have the foresight to record or remember them. For hours we would be engrossed as, in halting English, he would paint pictures in words, fantastic images of miracles performed and magic feats of wonder, and tales of the teachings and Tibet, all related as if it were as normal as putting the kettle on. We had no trouble following what he said, often offering the words that he didn't know in English. Julie would open her home to us, day after day, and deal with all our upsets and jealousies and excitements and experiences.

All of these memories tumbled through my mind, as she brought into focus the main point of being on the boddhisattva path, 'It's not about me.' Most of us don't know this when we are drawn to a spiritual path, and even when we learn it, it is often on an intellectual basis. Becoming a boddhisattva is the journey of putting into practice, every moment, the reality that 'it's not about me'. She also pointed out that, although we know that others also want to be happy and experience things as we do, somehow we don't truly realise that. We put ourselves first, completely unconsciously, because that is what we are mainly conditioned to do. Even when we put others before ourselves, most of us do it, not as a natural thing, but as an act of will. 'Oh, this person can go in front of me in the queue,' or 'I will share my food with this person,' or 'I will give my money to charity.' It's all referred back to 'me'. We don't realise that this person is the same as me and could be me or, in other words, is not different or separate from me. However, as Julie says, nothing happens without us automatically thinking, 'How is this going to affect me?' As Shantideva says,

> **What need is there to say more?**
> **The childish work for their own benefit,**
> **The Buddhas work for the benefit of others,**
> **Just look at the difference between them.**[2]

Julie's story

I was born in Dallas, Texas, in 1941, a couple of months before Pearl Harbour. Both of my parents were actors. Then, during the war and after, my father worked in the aircraft industry and became an engineer. My mother went back to school and took degrees in sociology and psychology and later she became a body-oriented psychotherapist. One of the things that I enjoy the most about my parents is that they supported and had an interest both in science and the arts. That goes back in my family three generations. I have also followed them in allowing both arts and sciences to influence each other.

I've been interested in a lot of people and things in my life and studied them all intensively, but only because they touched love in me. Somatics and Tibetan Buddhism came together for me at the same time, October 1975. I still find it amazing and non-coincidental that in the same month I began studying somatic psychotherapy, I also met a Tibetan teacher, Tarthang Tulku Rinpoche, and was strongly influenced by him. So I find it's almost impossible to separate these two influences, somatics and Tibetan Buddhism, in their effects on my life and experience.

Between 1975 and 1990, I worked combining three kinds of Western psychotherapy: redecision therapy, which I studied with George Thomson; Ericsonian hypnotherapy, which I studied with Milton Ericson himself; and body-oriented psychotherapies. In the last nine years, I have been more and more inclined to study and teach somatics itself rather than a kind of psychotherapy influenced by awareness of the body. I call it an exploration of the practical implications of being a body and being also aware. Western science hasn't yet addressed that simultaneity of body and awareness to my satisfaction.

Anyway, from the time I met Tarthang Tulku Rinpoche and received that seminal transmission from him, I didn't have any further contact with Tibetan lamas until I had finished writing my book, *The Lover Within*, that is, until I had integrated and expressed that first transmission. In 1985 I moved from the United States to live in Australia, largely because my work was being met with enthusiasm and appreciation here. I lived here until 1993, when two of my heart teachers pointed me back to the United States. Between 1985 and 1988 I met many impressive Tibetan teachers from whom I received instruction, including Sogyal Rinpoche, Namkhai Norbu, Chagdud Tulku, Gyalsay Tulku, Chökyi Nyima Rinpoche, and His Holiness Dilgo Khyentse. In 1988 I also met the Gyalwang Drukpa and his father, Bairo Rinpoche.

Waking up

The first time I met the Gyalwang Drukpa was at Sydney Airport with a friend of mine who had been his student for five years or so. I remember I took a lot of photographs. However, I really met him down at Bendigo, outside Melbourne, where he was doing a ten-day teaching retreat on Mahamudra. I don't know why I went to the teaching. My friend was going and he was very enthusiastic. For myself, though I was impressed with the teachers I had met, I wasn't that interested in Buddhism. I am still largely uninterested in the written teachings.

During that retreat, the Gyalwang Drukpa leaned forward somehow through the air and spoke, as it seemed, to me alone. It felt very intimate and riveted my attention to him. I felt a tremendous movement in my heart. My mind and heart opened to the real possibility of 'waking up'. I felt the promise of that possibility. It had been thirteen years since I met my first Tibetan teacher and even though I had been enormously impressed by them and really loved them, I had managed not to notice the point — that it was possible to 'wake up' in a way that would spontaneously benefit all beings.

Being 'awake' is difficult to describe, difficult to evoke. What I can say is that a person who is awake doesn't have the same limits on perception that we normal human beings do. It is impossible for us to perceive things as they actually are. Normally we perceive as our bodies, the 'perceiving instruments', are able to perceive. What a cockroach or a puppy can perceive is clearly different from what we perceive. But, though we assume correctly (I hope) that we can and do perceive more than either a puppy or a cockroach, it is folly to assume that what we do perceive is all there is. By enhancing our bodily perception with microscopes and telescopes and PET scans and so on, we can now perceive phenomenally more than we could before. Still, even that very much broader range of perception is limited and shaped by the form of the perceiver.

This whole arena is one I hope somatics will investigate. In the West we haven't actually studied the implications of the effects of form on perception, except for other animals, so we don't yet have a working vocabulary to open the door of discussion. One thing I am trying to do is to develop a way of talking about these things in English or at least pointing at the issues conceptually, even though this is difficult enough. To evoke or induce actual recognition of more open, relaxed and flexible states of perception may be impossible without a practice and a teacher to model how it's done.

We are all certainly familiar with the fact that we tend to think and feel certain things over and over again. This is the common run of human thoughts and feelings. Then, within that range of normal human thinking, feeling and sensing, we also tend to have personal habits accumulated from our experiences growing up. Those thoughts and feelings are often not about what's happening now, but are more like layered reflections of previous experience. One of the characteristics of being awake is the willingness and the capacity to notice and respond to what's happening in the present rather that to re-run the past rather compulsively.

Stripping away the layers

Anyway, after that experience of feeling invited to a new level of teaching and practice by the Gyalwang Drukpa, I felt like I might actually be willing to take refuge. This is considered to be the first thing you do if you have any interest in being a Buddhist. What refuge means varies a lot with your own understanding. I had felt for all those years that there was no reality to refuge or that I would be losing my freedom or it was a mechanical system I wanted no part of. Having been so deeply and impeccably touched by the Gyalwang Drukpa, all the old trust issues were swept aside. I felt willing, at least superficially, to go beyond 'What about me?' to make the wellbeing of all beings more important to me than myself. I realised I was willing to say, 'OK, I will live my life so that it is about more than me.' That was scary.

I did decide to take refuge though and it meant far more to me than that initial step. It was more of a risk. I gathered together some offerings, wildflowers and incense and a khatta [a white silk scarf] and went to knock on his door. I was told he was with somebody, so I sat on the bench outside his room. I was sitting there with my mind rather expanded but also in turmoil because I felt I was making a big decision, a life-changing decision, as it turned out. Then, as I sat there, the other door opened and Bairo Rinpoche, his father and also a great teacher, came out and sat beside me, keeping me company. In fact, it's clear he literally offered me refuge by being there with me, and I felt it, but it took me a couple of months to recognise what he had done.

Anyway, I went in and asked if I might take refuge. The Gyalwang Drukpa asked what day it was and I told him the thirteenth of November. He said 'No, what day in the Tibetan calendar?' When we checked the Tibetan calender, it turned out to be dakini day [a feast day]. That being an auspicious day, he gave me permission to take refuge later in the day. Even from the beginning, layer after layer of my expectations began to be stripped away. My first expectation was that taking refuge meant nothing. Despite the fact that I was quite agitated, nevertheless, to protect myself from disappointment, I decided it didn't mean anything. Immediately after taking refuge, I convinced myself that there was no real connection and nothing to rely upon.

What I discovered was Rinpoche's persistence in restoring the connection. He was very generous, patient, incredibly skilled at teasing my heart back open and very willing to reach out past my fears. He had a remarkable generosity that kept pulling me out of what I would call my ordinary, everyday mind. Westerners have a tendency to suppose that their emotional tides have some sort of intrinsic importance, especially the habitual ones. After some time with high lamas, it becomes clear that all these dramas are quite secondary. They begin to be less convincing.

My experience of my teachers is that they are love and clarity embodied. Love and clarity without limit, or at least any limit that I can find. I don't know how to talk about these things without sounding loony. It's not usual. I mean, you don't usually meet people who are evidently wise and loving and playful and generous and full of laughter. They are utterly entrancing. Even the tissues of their body are happy and aware. It sounds extraordinary, it is extraordinary. As a somaticist, these are the sorts of things I am inclined to notice. Other people might be more likely to be drawn in through other means. I realised that if I wanted to learn about these things, how my teachers came to be what they are, then I would do well to hang out with them. I wanted to know how they became so fully happy and loving and present and wise, unbelievably wise, in the most ordinary way, not at all pompous or arrogant. They just simply, moment by moment, respond accurately to what is arising and what is needed.

When we started, I was sure it would be difficult to talk about devotion, but now it seems simple enough to say that devotion is the progressive willingness and capacity to pay attention to the awakened state and be changed by it. In this process, the awakened state is modelled and demonstrated and induced by the teacher. As a somaticist, I am interested in what my teachers show me bodily and energetically, as well as by and through my mind. My teachers, however, are far more interested in drawing my attention to awareness without limit. It is important to be willing to be moved and touched by your teacher. This requires you to be aware and alert and relaxed and to allow the habitual patterns — of body, energy and mind — to ease and open and dissolve. The traditional Tibetan suggestion is to let your mind mix with the mind of the teacher, like water in water. My experience is that the effects go far beyond what we commonly consider to be mind.

Freedom from 'me'

From the beginning, I was aware of the Gyalwang Drukpa and his father pretty much all the time. I remember saying, 'I think about you and your father a lot.' 'Yes,' he replied, 'I know.' This was one of the early surprises to my mind, that he could know where my attention was placed and would say so. I don't want to imply it was a romantic sort of infatuation because that is misleading. It wasn't that I thought they would marry me. However, one of the things that inevitably happens when your mind begins to relax, when its contours of perception open and loosen up, is that the attitudes about life that you have tucked away start to surface, especially if you had hoped never to encounter them again. As Westerners, we have our own particular brand of hopes and fears, attitudes and expectations about the people we love and who love us. Nothing is more startling to the mind and heart than to feel truly loved. As women in the West, we may have been brought up to assume that someone who loves us will rescue us from our troubles, save us from ourselves and others, make all the difference between mere survival and flourishing. At some deep level, no matter how well we understand the matter of projection, we are likely to feel that we are going to suddenly and radically be 'all right' just because this love is there, just because we have met embodied love. Many of these feelings were there for me even though I understood them very well.

It has been my experience that most of us go through life yearning, or pretending not to yearn, for our heart's desire. When we meet someone who seems to hold the promise of the resolution of our yearning, then many things are stirred up. So I felt, 'Now everything will be all right. Now the wounds in my heart will be spontaneously healed.' There was the effortless ease that we feel when we are in love. In fact, I am happy to use the expression 'in love' in the specific, almost technical sense of being in the presence of 'Love', rather than being infatuated. As this opening, loosening and cleaning up progresses, I am more able to rest in present loving awareness without so much fascination with personal baggage. In the beginning, understandably, I thought that 'waking up' was about me. I thought I was going to get better and better until some critical point at which I would be perfect, and that would be 'awake'.

However, waking up is not about 'me' at all. Every twist of the mind that brings experience back to 'me' is going away from waking up. If you could make a map of practice, it might look like switchbacks on a steep grade. Radically, waking up is about freedom from 'me'. One of the things that people routinely report in the work I do is that they don't know who they are any more. This means that the 'I' they are used to has loosened up enough that their old map of expectations and sensations doesn't fit any more. I say to them, 'You are becoming somebody else and you need to take the time to find out who that is.' There is less concern for maintaining a particular self and more willingness to rest in present being. It's very difficult for us as human beings, as embodied beings, to relate to anything at all except as it relates to us and affects us. That's so intrinsically the case it's almost impossible to imagine it being otherwise. Whenever we relate to a person or event only as it influences us, then we are actually not in relationship to what is happening at all, but only to our own reactions. Then it's always how *I* think about things, how *I* feel about things, the sensations that *I* experience and the stories *I* tell myself about it. It's all me, me, me. *My* thoughts, *my* feelings, *my* body, *my* sensations, *my* experiences, *my* stories. You, as 'other', have very little part in that, except as part of my parade.

Flipping the card

Devotion flips the card of attention. Deflecting attention away from me, me, me, and resting it instead in that awakened state we mentioned before, as much as we can, for as long as we can. Initially, when we meet this state in another being, we may indeed be thrilled for us, again me, me, me. How marvellous for me that love is real, how marvellous that love and wisdom are paying attention to me. Fortunately, as we soak more and more in the presence of this state, we begin to be changed by it (as we are changed by whatever we pay persistent attention to). Gradually the whole process becomes less about us and what we want and more about what our teachers care about. My teachers care about waking up. They care about clarity and compassion. They are not thinking about themselves. They are concerned with the wellbeing of all beings, practically speaking, a very radical position, compared with what most of us are doing.

So, it can happen that, through love of them and what they are, we make a decision now and then to give over the song and dance of me, and let a few other beings be almost as real to us as we are. To let even one being be as real to you as you are to yourself is so rare and difficult that there are sayings about it, like 'Greater love hath no man than this, that he give up his life for his friend'. The shift of attention is immediately of benefit. It benefits us, no doubt about that, but it also benefits other beings as well, spontaneously, without any other action on our part. We recognise more deeply that others experience things as we do. They also have sensations, have stories, wish to be happy and loved and to have an easier life. That they are happy begins to matter to us, not just conceptually, but as a real heart wish.

How we learn from our teachers is similar to how children learn from their parents. Kids soak up huge amounts of information about everything, very little conceptual, very little of it about what their parents say. Even in adult communication only about thirty per cent of meaning is conveyed verbally, and the rest of the meaning is carried by non-verbal signals. While I am digressing here, we know that the brains of children up to five years old and adolescents consume much, much more blood sugar than either adults or middle children, apparently because of the massive amount of learning, changing and integrating they are doing. I would suggest as an interesting research project to test the brain blood sugar levels of practitioners getting close to waking up. I'll bet the levels will be significantly higher than normal. The things that children learn most deeply from their parents are the things that their parents are persistently being and doing. So if your parents are interested in learning, it is going to be a lot easier for you to be interested in learning. If your parents are compassionate to the spiders in the house and take them outside instead of killing them, then compassion for insects is going to be easier for you. If your father is a carpenter and gradually, according to your capacity, shows you how to hammer and saw, then you will learn that more easily. This is because it is something that your father really knows how to do, and his sharing it with you is an expression of his love for you. In the same way, by watching and absorbing and practising, we can learn to embody some of the qualities of the teachers we spend time with.

Being special

The question often comes up, 'What is the difference between doing therapy and meditating?' or, as we have been talking about here, practising devotion in the form of Guru Yoga? I'll say more about that later, perhaps, but here I'd like to emphasise again: both therapy and spiritual practice are about relieving suffering and supporting happiness, but therapy is pretty much exclusively about rearranging you or improving you or relieving you. (There's no reason it shouldn't be.) Devotion is never only about you, but about helping you to wake up. I can tell you a story about an intervention one of my teachers made with me that is a very good, though mildly embarrassing example, where he clearly reflected me back to myself.

Once I bought a shawl in Nepal with a pattern that indicated that it belonged to a ngakpa, an advanced practitioner who isn't a monk or nun. I thought the shawl was beautiful, cream and magenta and dark blue raw silk from Bhutan, though a friend advised that I shouldn't buy it because I wasn't ngakpa. I put it away because I wasn't sure I should use it, but just looked at it now and again. Later, my friend Tony came to visit and I thought, 'I know what I will do. I'll ask Gyalsay Rinpoche if it is all right for my friend to have it and, if it is, I'll give it to him. I wasn't alert enough to recognise that underneath was the hope and wish that he would say, 'Oh, it's OK for you to have one.'

So I explained the background to my teacher and he said, 'Oh yes, it's perfectly wonderful.' He even made up an elaborate little ceremony to give it to my friend. As the ceremony progressed, I was getting more and more distressed and then Rinpoche started to tell a story about some people who wanted their son to be admitted to his monastery. They came to visit him with the son and brought many gifts, which were actually bribes, so that he might be taken into the monastery. One of them was a watch.

He said, 'I still have the watch.' He went upstairs, brought it down and showed it to me. It was actually quite an ugly watch, very tacky. But my heart leapt up. This was to be my consolation prize. Of course that thought wasn't clearly formed, but that was my feeling. This really ugly watch, which I wouldn't want in the first place, is nevertheless a gift from Rinpoche and my prize. I may not get to have a special ngakpa shawl, but he is going to give me the watch and that will console me. I blush to remember myself.

So Rinpoche finished the story saying that he didn't admit the son, but he did accept the offerings they gave to the monastery. He added, 'It's not a bad watch. It just has a few screws loose.' Then he asked me to take it to the jeweller to have it fixed. So I took it to the jeweller who was very kind and said if he touched it he would have to charge me, but told me how to fix it with superglue. I took the repaired watch back to Rinpoche and left it outside his door. His surgical strike at my grasping was complete. My friend, on the other hand, was completely enraptured for a few hours and came back from that meeting in a state of total inflation, completely drunk with approval and specialness. It took us both a couple of days to settle down.

That's one of my favourite examples because it is so accurate, minimalist. The metaphor of having 'a few screws loose' was absolutely precise and very funny. My experience is that as I continue through the process, my projections and insistences are gently loosened or, as in this case, radically stripped away, and all manipulation fails. Simple presence is always profoundly met and received but any manipulation on my part has been refused with knife-edged sharpness. In this case, Rinpoche helped me to realise that deep down I did want to be treated as special, to be the favourite daughter and to be saved. Part of my survival strategy all my life had been to work out what people wanted and then to do my best to be what they wanted so that, in the end, they would do what I wanted. With my teachers there were no hooks, no preferences, no clues to follow so I couldn't distort myself into what I thought they wanted.

Annihilating the ego

I was brought up on the notion of romantic love. In my generation of Western women, we were culturally prepared to save ourselves for the perfect man who would care for us and satisfy us in exchange for adoration and sexual treats. That was the story. I don't recall it ever working out that way, but the training was very powerful. I am sure that men have similar patterns, maybe about being the chosen sidekick, the special attendant, the one student pure enough or powerful enough to serve and then take command. 'I will be the first lineage holder in the West.' Whatever our gender and our storyline, however, I'm pretty sure that people have no idea in the beginning how uncomfortable it is going to be to expose this 'I' to the dissolving of what and who we think we are. Dzongsar Khyentse Rinpoche says that Guru Yoga is hiring someone to annihilate your ego. It's an operation without anaesthetic. Even when we hear these things, we still feel that there is something essential that won't be stripped away.

The 'I' of us is made up of an incredibly complex lamination of sights and sounds and thoughts and sensations, inner and outer experiences, that are awareness as body. We gradually learn to experience that agglomeration as what we are. The process of letting go of the conviction that we are the thoughts, feelings, sensations, history and experiences, can be vividly painful. Eventually, no matter how committed and enthusiastic you are, you are almost certain to run across one or two 'aspects of self' that you feel justified in hanging on to. That bit will be painful, no doubt about it. It's complicated by the fact that we don't have a tradition for this practice. In fact, it clearly cuts across most of our cultural development for the last several centuries. (Of course, our cultural parameters don't include waking up as a real option either.) Nevertheless, I don't think it is only our difficulty.

I doubt there are many people in the East who are really doing Guru Yoga. It's too hard. The balance between trust and surrender, on the one hand, and self-responsibility, on the other, is just too challenging for most of us. Your teacher isn't your mother or your father or your therapist; not your saviour, your brother, your lover, or your friend. What the teacher is blows apart all the models that we carry with us. Nevertheless, we use those models because they are the ones we have, and we relate mostly through roles, not reality. We try them, one after another, until we find out that none of them apply. If we keep on letting them drop away, eventually we will rest attention in openness. The moment we are willing to let the mind rest, when we are not insisting or trying to get it right or grabbing at something, then openness comes simply and effortlessly. That's one of the lovely things about telling guru stories — it reminds the heart. Telling these stories, just as we are doing now, reminds us of what's possible.

Making the extraordinary ordinary

How do you make the extraordinary ordinary? By embodying this practice of loving presence in the present moment. There are simple exercises that help a great deal if you are persistent and consistent about doing them. Gradually and spontaneously you become more open, clear, and more loving. Awareness of self eases and becomes more cellular. The fast track is to let yourself rest in awareness of your teachers, in their clear, laughing vastness. If you do that, inevitably you will be touched by them and influenced and changed by what they are.

When I remember them, I am eased. They are — that's central. It's a relief to my heart. When being feels too hard, just to know that they are possible eases me.

The brilliance of the sun shines upon all,
but I always want to bask in its glow.
I pray for my motivation to be perfectly pure,
yet still I think it's all about me.
Teach and transform me and all those like me
who wish to step into the source of the light,
So we may cut through our pride and radiate
with virtuous deeds.

THE FUNDAMENTAL STATE

THE NON-EXISTING DEMONS

A meditator undertaking a retreat was endeavouring to realise the nature of emptiness. He was attempting a practice to conquer the projections of his mind, in the form of demons. One night in the dark, he returned to his hut, not knowing that his sister had visited and left him a jug of yoghurt. He mistakenly thought he saw, by the faint glow of a butter lamp, the large eye of a demon, which of course was merely the top of the yoghurt pot. Deciding not to be afraid, demon or not, and convincing himself that demons were only in the mind, he yelled and hit the demon. The yoghurt spilt everywhere and suddenly, in the dim light, he thought that there were now many demons staring at him with their white eyes.

Determined to overcome his terror at the thought of numerous demons waiting to attack him, he kept hitting them all with his shawl but they kept multiplying. Suddenly, cutting through everything, as his meditation practice had taught him, he realised he had yoghurt on his hands and stopped and laughed. There were no demons to destroy and the whole episode had been created by his overactive mind and foolishness.[1]

Michael Kern is an osteopath, craniosacral therapist and naturopath, and runs a private practice in London. He also teaches and lectures, and is presently completing a book on craniosacral therapy. He doesn't see his work and the Dharma as being separate; the benefit he receives from his meditation practice gives him support and a foundation in his work and daily life.

He is one of the coordinators of the Drukpa Kagyu Trust, a charity founded by His Holiness the twelfth Gyalwang Drukpa, the head of the Drukpa Kagyu lineage. The Trust was set up in 1992 to support Tibetan culture and spiritual teachings. It has three main areas of activity: inviting Tibetan teachers to visit the West to give teachings; a sponsorship scheme for children, nuns and monks, mainly in Ladakh, but also in some of the other Himalayan regions to help them with their basic needs and education; and the Ladakh School Project, which aims to build a school for local children to provide a comprehensive modern education that is also based in their indigenous culture and spiritual traditions.

1. Dilgo Khyentse Rinpoche — One of the teachers of Sogyal Rinpoche, Dzongsar Jamyang Khyentse and His Holiness the Gyalwang Drukpa

2. His Holiness the 14th Dalai Lama of Tibet

3. Jamyang Khyentse Chökyi Lodro — One of the teachers of Sogyal Rinpoche

4. Khandro Tsering Chödrön — One of the foremost woman spiritual masters in Tibetan Buddhism and spiritual wife of Jamyang Khyentse Chökyi Lodro

5. His Holiness the 14th Dalai Lama with His Holiness the 12th Gyalwang Drukpa

6. His Holiness the 14th Dalai Lama and Dilgo Khyentse Rinpoche

7. His Holiness the 12th Gyalwang Drukpa

8. Sogyal Rinpoche

9. Dzongsar Jamyang Khyentse Rinpoche —
Reincarnation of Jamyang Khyentse
Chökyi Lodrö

10. Dudjom Rinpoche — grandfather of Dzongsar Jamyang Khyentse
and one of the teachers of Sogyal Rinpoche, the Gyalwang Drukpa and
Dzongsar Khyentse Rinpoche

11. Kalachakra mandala for world peace

12. His Eminence the 2nd Thuksay Rinpoche — Reincarnation of His Eminence the 1st Thuksay Rinpoche, one of the teachers of His Holiness the Gyalwang Drukpa

MICHAEL KERN

Michael's story brings out many key points. He talks honestly about his short retreat in a cave in the Himalayas. As Westerners, we are really not used to extremely basic living conditions. However, the Tibetan lamas are totally at home in any sort of setting, no matter where they are. They seem to have the ability to adapt and be happy in the most basic circumstances as well as in comfortable surroundings. They really do put into practice the sense that everything is the same, meaning they have no attachment or aversion.

I have seen the Gyalwang Drukpa in his monastery in Darjeeling in a highly traditional setting, with Tibetan horns being blown and people prostrating every time they saw him. I have also seen him in his robes walking through the West End of London on a Friday night, among drunken office workers and gangs of youths, and on a harbour cruise to see the Opera House in Sydney. He has walked through frosty fields in Brittany to conduct a fire ceremony and travelled through the outback of Australia to visit an Aboriginal community. As Michael points out, he is equally at home in his monastery in Ladakh or mixing with the rich and famous in Europe.

Michael also talks about how His Holiness embodies the quality of treating everyone equally and how he is always teaching in every situation. Even stepping off a plane after a long flight, to meet yet another group of people in another country with a totally different culture, he remains the same. He is always calm, courteous and at peace, warm and friendly, treating each person with as much importance as the next. Day after day, for twenty hours, he receives an ongoing stream of people, all wishing to see him. Even when it is obvious that he is tiring or not so well, he just quietly continues to serve.

Michael also addresses one of the most important points about devotion, which is often misunderstood — that devotion is not emotion. The Gyalwang Drukpa says that Westerners tend to either 'fall in love' with the lama or are just desperate and do not really spend the time necessary examining the teacher, committing to the guru–student relationship.

Despite the fact that His Holiness is the head of the Drukpa Kagyu lineage of Tibetan Buddhism, sometimes it takes time to realise who he actually is, as Michael recounts. This is because he is so natural, never 'standing on ceremony' or making you feel that you are less than him. It is easy to forget what a high and great lama, how extraordinary, he is. He has such a humility and ease about him, as well as a natural authority. He writes:

Since so many past teachers have said,
'All appearance and existence should be seen as teaching,'
I need to really think about the meaning of this,
Even though I don't have the sharpest of minds.
Yet knowing my own emotions create both pleasure and pain,
With conditions and companions always changing,
Impermanence and suffering, karma and its results,
Interdependence and the union of appearance and emptiness —
These I know as true teachers, showing what's real.
These I know as true teachers, pointing out defects.
These I know as true teachers, crushing arrogance.
These I know as true teachers, driving one toward Dharma.
These I know as true teachers, causing compassion to grow.
When I sometimes have a bit of insight about this,
According to my training, I feel this truly
Receiving the Guru's blessings.
So to the Gurus I intensely pray
And am quite happy when I feel their kindness.[2]

Michael's story

I met His Holiness the twelfth Gyalwang Drukpa in 1983 while I was travelling in the Indian Himalayas. For many years I had been practising different forms of meditation and been interested in the philosophical teachings of Helena Blavatsky, Alice Bailey and Nicholas and Helena Roerich. They had written books starting from the end of the last century up to about the 1950s, about their spiritual connection with some of the Himalayan masters. Visiting India was really like going on a pilgrimage to see some of the places that I had read about and had fascinated me for many years. I was interested in the culture and the traditions of the whole region, having studied some of its spiritual traditions. However, I certainly wasn't looking for a teacher or a guru.

I guess I had started dabbling in meditation out of desperation. In my teenage years I was quietly confused. I had a group of friends in London and we were all into rock music, yoga and spirituality. A lot of young people in England were following in the footsteps of the Beatles and we were exploring different lifestyles, beyond the materialistic life and expectations that were being presented to us at the time. Music and drugs were an escape for us into another reality, or so we thought at the time. I guess we thought we were rather 'alternative' at the time and maybe we were.

However, the net result of all this for me was great confusion. I discovered I wasn't the person I thought I was, but I also didn't know who I was. The concepts and ideas I held about myself were quite challenged. What I thought I wanted to do in the world and what I expected had all changed. On the surface I appeared to be doing all right, but inside there was a volcano of unresolved emotions and a confusion about how to live honestly and authentically. For many years after that, I was searching and looking at different psychotherapy models, bodywork therapies and meditation.

On my journey to India, after being thrust into the mayhem of Delhi, I travelled up into the foothills of the Himalayas and, after an amazing set of so-called coincidences, arrived in Ladakh. I stepped off the plane into this extraordinary haven in the mountains, a plateau at about 11,000 feet above sea level. It is an old Himalayan kingdom surrounded by some of the biggest mountains in the world, and has remained relatively cut off from the rest of the world for many centuries. It has developed a very deep and extraordinary culture and spiritual tradition, which is still part of the fabric of social life, even to this day. However, since the late 1970s, when Ladakh was opened to tourism and foreign influence, it has become a culture under pressure.

The heart of Ladakh

I was very touched by the beauty of the country and of the monasteries, but also by the sheer beauty of the people, who were vibrant, warm, generous and friendly, with a 'presence of being' that I had rarely come across before. This presence seemed generic through the whole society and uplifted and inspired me. At the time I was reading a book by Andrew Harvey, *A Journey in Ladakh*, in which he describes travelling in this area and meeting some of the region's Tibetan lamas. One day I was visiting Hemis Monastery about forty kilometres from the main town of Leh. I had just been reading about a young lama in the book and someone then told me that he was in Hemis Monastery at that time. In a way I was there as a tourist, but in my heart I wasn't there just for tourism. I wanted to go deeper into the spirit of Ladakh and felt that meeting the head lama would be a way of connecting with the spiritual heart of that place. I asked if it was possible to have an audience with the young head lama and was told that I could see him the following day. As Hemis Monastery was a long way from the town, I decided to stay the night there and found a tent to sleep in.

An old friend

I awoke the next morning, remembering a strong, clear, vivid dream. I'm really not a person who has dreams or visions or wonderful spiritual experiences that some other people seem to have. However, the young head lama appeared in this dream. He told me that I had been a friend of his in a previous life and I woke up with a very strong feeling from the dream. After breakfast, I waited for a while and was then ushered into his room. There in front of me with a big smile was the lama I had just dreamt about the night before. It was the same person. It was truly like meeting an old friend. He was very warm and welcoming and we talked for a few hours together. His English was quite good and he was very interested in hearing about life in England. In return, I asked him some questions about his life.

After our meeting, I went back to Leh, the main town in Ladakh, and about a week later decided to return to Hemis to revisit His Holiness the twelfth Gyalwang Drukpa. Luckily, he was able to see me and invited me to stay for a ceremony he was performing in his room. I sat down in front of the monks, who were chanting and praying, and I remember being extraordinarily struck by it all. From this remote place, in the middle of the Himalayas, these people were offering prayers and sending love to all of us in other parts of the world. I felt there was a real spiritual presence being generated, full of love. It touched me very deeply that they should care. After the ceremony, His Holiness invited me to stay for tea, and it was one of the few times on that journey I was given sweet tea rather than the traditional salted butter tea.

I was grateful for that, being an Englishman abroad! Before I departed, I gave him my address and invited him to visit England, but never thought for one moment that anything would ever come of it. I then returned to London and started my studies. A few months later, out of the blue, I received a Christmas card from His Holiness the Gyalwang Drukpa and, in return, sent him a Tibetan New Year card. For a few years we kept in contact by letter, a couple of times a year. It always made me feel very happy to receive his cards from the Himalayas.

On equal terms

Three years after we first met, I was at home and he phoned from Paris, saying he would be visiting England. So he came to stay at my home. I was rather delighted and taken aback to hear from him but it was a great pleasure to have him here. It was like the heart of Ladakh coming to London. His Holiness was accompanied by an attendant monk who would wash his maroon robes and hang them out of the window to dry, which fascinated my neighbours. However, I still wasn't, in any way, consciously looking for a guru and regarded him as a friend.

About a year or so later, in 1988, he visited again, this time with his parents and another monk. I was rather concerned about how we were all going to fit into my rather small flat. His father, His Eminence Bairo Rinpoche, I discovered, is one of the leading Tibetan lamas in the Nyingma tradition of Tibetan Buddhism. During this visit, I began to realise what an amazing person His Holiness was. I saw how he always had time for people, no matter how busy he was, that he was never flustered by anything and that he dealt with everybody on equal terms. Everybody and everything was important to him.

Simple chitchat

I had some neighbours, a middle-aged couple and their elderly mother who had lived in India for some time in the days of the Raj. They invited all of us for tea one evening. I was silent, listening to the conversation between His Holiness and my neighbours, who were a pleasant ordinary English family. As far as I was concerned, the conversation was quite boring with my neighbours talking superficial chitchat, about how India has gone downhill since the British left and how no one looks after the gardens anymore and how much the cost of food has gone up and so on. I was sitting watching all of this and observing how His Holiness handled it. He met them exactly where they were, saying things like 'taking care of flowers was really important as they made people happy' and that 'it was the same in Ladakh with the price of barley going up'. I witnessed how His Holiness engaged these people in an utterly wonderful way. After a while, the whole room just fell quiet, as if all of the questions and the chitchat had been said. A deep silence came into the room, probably for only about thirty seconds, but it felt a very long time. It was as if everybody had felt heard and there was nothing more to say.

Then His Holiness said, 'I really shouldn't take up more of your time. Thank you for your hospitality,' and we left. As we came down from upstairs, I said to him that he had really taught me something that night. I get very impatient with chitchat like that and would have changed the subject or wanted to talk about something more important. He just laughed and said, 'No, I enjoyed myself.'

Living-room prostrations

Some Buddhist students came to visit him at my house. When they arrived and saw him sitting on a chair in my living room, they prostrated themselves full length before him. It seemed very strange to me that people would prostrate themselves on my living room carpet. I didn't really understand what that was about, but nevertheless thought it was interesting. I guess at the time, I was at a spiritual crossroads so I decided to ask Gyalwang Drukpa for some advice about how to progress. He talked to me about what it means to take refuge, putting my confidence and trust in the Buddha or the nature of reality, of following the teachings of the Buddha and cooperating in the community of people who are sharing the journey with you. This explanation felt like something very natural for me and an affirmation of what I already believed in, even though I had no particular interest in Buddhism as a religion. Somehow it also didn't conceptually challenge me, so I felt comfortable in going through the formal refuge ceremony with His Holiness a few days later.

In 1992 I attended a big festival in Ladakh that His Holiness was presiding over. This celebration occurs every twelve years and, for only the second time in his life, he was giving a public blessing with the Vajrayana ornaments of Naropa, who was a great master from the twelfth century. His Holiness is regarded as the current incarnation of Naropa and these bone ornaments, called 'the six bone ornaments of Naropa', are the actual objects that Naropa used when he initiated his disciples. Anyway, I had been working very hard in London and felt like stepping back from my busy life for a while. So I decided to go to Ladakh for a few months and His Holiness suggested that perhaps I could undertake a retreat.

Recognising the guru

The day that His Holiness arrived in Ladakh, there were extraordinary scenes in the streets. The whole of the local population came out to meet him. The streets were lined with throngs of people trying to catch a glimpse of him, offering flowers and incense. The devotion, respect and happiness of the Ladakhi people towards His Holiness was something that I had never witnessed before. I joined the entourage of jeeps that were following behind him and for the whole forty kilometres to Hemis monastery villagers were standing beside the road, bowing their heads in reverence to receive a blessing as he passed. In their eyes, he is not an ordinary being, but a living buddha. The ceremonies began and approximately 30,000 people came for the main initiation. The local people all pushed and shoved to try to receive their blessing. Witnessing these extraordinary scenes I felt incredibly confused and I shared this with another student of His Holiness. I felt that I didn't know how to relate to His Holiness anymore because, in my eyes, he was still just a friend and suddenly I was seeing all these people throwing themselves at his feet and treating him as if he were a living god.

The next time I saw His Holiness in his tent, he said, 'I understand you've been experiencing some problems.' I explained my dilemma and he calmly replied, 'As far as all this guru business is concerned, it's just that we don't know ourselves, who we really are. However, the guru is in touch with himself. So we need the guru as a kind of bridge to help us to get closer to ourselves. The guru is able to guide and support us so we can become more understanding of our own nature.' He only spoke for a few minutes but during this time my whole mood changed from worry and concern to a tremendous feeling of warmth and reassurance. He continued, 'The test of whether a guru is genuine is, if he helps you to get close to yourself, then you can call that person a guru. If a guru doesn't help you do that, it doesn't matter how famous or well-respected they are, they're not your guru.'

I looked at His Holiness and felt such a deep sense of peace inside that I realised, by this definition, he was my guru. I had been feeling so confused and now I felt right back in touch with myself. Sitting in front of him I felt connected, present and integrated in my thoughts and emotions and no longer felt isolated, worried or alienated. So it finally dawned on me, probably six years after I first met him, that he was my spiritual teacher.

Silent retreat

I started my retreat according to the advice I received from His Holiness. It's interesting that my concept of a monk or spiritual person was maybe someone in a cave or monastery, perhaps remaining silent, abstaining from contact with the outside world and experiencing deprivations. I had been surprised at how much in the world these Tibetan lamas could also be. It seemed to me that they were equally at home in the middle of Piccadilly Circus as in the sanctuary of the temples in the monasteries of Ladakh. However, here I was, about to enter a one-month silent retreat.

I must admit I was nervous about this, but also interested and excited to discover how I would cope, being on my own and staying in a cave in a remote part of the Himalayas. I collected my food supplies and borrowed a couple of donkeys from a nearby village, and wound my way up the path to a small derelict building that had been built around a cave in the mountains. It was actually just next to a holy cave where one of the great Tibetan yogis, Gotsangpa, had practised many centuries before. It was also in this cave that His Holiness the Dalai Lama and His Holiness Gyalwang Drukpa received a vision confirming the whereabouts of one of the great masters of Ladakh, the reincarnation of Thuksay Rinpoche. (Thuksay Rinpoche had previously been Gyalwang Drukpa's main spiritual teacher.)

I have to be honest and say that when I walked into the house that had been built around the cave, my jaw dropped. It was filthy, with thick black dust and gaping holes in the walls. There was very little light and it was dark, smelly and dirty with no electricity. One of the monks from the nearby hermitage tried to reassure me, saying he would help clean it up a bit. As I looked through a small window I could see across the valley and just up above the cave there was a view of the white peaks of the mountains towards Chinese-occupied Tibet. I did what I could to set up home and His Holiness had given me a program of daily meditation practice. My days were well structured, but I was totally on my own and silent for a month. I felt the contrast between my busy life in London and this cave and it took me at least the first three weeks just for my mind to quieten down partially.

Rats, mice and me

On the first night, after blowing out the candle, I heard little shuffling sounds in the cave. I turned my torch on and finally caught the sight of two mice running around near my food. So I got up to seal everything, then tried to go back to sleep. The shuffling sounds continued, this time just above my head. To my horror, when I switched on the torch, I saw a large rat dart across the rock above my head. This really frightened me and I didn't get any sleep. The same thing happened the next few nights and I felt very challenged to be sharing my sleeping space with these animals. I couldn't change my concept about rats being vermin and carrying disease, no matter how hard I tried. Yet I also didn't feel like just giving up and quitting because of the mice and the rats. I resolved to stick it out and stay there.

Some days my meditation would go quite well, but on other days I would be overcome by feelings of loneliness and isolation and would question. 'What am I doing here?' Then I'd go more into meditation and feel a deeper level of calm. I vacillated, but through it all, I started to recognise how busy my mind was and how hard it was to slow it down. I did eventually settle somewhat, even with the mice and rats, though I never got completely used to them. From that time onwards, I think I could have stayed a lot longer, even three months or three years. I did come out, though, after a month. At the end of the retreat, I felt some sense of achievement, although this was probably just my pride and ego, especially as I managed to stay silent for a month. There was also, though, an indefinable sense that I had moved through some barriers or limitations within myself in terms of what I felt I was capable of doing. I was left feeling a little more open and quiet inside.

Learning a lesson

Being with the Gyalwang Drukpa is always a teaching, no matter what the situation is. Once he asked me to accompany him on a drive from Delhi back to Katmandu in Nepal. I finally managed to get a flight from Nepal to meet His Holiness in Delhi and tried to contact him on my arrival. He was staying in one of the larger luxury hotels but when I called he was out. I was asked to call back in the morning, so in the meantime I booked into a cheap guesthouse near New Delhi railway station. It's an atmospheric area bustling with markets and street life. Apparently, though, His Holiness was wanting to start the journey very early in the morning, so he and a couple of monks came to look for me late at night, in various hotels in the area, but couldn't find me.

When we left in the morning His Holiness told me they'd been looking for me the previous night. He commented that the area I was staying in was very interesting and lively with so many people on the streets so late. I explained that was why I like the area. When I stay there, I know I'm really in India rather than staying in an expensive modern hotel where I could be anywhere in the world. He then said, very thoughtfully, that he would also like to stay in an area like that sometimes if he had the choice, but that people expected him to stay somewhere nice, as he represented the lineage and the teachings. I was surprised at his reply and argued that this was just their concepts and it would probably be a good teaching for people for him to break their expectations. He agreed, but wondered if people would really understand this or if it would just confuse them.

This conversation continued for quite some time and into the next day. He said that it was important in this day and age to meet people where they are and that it was a very different situation now to how Tibet was a hundred years ago. I found this idea hard to accept as I didn't see why my teacher should be bound by all our expectations. I maintained that part of the teacher's job was to challenge our expectations and, as he looked at me with a wry smile, he replied, 'Well, when I first met you, you didn't know anything about Buddhism.'

I continued to disagree with him on the subject, and on the next night something happened that I was quite unprepared for. We were driving on one of the main roads in the north of India and suddenly His Holiness stopped the car and said that we would stay there for the night. I looked around and we had pulled over by a truck stop where there were a few matted beds on the floor, a kiosk selling rice, with Hindu music blaring out, and trucks roaring past every few minutes. I told him very nervously that there was a town only a few miles up the road where maybe we could find a nice hotel to stay in. He said, 'No, look we have a nice bed here to sleep in, there's some food and it's very atmospheric.' It was the middle of summer, hot, humid and sticky, and the place was dirty. I stuttered, 'There's lots of mosquitoes here too.' He pulled out some insect repellant and told me to put some on. It was only after about fifteen minutes of this that I started to realise what was happening. The fact of the matter was that I really did not want to stay in this place and I was complaining. I was the one who had complained about him staying in the hotel in Delhi and now I didn't want us to stay here either. His Holiness had no problem with either, a hotel or a truck stop. I was the one who had the problem. When I realised the predicament I was in and what His Holiness was teaching me, I promised that I would never criticise him again.

This is an example of why I feel such strong devotion towards His Holiness. There was no verbal teaching in the situation and he never said to me what I should or shouldn't think. It was a powerful teaching through my experience of his demonstration of equanimity.

The flow of life

I have never really had a conflict between being involved with a spiritual practice and getting on with my life. Feeling connected to oneself isn't about just 'staring at your navel'. It's about being present and whole in whatever we do in our lives. My experience is that the help and support I have received from my teacher has helped me be more patient and effective in the world, in my job and my relationships. However, I feel the real aim of spiritual practice is not to be more successful in the world, but to gain realisation of who we really are. This process is not just about placing attention in ourselves and ignoring the rest of the world. By connecting into deeper parts of myself I can hopefully connect more to others and be more helpful.

I think particularly the teachings on kindness and non-attachment are where I continuously draw inspiration from. These teachings help me enter into a greater and more engaged flow of life, where caring and compassion have a vital role to play. The Dharma for me is about constantly working with myself, with my shortcomings and ignorance, in order to enter into a deeper stream of life. It's not necessarily easy and sometimes can be very challenging. To be with my teacher often means to have a mirror very clearly held up in front of me. This often reflects my shortcomings and idiosyncrasies. It's not a cop-out from life, but a cop-in. The more I progress, the more I realise my own limited habitual patterns and the reality of my situation. That can help because then I don't take it all quite so seriously and I can find a relationship to my problems. Then I can work with my difficulties rather than being consumed by them. It may then be possible to move beyond my unresolved issues into greater understanding.

Beyond our conditioning

The spiritual teachings and practice can also bring our unconscious patterns of thought and behaviour into awareness and this is where I sometimes feel the challenge and friction. That's healthy though, because the friction is necessary to produce movement and change. The key to Dharma practice, for me, is that it goes right to the fundamental state of my being and works to facilitate and encourage the emergence of that fundamental state. Dharma deals with the very core and structure of the mind, while many therapies tend to engage more with the contents of the mind. There are, of course, therapies that acknowledge a fundamental state of being, but they generally work with our conditioned patterns of experience that overlay this state. What is unique and explicit about the Dharma is that it contains an ultimate teaching on who we really are, beyond all our conditioning. The Dharma is concerned with how we manifest our fundamental nature in all aspects of our lives, in therapy, business, teaching and so on. Dharma points the way to a quality of presence that we can bring into everything we do. It provides the root for everything I do.

Devotion, for me, is an experience of a naturally arising joy that springs from something being understood. There's a difference between emotion and devotion. Devotion is not a feeling of whether or not we like someone or feel good about them. It carries something that is far weightier, with more depth to it. This springs from a profound place within one's heart where you experience the joy of glimpsing something of the immutable nature that underlies our thoughts, concepts, projections and emotions. Underneath our conditioning is a state of reality of our own mind or truth. The teacher plays a vital role in helping to introduce us to our real nature, which has always been and always will be with us. The spiritual teacher helps create the opportunity or makes the space for us so that we can get a glimpse of who we really are. When we understand that's what the teacher can do, then the naturally arising feeling is one of profound gratitude and devotion.

The sound of silence roars like a lion in my ears,
yet I am still full of my own opinions.
I wander the empty rocky mountain hermitages,
but solitude and peace run away like the deer.
Teach and transform me and all those like me
who seek to have gratitude to the supreme lama,
So we may appreciate the innermost treasure
of simplicity of the heart.

THE PLACEBO EFFECT

THE MESSIAH IN US ALL

Once there was a monastery that had become dilapidated and deserted and only five old monks remained. Fearful of the apparent ending of his monastery, the head monk decided to consult with a rabbi who sometimes undertook a retreat in the forest nearby. They met, talked and studied together and consoled each other about the general decline in spirituality. Finally the old monk asked the rabbi again whether there was any advice he could give to try to save the ailing monastery. The rabbi finally replied that he did not really know but that one of the remaining monks might be the Messiah.

On returning to his fellow monks, this was related to them and in the months that followed, each monk began to examine and contemplate that possibility and who it might be. Although each monk had his faults, they started to focus on the positive qualities of each of them and to treat each other with the greatest respect, in case one of them was indeed the Messiah. People who still occasionally visited the enchanting forest and monastery to meditate began to feel an extraordinary presence and respect flowing from the old monks and, without even knowing why, began to feel compelled to go there more and take their friends and acquaintances. Some of the young men talked with the monks and, as time passed, many decided that they wanted to develop this extraordinary quality they perceived and asked to join. The monastery flourished and once again took its place as a centre of learning, wisdom, peace and spirit.[1]

Regina Weilhart, was totally unexpected. Suddenly there she was in Sydney in March 1999, to see Dzongsar Khyentse Rinpoche, while he was completing his new movie, *The Cup*. I was just about to leave for London and our paths crossed briefly, just enough time to sit together in a coffee shop in the middle of the city, with buses roaring past the door outside and pop music playing in the background.

I had met her briefly in London during 1994, while Rinpoche was there, and I remember being incredibly impressed with her. She is an extremely artistic and talented woman, with a successful career working all over Europe in costume design for theatre,

REGINA WEILHART

opera and film. She was born in Munich, Germany, is fluent in several languages and has lived in London, Brussels and Geneva, and is just about to move to Nice, in the south of France. Her profession and her passion have always been connected with fashion and fabrics and design. She developed a strong fascination for Asian textiles and her work is a great source of inspiration, through which she also reconnects with herself.

She is quite tiny, physically, with a fineness and delicate quality about her, which belies her achievements. She also manages to appear quiet, yet vivacious and fiery, all at the same time. She was unsure about her contribution, because she feels she still has so many doubts and questions about devotion. I felt that her comments were very useful, because she is one of the few courageous enough to express what we all feel at different times, but often don't say.

This was, in fact, immediately proved to be the case as other students discussed the impact of her raising the issue that perhaps devotion was like a placebo. In other words, as Regina sees it, if you believe in devotion, which is having deep faith in the teacher and the path, it works. Through devotion towards the teacher you profoundly open your heart, and get more and more in contact with your essence. This is a long and often doubtful journey — a journey which will unroot many concepts and habits. It can be frightening, uncomfortable and annoying at times. Therefore it is important to have someone you can rely on, and even project onto. She questions whether it is a skilful method on the relative level to encourage people to stay on the spiritual path until enlightenment. A friend then said that to think of devotion in this way was insulting, and a debate followed. It seemed to me that she was, without even trying, producing a healthy conversation where people could express their own different views, without having to follow one way of thinking. Rinpoche says himself that people don't somehow stop having doubts, just because they are engaged in Buddhism. The Buddha was very clear that people shouldn't believe him just because he said things, but must question and find out whether what he says works for them.

It is also obvious that Regina is totally devoted to Rinpoche, even if she herself has doubts about how genuine this devotion is. So, is it possible to be so devoted and yet not recognise it in oneself? There are many different forms of devotion that do not all look or sound the same, or manifest in a traditional way, especially with an unconventional teacher, like Dzongsar Khyentse Rinpoche. As she talked about recently spending time with

Rinpoche in Bhutan, her whole face lit up and her voice changed, even to the point that a friend who transcribed the tape of our conversation commented on how devoted she was. It reminded me of a traditional teaching that says:

> If you see your teacher as the buddha,
> you will receive the blessings of a buddha.
> If you relate to your teacher as a spiritual friend,
> you will get a friend.
> If you relate to your teacher as an ordinary person,
> you will receive the blessing of a human being.

We can read this in many ways. It could be that it does work because we believe in it, as Regina ponders, so, if we believe in the Buddha or a friend, we receive that experience. Another way to see it is that the teacher is merely mirroring what is in our mind and responding accordingly. Is there any difference between having a Rinpoche as a teacher or someone else who is just a good role model? These questions need to be asked and answered to every student's satisfaction, before they can truly cast aside their main doubts and commit themselves to a teacher. Guru Rinpoche said: 'Complete devotion brings complete blessing; absence of doubts brings complete success.'[2] Vajrayana teachers themselves ask people to err on the side of caution and advise that we take many years before making a final commitment to follow a teacher.

Juxtaposed with all these dilemmas that we love to discuss, is then Regina's example of the Bhutanese people. She describes their simple, yet unshakable, faith in Rinpoche, travelling many days and nights, by foot, through difficult terrain, waiting sometimes just by a bend in the road at night, because they know Rinpoche will pass that way. Just to have a glimpse of him or receive a blessing or walk around his tent is not only enough, but is a moment to be remembered and treasured all their lives. For them it is completely obvious, with no doubt whatsoever, that he is the living buddha. We then have to ask ourselves, 'Is this really placebo?' or is it that, for all our education, knowledge and cleverness, these people know something that still eludes some of us in the West. Is this faith and trust simply beyond us? We keep looking for answers, yet, when they are in front of our face, we miss them completely. We become so full of our deepest fears, attachments, expectations and doubts that we cannot just trust.

Regina raises some of these issues and the possibility that getting caught in the placebo argument is also missing the point. Traditionally the student is regarded as having a sickness, the teacher is seen as the doctor who knows and then prescribes the correct medicine, which is the teachings. Surely the point is whether the patient is completely cured, not whether the medicine is real or a sugar pill.

Regina talks about a prayer of the guru breaking your heart. It reminded me of a question I once asked Rinpoche about why, in the path of devotion, your heart had to be broken. The answer was that, every time your heart is broken, it gets larger, until your heart is so big that it encompasses all beings, not just one or two. By being with a teacher and expressing and then letting go of our doubts, it enables us to grow a bigger and more unprotected and open heart.

Regina's story

My first contact with the Dharma was when I was about nineteen years old. I met a Zen Buddhist teacher and loved Japanese art. I found, though, that Zen was reinforcing my already rigid tendency of being hard and tough on myself. So I totally stopped and went into therapy, which helped me a lot at the time. Then in 1988 I went travelling to Ladakh. I had seen pictures of a totally empty landscape at high altitude and was very drawn to it. My journey had nothing to do with being on a spiritual path and I didn't know anything about Tibetan Buddhism. However, I was very taken with the landscape and the culture and the friendliness of the people. They seemed to have a happy, vivid and lively attitude to life. Also I really liked the fact that I could travel there on my own, as a woman, and feel totally secure. I felt that this was a society where people were very much respected, self-confident and independent.

So I found myself in the middle of nowhere in an amazing vastness. I just wanted to experience this emptiness. I found everything there as I had hoped. I remember going over the high pass in the Himalayas that leads you into Ladakh. I felt an incredible sense of happiness, like I was coming home. I had one of the best times in my life, just being completely contented and wandering around meeting people. Some say it's like the end of the world but, to me, the vast empty landscape was a total relief. When I returned home to Germany, I was curious about the way I had felt in Ladakh and it made me wonder about the philosophy of the people. Also, I had seen some of the Tibetan paintings and felt that here was an ancient wisdom that knew how to work with people's minds, long before Freud and Jung had started working with psychology in our culture.

No reference

One day my boss at the theatre where I was working, who knew of my interest, told me that a Tibetan lama would be giving a talk. So I went along and saw Sogyal Rinpoche in Munich. I was so fascinated that I immediately signed on for a ten-day winter retreat. What he talked about really captivated me, as for many years I had been through several periods in my life where I had totally lost my orientation. I didn't know what life was really about or what philosophical structure I could believe in. I know that I had a strong reaction to reading Einstein's biography, where he came to the conclusion that there is no permanent or substantial truth to anything. At that time, I was looking desperately for something to cling on to, but reading that pulled the rug out from under me. I felt I had totally lost any point of reference. Later on somebody told me that losing your point of reference is a very important part of Buddhism. That gave me hope to know that there was actually a philosophy that takes losing the point of reference as a base. This is what pointed me towards Buddhism. Then hearing Sogyal Rinpoche teaching very deeply on ultimate truth, and that there is no permanent substantial truth on the relative level, helped me get back on track again.

That's me

There is a very strong link for me, between therapy and Buddhism. In a way, I still feel that undertaking therapy was almost like a preparation for Buddhism. I learnt that the whole way you see or experience the world is because you project onto the world what you've been taught or what you experienced so far. A very simple example is that, if you had a mother who was always very negative about men, then you are very much bound to see the men you meet as worthless. Your core belief system might be that relationships will never work out. Suddenly you discover that this is not the only reality and therefore there could be a way out.

In gestalt therapy, for example, you might try to enact a reality where your mother tells you that men are wonderful and life is great. Buddhism also picks up this theme in how we project onto things and this is why they are the way we see them. I think every one of us knows the experience of being in a bad mood and everything just feels black. Then, when we are in a great mood, things turn out wonderfully. So I came to understand that my reality depends on the way I look at the world, not the world itself. Realising this can help us on a day-to-day basis, in terms of how we relate to our friends and family, and in our work life.

Therapy helped me build up confidence, find my own value, become more independent from the past, make my own decisions and develop a stronger sense of 'that's me'. However, after a few years it became evident to me that you are still going to have times when you are unhappy or when relationships don't work out or people around you are unhappy. I came to a certain point where I knew I still didn't have the solution and there must be something else.

I sometimes see Buddhism as almost the opposite, in that you discover there is no 'me'. That is the reason you feel you are always banging your head against a wall, because you always think 'that's me'.

Knowing yourself

I studied with Sogyal Rinpoche for about two years and I still greatly appreciate what I received from him. I was really struck by him in the first encounter. This feeling can happen for me when I listen to incredibly beautiful music or if I see a beautiful piece of art or am standing on the top of a mountain. It's meeting someone and being deeply and strongly touched, happy, loving and joyful. I experienced him as very charismatic and the way he teaches Buddhism in a non-traditional manner made me realise that actually, deep down, I know myself. That is just so precious.

I started the sitting meditation practice and chanting mantras and sometimes, at the same time, I watched myself and thought, 'OK, what are you up to now?' At the beginning I had some difficulties. It was strange to find a mala [beads for counting mantras] in my hand. Also, because I love the Japanese style of simplicity and clarity, the Tibetan art, ritual and iconography just didn't appeal to me. I also love Jungian philosophy and believe we have deep inner pictures that are very much connected with us, but somehow all the images of the deities that were supposed to aid my concentration didn't work for me. I went through a period of doubt, being quite resentful and feeling that I should take a step back.

It's interesting because now I regard myself as having been very fortunate. I could be close to Sogyal Rinpoche as his attendant, helping to serve tea or packing his bag or just generally assisting in whatever way I could. I still treasure those moments because this is one way that Sogyal Rinpoche teaches his students to be aware and present. It helps us not to always be in our own thoughts with our own 'cinema' running, thinking, 'Oh, this situation should be like this or that.' It shows us what the present situation actually is, rather than how we think it should be.

Speaking out

I met Dzongsar Khyentse Rinpoche in London in 1992. I had made a coat for him and was delivering it. At that time, I was experiencing a lot of difficulties and just found myself talking to him about all my doubts about Tibetan Buddhism, the art and ritual and how people behave towards their teacher, making a fuss and so on. It just all came out and it was such a big relief to say what I felt and thought, without pretending. From then onwards, what I loved about Rinpoche was that I could be totally outspoken and say what was true for me. Actually, in the beginning, I regarded him as a very good friend. Only after months of discussion with him, did I start to develop more respect for him and his great wisdom. It just grew in me until I realised that he wasn't just a friend, but that I actually wanted to learn from this person. Sometimes I contemplated for days on a remark he made. Once, when I told him that I didn't relate to Tibetan art, he said, 'Oh exactly, I don't think you should be relating to it. You don't have to like it.' That was a big relief to me because it meant I didn't have to be what I thought was a 'good student'. I could say if I didn't like something and still be perfectly accepted.

My honeymoon

It's always been my dream to go to Bhutan, probably similar to the dream I had with Ladakh. The first time I was in Bhutan was 1992, for the cremation of His Holiness Dilgo Khyentse Rinpoche, who was one of the most renowned and great Tibetan masters of this century. In Tibetan Buddhism, cremation has very different significance than in the West. It is very auspicious to attend, especially when it is a great master. It is not a sad end of life, but just another step, a transition in the whole circle of life, death and rebirth.

This was actually my honeymoon, which may sound a little strange, considering the occasion, but I was just amazed to go into a country where Tibetan Buddhism is the state religion. There is almost no Western influence whatsoever and no advertising. People still wear their traditional costumes and even petrol stations are built in typical Bhutanese architecture. It seemed very familiar to me because the landscape is almost like Switzerland, with deep valleys, some very high mountains and quick changes of altitude over very short distances. I felt very lucky to go, as Bhutan at that time was even more difficult to get into than it is these days. The Bhutanese government had given permission for a couple of hundred foreigners to enter the country for this event. What touched me was that it was actually a state ceremony, a public event. The cremation was reported at great length in the newspaper of Bhutan and I almost felt jealous in a way. Those of us who follow Buddhism are regarded in the West as doing something a little bit exotic. The Bhutanese, however, can be totally open as it is part of their culture. At the time, I probably idealised it, but there was this large crowd of people in colourful costumes who had come from all over the country to see the cremation. It was a very friendly, peaceful and devoted atmosphere.

Travels in east Bhutan

I am still fascinated that this is now one of the few countries where Tibetan Buddhism is very much alive, and returned in February 1999 with Dzongsar Khyentse Rinpoche. I found the circumstances very little changed. It was really amazing for me travelling with Rinpoche, seeing him in his traditional role, away from the West. It started with Rinpoche, two monks and I being picked up from the airport by the Chief of Police of

East Bhutan, who is a very devoted practitioner of Buddhism and student of Rinpoche. As we crossed the border there were over one hundred people lined up on the road, all dressed up and holding white traditional scarves, waiting to greet Rinpoche. He stopped the car and gave everyone blessings. People have the greatest respect and regard for Rinpoche and see him as a totally enlightened being, a living Buddha. I am so amazed by their devotion. People will walk for days just to get a glimpse of him and receive a blessing and then go home again, happy and contented.

We continued to his monastery in east Bhutan where he was leading nine days of prayer, which is conducted twenty-four hours a day. At four o'clock in the morning, Rinpoche with all the monks would be doing a very elaborate practice that included exactly all those Tibetan rituals I had disliked all those years ago. I never thought I would be doing them. I surprised myself, getting up so early to sit in the tent, seeing Rinpoche in a more formal setting. I didn't even want to travel too far to other places. The day after, though, Rinpoche, in his funny kind of smiling way, said, 'Well, I think you should be going, I'll organise something for you.' Maybe he thought I would get bored and that I should see something of Bhutan. Then he called one of his monks and had a little discussion with him. The monk gave me this big smile, left the tent at the tea break and returned saying, 'There's a car waiting for you, just get your bag as you're going to go away.' I didn't know where I was going.

So I just got my things and found myself, a few minutes later, in the car of a shopkeeper from a town north of Rinpoche's monastery. Rinpoche had asked him to drive me there and bring me back the next day. The whole trip was pretty magical. However, I had forgotten to take my passport with me so when we came to the first checkpoint and they asked for my passport, my driver just said, 'Well she's a student of Rinpoche and Rinpoche has asked me to bring her to the north.' The police opened the gates and let me go through because I was a student of Rinpoche's. When we came to a restaurant, people treated me with great hospitality and I could see the driver was proud of having the task of driving Rinpoche's student around. In some ways it made me giggle but I was also embarrassed about it. At the same time, it revealed to me how much devotion Bhutanese people have for their teacher and how important Rinpoche is to them.

In the evening we stayed at a tiny little house. They made me the most incredible bed, piling up all their mattresses one over the other, with lots of cushions. They installed a little electric light bulb in the sleeping room because there hadn't been any light there and I went to bed with five people watching me from the door because they wanted to make sure I was really comfortable. It was really touching. The trip itself was quite tiring, we travelled on tiny little mountain roads on which it takes hours to move any distance. Sometimes we would cross landslides on the incredibly narrow curvy roads, with beautiful little towns on each side. When you travel through India, sometimes you visit quite dirty places. I felt wherever I went in those two weeks that everything was so well taken care of by the Bhutanese people. It's very clean and they have little flower pots everywhere and everything is decorated so you feel they are well off, even if they are very poor. Bhutan is a country very much about strong images, beautiful landscapes and colours. It was a very visual experience and the encounter with people was incredible. Even though people didn't speak much English, I could tell they had a great sense of humour and were very down to earth.

Another striking event for me was being invited to the twenty-fifth anniversary ceremony of the technical college of Dewathang. The Foreign Minister of Bhutan was there. He gave a short talk about the importance of the college for Bhutan because it's the only technical college. He then talked about people needing to keep their values against corruption and the laws of cause and effect. What really struck me again was that a political minister was talking about Buddhist values in a public setting. I know that Bhutan has been criticised by some international press over how Nepalese immigrants are treated, but I found the sincerity and devotion of the minister in this particular situation towards Buddhism inspiring.

Fairytales for adults

A couple of days later I went to the place where Rinpoche was discovered, a very small remote place where his grandfather had been living. Sonan Zanpo was regarded as a great yogi and highly accomplished practitioner and his name has become legendary. Visiting the actual place made it all very real for me because sometimes I think it's almost like hearing fairy stories. Maybe that's why we like it because it's fairytales for adults and we can indulge our imaginations — far-away Tibet, high mountains, remote cultures and strange ceremonies. For me it has been something between fairytale and reality. Going there and seeing the people who actually knew these masters and the places where they lived made me feel very fortunate. There are still yogis who do nine-year retreats, and this is still a normal part of Bhutanese life. I feel those people have a much more steady attitude and unwavering belief that we in the West don't know how to have.

They have so much devotion, but they don't talk about it like we do. It's part of their tradition and their life and what they do. In fact, one of my concerns of Bhutan becoming more open to the West is that they may start losing faith and no longer follow their traditions. This is especially true of the younger people, who are drawn to what they see as freedom, when, in fact, they have the true strength already within their culture. It seems really important for young people to start studying Buddhism now, so they don't view their heritage as an old-fashioned tradition to get rid of because they want to be more Western and materialistic. I think conviction can only be obtained by studying.

There is something deeply inspirational about people who have such a strong belief that they are happy to walk for days just to see Rinpoche, circumambulate the tent for the next few days because they feel it is going to give them incredible blessings and then walk off again. They rarely even ask for teachings because studying Buddhism was traditionally in the hands of the monks, whereas Westerners would probably have far more expectations, ask for much more and know more, and yet experience tremendous difficulties in being devoted.

Being honest

I often feel that I don't have true devotion. I still go through periods where I am not convinced that the teacher has done something in the best way. I can't say I don't have any devotion, but at the same time I can't say I have any either.

Actually, for me devotion is something that changes all the time, rather than being stable. I guess, if I'm honest, things have been up and down for years. Often I'm convinced that the Buddhist teachings and discovering the truth is the most important thing I have in my life. At other times I think I'm never going to realise anything in my life anyway and I just want to have a good time. These are the moments where I am not particularly devoted. However, I think that it's important to be able to express doubts and criticisms and not just become all holy without your feet on the ground, so to speak. I can't see the point of just saying, 'Yes, Rinpoche,' if deep down you are feeling, 'No, Rinpoche.'

If you don't really feel it inside, just don't do it. It's important to me to be honest and not pretend. It becomes difficult in a group if people can't stand up and say they don't agree with something or support their private needs. From my own experience, these were very special moments whenever I dared to do this, because either the teacher showed me my projection or it was resolved. Devotion doesn't mean losing your sense of responsibility or handing over your decision making to the teacher or running away from the world.

One person to rely on

It's essential we also get on with our lives. I don't think I'll get enlightened in thirty days, and I actually do want to enjoy life, travel and do totally mundane things as well as focus on Dharma, and one certainly doesn't exclude the other, but they rarely enhance each other. Yet, when I look back, I can see that since I met Rinpoche, whenever there was a key situation in my life, happy or difficult, there was one person I could totally rely on and that was Dzongsar Khyentse Rinpoche. The longer my life goes on and I see all the waves I go through, sometimes not seeing him for months and then being able to travel with him and feeling close, then being fed up with him, then going away, practising meditation and then not practising, within all of this, there is this one stable relationship that remains. The longer I know him the more it amazes me. I feel a great sense of gratitude for that.

It's like a decision I renew again and again. When I see other people trapped in situations or that ordinary solutions don't work, I feel lucky that I have the teachings to refer to, because they do definitely help. This is the reconfirmation of what is really the most precious thing I have in my life. Even if someone is very nasty to me now, I don't get totally depressed about it because I have more tools to work with myself. I have a framework and a means that 'gets me back in shape'. It's not so much returning to my old rigid form, the way I used to be, but it allows me to have something inside that I can hold on to. That actually makes me more independent.

There is a prayer of devotion that touches me deeply whenever I hear it. It says, 'Pray to the Guru to break your heart, and make sure that it is never repaired again.' This appeals to me because it's totally opening up your heart and finding truth, joy and love for yourself and others. Then to pray that you are never going to close it again, means that you're never going to develop a hard, protective shell around your heart.

Rinpoche himself has been through years and years of really tough training, and part of the tradition is that he still has teachers himself. He continuously acts in a perfectly appropriate way and is incredibly wise and skilful in handling all types of situations and people. What has had the most impact on me is the non-formal teaching. Just by being with my teachers and them pointing out the key issue in one sentence to me, or undermining my expectations of what I think should be happening, or not behaving in the way I think they should. When I recently learned that my work contract was ending early, because of a difficult situation that had nothing to do with me, I panicked and phoned Rinpoche to ask him what to do, hoping for a very wise answer. He said to me, 'Don't do anything.' This left me totally puzzled and a little annoyed. It certainly wasn't the answer I was expecting. Suddenly

I realised it was a great idea because I could surprise people by not reacting in the way they thought I would. This then gave me a greater sense of choice. By not engaging, the story didn't last longer. It was like a glass of bubbly, sparkling mineral water and I just watched how it sparkled without putting my finger into it and causing more bubbles. This attitude then helped me remain quite calm.

It reminds me of the teachings on impermanence, that tomorrow everything can be different. You'll never know and it always takes you by surprise and you always fight against it. It's like losing your job or needing to move and you don't want to cope with it. It's going to end one day and the fact that you can end it in a very nice or nasty way doesn't alter the fact that it will end. So again I saw how perfect Rinpoche's advice had been.

So even though I still think it is important to be honest with yourself and ask questions, I also have the utmost admiration and trust in Rinpoche. He is a person I can totally rely on, knowing deep in my heart it is not only him as a person, but that he represents the teachings and the path to realise ultimate truth.

The flowers raise their heads to the sun and rain without bias, welcoming both to grow strong.
I too invite the elements of transformation,
but am imprisoned in prejudice.
Teach and transform me and all those like me
who wish to plant the seed of impartiality,
So we may ripen and blossom into the infinite void.

NOTHING TO PROVE

THE LEPER'S GIFT

A monk called Geshe Chekawa came across a verse:

> **Give all the profit and gain to others
> and accept all blame and loss.**

Geshe Chekawa was so completely amazed at these words that he decided to make them his life's path and to discover who had written them so they could teach him the truth and reality of these two lines. He travelled, asking many people who had composed these inspirational thoughts, only to finally discover from a leper that they had been written by Atisha, a great master who had died one hundred years previously. Determined not to give up, he finally found a disciple of Atisha called Layman Drom. He committed himself to study and practice so that he could attain the realisation of these words and, in doing so, also attain limitless loving kindness and enlightenment.

Initially Geshe Chekawa did not reveal what he had learnt but, after many years, some lepers approached him and asked for teachings. He felt such gratitude to the leper who had assisted him, he began to teach them. After a while, there were stories of extraordinary healing. His brother, who had always been very skeptical and cynical about Buddhism, saw the healing among the lepers. He secretly began to practise the mind training of the Tonglen practice of giving and receiving, which his brother was teaching, while still pretending that he had no interest. After a while, he had changed so much that even Geshe Chekawa was surprised. Seeing that these teachings could transform even the most difficult person, he wrote down everything. These precious teachings are known today as Atisha's 'Seven Points of Mind Training'.[1]

Patrick Jacquelin was born and grew up in Kenya, Africa, with his European parents. They moved to Austria when he was twelve and he went to school in Vienna. He then studied history at Cambridge University in England, after which he completed his military service in the French army. At a fairly young age he attended a well-known business school in

PATRICK JACQUELIN

Europe, then moved to London in his twenties and worked as a management consultant with an American firm. He now manages his own business.

I hadn't known of Patrick until several people recommended him for inclusion in this book. I found myself on Easter Friday, driving across London in search of the elusive Patrick just before he was to fly to Hong Kong. When I met him for the first time, at his apartment in London, he immediately struck me as a stylish, sophisticated and elegant Englishman. This was very interesting in the light of him then saying that he had never felt like he belonged in England. People are often not who we think they are, yet we continue to assign certain characteristics and attributes to individuals and groups based on the flimsiest look or accent, clothing or sexual orientation.

The phrase 'appearances are deceptive' reminds me of the tradition of the yogis, who often travelled incognito, in the old days, as beggars, farmers or fishermen. Now, we can find teachers cycling in Japan, lifting weights in a gym, hanging out in the local coffee shop or sitting next to us on a plane. So how do we know who is a genuine teacher and who is not? Wearing robes does not necessarily make someone an authentic teacher or even a person who has no selfish motivation. How much more difficult to discover this, then, if the teacher does not appear in traditional form, as we project onto even ordinary people all our beliefs and prejudices.

Within this, Patrick then points out one of the dangers of exploring the spiritual path but not having any guidelines or knowledge about the different groups that proliferate in society today. He became caught up with a group of people and was aware he was not comfortable with them, even though he was drawn to their ideas. Luckily he managed to extricate himself, but many other people get caught up before they really know what they are engaging in.

In *The Words of My Perfect Teacher* Patrul Rinpoche gives clear guidelines on how to distinguish a genuine teacher and summarises the process:

> Before becoming committed to him through empowerments and teachings, you should examine him with care, meaning 'does he or does he not have bodhichitta (heart of enlightenment, no selfish desires) and do whatever is best for his disciples in this life and lives to come, and their

> following him cannot be anything but beneficial?' ... If a teacher's heart is filled with bodhichitta, follow him however he might appear externally ... But from the moment you follow him, learn to have faith in him and see him with pure perception ... For ordinary people like us, however, no amount of careful examination can reveal to us the extraordinary qualities of those sublime beings who hide their true nature.[2]

These words are from so long ago, yet still have as much relevance to us today as when they were first spoken.

Patrick also explains how puzzled he was when he first came into contact with the teacher. He couldn't understand why people were 'hanging around' the teacher. I have also heard a similar view expressed by people who simply cannot comprehend why people do this and tend to think that it is a 'cult' of the personality of the teacher. This is how misunderstanding and confusion can arise so easily. Patrick states that in the beginning his path seemed to consist entirely of hanging out with Rinpoche, and it took him a while to realise that there was an intrinsic value in this. He learnt by osmosis rather than formal teaching. Most students are probably surprised by the methods of a teacher who is skilful enough to assess what is appropriate to each person and their best learning style. We don't always get what we want, but rather what we need. For some, this might be what looks like friendship and informal socialising, whereas for others it could be a disciplined path of training. The Buddha taught 84,000 discourses to suit every sort of mind. The teacher is flexible, different and appropriate to each one of us.

Patrick then discusses openly his experience of being gay within the Buddhist community and says that this has been non-conflictual for him. However, discussion of religion, sexuality and homophobia can be a potent mixture. Being part of a minority in a mainstream culture can rarely be truly understood by those in the mainstream. The experiences that people live with every day are often marginalised, ignored, degraded or abused. Prejudice can be subtle or blatant, individual or societal, and is always contained within the conventional structures of the culture. Despite living in a multicultural society, we can clearly see, for example, in the Western cultures, how religions from the East are viewed with some tolerance, up to a point, but only when they do not overly threaten the mainstream religion. They are also often seen as strange, rather than different, and anything unfamiliar is viewed with suspicion. The example of prostrating oneself, or bowing down, which could perhaps be seen as reflected in kneeling down in Christianity, is something many people have difficulty with. In Buddhism this is an antidote to pride, and acknowledging our buddha nature, yet in our culture we are taught to 'stand proud and tall and bow to no one'. When we don't understand, we have a tendency to condemn the outer appearance. In a similar way, being gay in a hetereosexual society brings its own challenges.

However, interestingly enough, Patrick observes that, no matter whether we are straight or gay, sexuality and relationships are two of the main areas where we become caught up, preventing us from letting go. This doesn't mean letting go of relationships necessarily, but letting go of our concepts of how we think things ought to be, rather than how they actually are. It can be more difficult, though, when accepted mainstream societal values, individuals and institutions do not support, and in some cases condemn, a minority group. From what Patrick says, in Buddhism, sexuality is just another concept to be worked with in a similar way to any other.

Patrick's story

As I grew up in Africa, I think romantically it was somewhat idyllic. My parents were quite involved with themselves so I had a somewhat neglected African childhood and spent a lot of my time with black people. My first language was one of the local languages and I didn't speak a European language until later. It felt like my place and I was very close to Africa. That feeling has never left me, even though I didn't go back after the age of thirteen. As a consequence, I never really felt I belonged to Europe, especially England, where I arrived at nineteen. Africa left me with an affinity with underdeveloped countries and I've always enjoyed being in those countries because that is what I grew up with. When we moved to Europe, my parents divorced and that was quite difficult.

Coming out

Then there was me being gay and I think that, relative to some other people, it took me a long time to accept myself. I 'came out' in my late twenties. I grew up in a conventional environment and was in denial about my gayness. Having difficulty accepting myself, I formed a personality that tended to want to be in control. I learnt how to charm other people so they would accept me. At the same time, I never really trusted anyone and wouldn't let people come close to me. The whole ability to communicate and to trust myself wasn't there. I didn't have the language or the tools. So it wasn't that I was scared to 'come out of the closet'; I hadn't even reached that point and didn't know there was a key to open the door and step out. Finally, falling in love gave me the key. At that time, I was so much in love with the man, with whom I then lived with for seven years, that I had no doubt that this is what I wanted and who I should be.

By the time I met Dzongsar Khyentse Rinpoche in 1992, I think I was quite lost. Two years previously I had finished a seven-year relationship with someone who I had known most of my life and it left me shattered and confused. I was in denial about a lot of things. The end of this relationship was in some way a catalyst for my spiritual path. Before my partner left, he had been looking at different spiritual paths and I think I competed with him in this area. I guess I was trying to grasp onto that relationship, even though it was finished.

So I delved into all Jung's books and met a group of people, whom I now recognise as a sect and rather extreme. I was always rather uncomfortable with them, even though I was interested in some of their ideas, but never liked how they presented them, which was rather didactic and intolerant. Their approach reminded me of some of the worst episodes of European history this century. I remember I attended a conference of this group in Rome. It was sort of evangelical and I got really scared and I decided to just leave. It really wasn't for me. In fact, later they threw me out when I told them I was gay.

A friend of mine

I went to Thailand for two weeks to a small, remote island without electricity to do a short retreat, you could say, although I didn't really know what a retreat was. I got rather bored reading this one spiritual book I had taken to study, but I did find a book that is in Thai hotels, which is the Japanese–English version of the Buddha's teaching. It was rather simple, about the 'Four Noble Truths', and I enjoyed reading it. I met Dzongsar Khyentse Rinpoche two days after this in Bangkok. It's interesting to mention that, before I even met Rinpoche, I had always had a great sympathy for Tibet as a country and knew about its history and His Holiness the Dalai Lama. I don't know whether it was as banal as being a French child and reading all the Tin Tin books, like *Tin Tin in Tibet*, but I don't think so.

I knew Albert-Paravi Wongchirachai, who lives in Bangkok, and had been a student of Dilgo Khyentse Rinpoche, but I had never got involved with Buddhism at all. Albert rang me and said there was a Tibetan Rinpoche coming and invited me over, but I already had a prior engagement. However, Albert insisted, so I went to the hotel that evening. I was rather fascinated by Rinpoche and the people there who were having a debate about Buddhism, which I didn't understand a word of. Later we went to dinner, and at the time the whole event seemed to me like a social evening.

My first impressions of Rinpoche were that he was unusual and very interesting. I was curious about him and I liked him. What I actually thought was, 'This person should become a friend of mine.' It took me a long time to realise that, in fact, he is a lama and I didn't know then that he would become my teacher. Later I also realised that he is a very public person. So, rather selfishly, I thought he'd just be a friend, rather than balancing all those three aspects. Anyway, I have always had a very strong connection with Thailand and it has always remained very close to my heart. That evening, Rinpoche talked about how much he liked Thailand.

We went back to the hotel and Albert told Rinpoche about the Erawan shrine. When the Erawan hotel was being built, a series of disasters had happened, with people falling off the scaffolding and things going dreadfully wrong. They finally built a small open-air shrine and, from then on, everything went well. It became one of the most popular shrines in Bangkok and whenever I went it was always full of people making offerings. We walked back past it at ten thirty at night and it was closed. The guy who was washing the shrine opened it up, which was very unusual, so we were all quite surprised. The whole evening was enjoyable for me, and I remember being quite struck by Rinpoche liking and respecting Thailand and visiting the shrine.

Shortly after this I saw a lot of Rinpoche in London for a few weeks and it was fairly quiet with only a few people around. I don't really know what happened, but I found myself asking Rinpoche if he would teach me. He asked me why and I started telling him. As I was speaking I realised I was talking incomprehensible nonsense and stopped. He agreed and so I became his student. I don't really know why that happened. Even though it was premeditated, he had not talked to me about Buddhism and I honestly didn't know anything about it. In retrospect, those few days with him have never left me.

In the gateway

The first thing I would say about devotion is that I suddenly had a real feeling that I could trust this man. This was the seed that a flower grew from and has never withered. That moment of trust didn't grow overnight, but nevertheless, for me it grew quite fast. It's actually very unlike me, because in my life I'm usually untrusting and have boundaries that I don't allow people to cross. My natural tendency is to reject. With Rinpoche, somehow, I really knew that I could give myself, that I could place myself in his hands. He never allowed an opportunity to arise for me to act out my habitual tendency. I remember Rinpoche said to me, 'Keep your doubt. It might be one of your greatest treasures.' In retrospect, I think it was good to be aware of my doubt, as then I saw it change, and retreat and fade away.

The other strange thing that has happened, is that the relationship I have with Rinpoche has not really changed much since the beginning. I somehow thought it would change over time. I thought that maybe he would say, at some point, 'Now, it's time to go into a 500-year retreat' or something. What I find though is that my trust has always grown and been reinforced. When I was in Katmandu, for example, for the enthronement of the reincarnation of Dilgo Khyentse Rinpoche, I was going through a bad phase, resenting all the people around me, and feeling outside it all. When I saw Dzongsar Khyentse Rinpoche, he somehow managed to turn my mood round. It became apparent to me as I got closer to Rinpoche, that he was the one who was giving, not me, although I tried to. What struck me about him was how he always shares and gives what he's got. I mean, it's difficult sometimes because there are so many people. If you are not aware of it, you can feel hard done by.

He has given me so much, not only with the lineage and the treasure teachings but in the small things. He has taken me to places and I've met extraordinary people. Most of all he trusts you with large and small projects, like helping on his film, *The Cup*. He just leaves it with you. It's amazing to see the way he lets people do things. That's what he did with me and I suppose that's partially where the trust came from. It's not a question of performance; it is more about a relationship. At the start it was definitely Rinpoche, not Buddhism, for me. It was he I met and he that I trusted. Now it's different, but my path up to then was Rinpoche. He was the entry point and I was still in the gateway. I remember feeling scared that suddenly he would go, and I remember when he went into a one-year retreat and I thought how terrible it would be if he wasn't there.

Part of the family

I went with Rinpoche to the naming ceremony of Yangsi Rinpoche in the cave at Maratika. This is the cave where Guru Rinpoche and his consort spent some time in the ninth century. The Hindus worship it as a fertility shrine, but it is still a very famous Buddhist shrine as well. The ceremony was really the formal recognition that this little boy was the reincarnation of His Holiness Dilgo Khyentse Rinpoche and preceded his enthronement.

The cave is in Nepal and we flew by helicopter because it's pretty inaccesible. It's madly romantic, in the middle of nowhere with only a little gompa [temple]. There are spectacular caves there and it feels a bit like *Raiders of the Lost Ark*. The main cave is very beautiful and dramatic with spectacular light and many bats flying around. Being in this setting with the monks and lamas dressed in red performing a ritual was amazing and inspiring. All the lamas presented the little lama with scarves and I was very moved by the whole atmosphere. It was really the unspoken and unseen things that touched me so deeply.

The two days I spent at Maratika were very moving. In particular, I felt honoured because it was like being part of a large family. The Tibetans do this to you. Being there with Rinpoche made me realise that much more was being offered than I had known. This wasn't a passage together in a limited sense but for the duration. I thought I was just a visitor who was lucky enough to be there but, as far as they were concerned, I was there to stay. There was no door that was going to close behind me and I was very happy about that.

In fact, I met Dzongsar Khyentse Rinpoche just after His Holiness Dilgo Khyentse Rinpoche died. I told Rinpoche a few years later how sad I was that I had never met

Dilgo Khyentse. He replied, 'Oh, you will.' I didn't know what he meant at the time. At the enthronement in Katmandu, which continued for three days, I went to see Yangsi Rinpoche twice. That ceremony was one of the first times since 1959 that the Tibetans were able to put in place a proper enthronement ceremony. What was incredibly beautiful and clear was the devotion of everyone. It was like the devotion was on display, but it wasn't a show or light entertainment.

No big deal

One of the things about being gay in a Buddhist community is that I can't really separate it out. I have found it very unconflicting. This is because neither Rinpoche nor anyone else has never made an issue out of my being gay. From the beginning Rinpoche was the one who made me avoid making a problem out of it. With him, being gay does not seem to have any central role, but is treated as just a facet of my personality. That was quite a rare experience for me. I think I did try to make it an issue at one point, but he wouldn't let me. He signals very directly and honestly that you're on a non-issue.

It's interesting because I think that if I were to be a gay activist now, I could be more effective than before. I would achieve my objectives more easily by not being so emotionally attached. I've learnt to accept things more as they are and move at my own pace. Having something to prove often results in internal conflict, taking positions and getting stuck. It's like two deer with antlers locking horns. Being gay is important, but it's just there. Making a big statement about it is like locking horns again. I'm much more comfortable now about letting things be.

Buddhism has changed my views in that it took me away from being immersed in the basics of sexuality to understanding something more complex about human relationships. Heterosexuals have very difficult lives. They often think they're simpler because there are conventions around them. Ultimately, though, all these sexual and emotional ties are in some way illusion.

The events of your life or the path you go down is supposed to be some sort of mirror. Part of this is the way you imagine or identify your sexuality. If people put a lot of obstacles in your way because of convention, then I think that has to be faced. People who are not gay often do not see the enormous traps that they fall into. It's easy to see how women are still poorly treated. Even more simply though, because of expectations, people go into marriage quite blindly, without having explored what they want from relationships. Then they find themselves caught in the most painful traps.

In a similar way it reminds me of friends watching me in my late twenties, seeing the mistakes I was making in going against convention. I had to face the consequences, like the difficulty of establishing long-term relationships in a framework where there was no role model — in fact, the complete opposite of the trap of the heterosexual. Also thinking I could just imitate that, but finding that without the support of the structures like the family, society, the tax system, it's more difficult.

I think that in all relationships, whatever their nature, we tend to project ourselves onto other people. For example, if we try to make ourselves attractive and sexy, we can get caught in that. You can't see the other person because you get trapped in seeing how they react to your projection or seduction. So you inevitably end up being stuck. The alternative is to try not to project or prove. Just see the other person, let things happen and allow things to be. It's not easily done, but I think if it can be done the scope becomes much greater.

I think though that my association with Buddhism has led me to see sexuality as related to the ego. Before, I gave it much greater importance, whereas now it seems not so much of the essence, so ultimately it doesn't matter at all which way you are inclined. The thing is just to get on with the path. On the other hand, sexuality is also a very important thing because it is so powerful in life. You can't repress sexuality without repressing other elements in yourself. So it will be a central element to any path. So it's like the Zen koan. It's not of the essence at one level, yet it's still important to work with. I think I should make it clear these thoughts are aspirations rather than achievements.

Being myself

Rinpoche also encourages me to be outrageous, although I can never really do it. I understand why he encourages us to make fools of ourselves. It's so healthy because of pride. Also we are all fools anyway, but we refuse to believe it and we put on all these acts of dignity. By teasing us, I think he's telling us to get the childish rubbish out of the way. It becomes clearer and gets much lighter if you take the seriousness out of it. Westerners are incredibly serious about relationships and religion. Meeting Rinpoche has begun to change my view on all these things. It feels more real and also easier.

So much of the teaching for me has been in hanging out and being with Rinpoche. I didn't understand this at first and I wondered why I was doing it. Watching him and seeing how he handles his day and his life has been a revelation and a great role model. His ability to remain calm and not worry is admirable.

At one level one could see the relationship with the teacher is one for life. Actually, it's like a form of marriage. It's also reciprocal, mutual, not just one way. There can also be demands that have to be met to satisfy the relationship. That's where the trust element comes in. With Rinpoche, I've trusted him and the timing of demands. For example, it was a long time before I took any initiations and they have always been phased. Things have always come at the right time. In fact, instead of telling me to go and spend three years in a cave, he keeps telling me to concentrate on my business. So for me, the essence of devotion is trust. Opening to trusting Rinpoche has allowed me to open to trust myself and others. It is clear to me now that the point of devotion is that it benefits you, not the object of devotion. I am definitely the beneficiary.

I think that Buddhism and Rinpoche and the Tibetan tradition have begun to open the doors that have helped me to better understand reality. I didn't have that before. The ideas and concepts are clearer and more truthful than the alternatives that I've come across.

In my life I have been very intellectual, and in Buddhism I've tried to steer clear of that. It's only recently that I've even bought some books on Buddhism. It's been a singular experience for me, as I met this man and I got closer to him. Trust followed and from that I started absorbing the teachings, even though I've hardly studied them. It's really been more osmosis.

Rinpoche has taught me the simplicity of awareness, just looking and seeing what I do and what happens. So, sometimes I slowly become more conscious and more aware of all the games I play. After a while I stop enjoying the games so much and then the benefit I get is that sometimes I may be freed from them. Of course, as a beginner, I then just fall into a new trap, but then I'm free of that one until, finally, the bank of habitual patterns becomes lighter. My hope is that bit by bit the account may become lighter and replaced by something much richer. You begin to realise how ephemeral everything is and have a much greater acceptance of change. Then you have the freedom of realising that the roles you were playing weren't that important. Life becomes more fun, we gain more confidence and flexibility and we can face life more.

Floating forward

My understanding of Buddhism is that there is no target. Therefore, enlightenment is not a goal to be striven for, in the way we normally understand being goal-oriented. I think that as soon as you start setting targets, you've gone off the path and that striving leads nowhere. It's difficult to understand, and I have found it difficult myself, but as soon as you have a goal in spirituality, you are no longer floating. Floating is the only possibility of moving forward. It's about respecting that things happen at their own pace and the teacher is an influence. The old tools that we use are meaningless in this setting, because we are talking about losing the ego. I am only just beginning to take the first steps towards learning and understanding all this.

My whole relationship with Tibetan Buddhism and Dzongsar Khyentse Rinpoche has been like rain falling on a petal. It was never forced on me in any way and I never accelerated it. It just rained and I was there and I took it in.

I pray for protection and wisdom,
but am enslaved by my past.
The clouds of change invite me to grow,
but I'm unable to take the instructions to heart.
Teach and transform me and all those like me
who wish to taste the supreme nectar,
So we may practise with unstinting perseverance
and secure the ultimate fruit of wisdom.

PARALLELS

ATTENTION

A Zen Buddhist master was dying and her students asked her for her final teaching. She said one word, 'attention'. However, they were all expecting something more, profound words of wisdom or a poem or stories. They requested again for her to give them the essential wisdom, the pith instruction to help their realisation. Again she answered, 'Attention.' They still felt dissatisfied and wanted to know to what or whom to give their attention. They supplicated to her for a third time, saying, 'Please reveal to us the innermost truth of the Buddha's teaching.'

As she died, she said, 'Attention.' This was her precious last gift to her students, who were unable to recognise the treasure she was bestowing upon them. Their own complexity had distracted them from being in the present moment, being concentrated and focused, and through meditation being totally at one with themselves and everything around them.[1]

Harry Lee was born in Hong Kong, presently lives in London but has spent most of his life in America. He has worked in hotel management and, ten years ago, started to study singing and is now an opera singer. When I met with him in London most of the time I was either laughing at his great sense of humour about himself and life in general, or being amazed by his passion, dedication and devotion to the subject and experience of singing. Harry seemed to embody the very subject of letting go and not trying to manipulate or change anything. He had no interest in seeing the outcome of his story and was totally unconcerned about the final result. He was completely in the moment, didn't need any prior information and let it go as soon as he had finished talking. He lives his life as he describes the best singing, that which is totally spontaneous.

He is amazingly honest in talking about his first contact with the Buddhist teachings, saying that he thought they were boring, didn't think much of the students and only hung around because he couldn't change his airline ticket. He also only wanted a meditation practice because others had one. I think, however, that he is rather underplaying himself and it is obvious that he has a great deal of love and devotion towards Dzongsar Khyentse Rinpoche.

HARRY LEE

This becomes even clearer when Harry begins to talk about his passion in life for singing and singers. He describes it in almost devotional terms as if he is transported to another world that is not at all ordinary. As with any artistic endeavour, there are many similarities or parallels between training to be a singer and following a spiritual teacher and tradition. You need a huge amount of discipline, perseverance, patience, dedication, hard work and trust, to name just a few qualities, to train your voice to perfection. You also require the equanimity to survive the disappointments, hopes being dashed in an instant in auditions. Having unswerving faith and not giving up, continuing your efforts until some results are reached, sounds very much like a devotional path.

Harry feels that the beauty offered through the voices of our finest singers also indicates a great deal of mental generosity. The subject of reaching perfection leads him to discuss a major issue of how Westerners expect their spiritual teachers to be perfect. We do not expect or want the teacher to have a personal life, and become confused between this and the teachings.

We think that if the teacher is the vehicle through which the teachings are transmitted, then somehow they are not allowed to be human. Traditionally before a teacher mounts the throne or seat upon which he sits to give teachings, he prostrates three times and then snaps his fingers. This is so that he 'leaves himself behind' and becomes, in that moment, a pure vessel or conduit through which the teachings flow.

In Harry's world it is similar to a singer who, while he is performing, is divested of his ego so that he may perform purely and at his best. The performer does not get in the way of the performance and therefore the singing is heard in its pure tone. Of course, often with singers the ego reasserts itself when the singing stops, unlike a teacher with enlightened mind, who has no ego. Having no ego, though, does not necessarily exclude having a private life. There are actually many points here that need to be disentangled from our cultural and psychological ideas.

First, we come from a culture where 'religious' figures are seen as celibate and in robes. Therefore we assume that anyone wearing robes is a monk, but this is not necessarily true. Harry himself states how he was initially confused by the different roles Rinpoche has, in being the teacher, eating meat, drinking alcohol and answering questions on sex. It is often unknown to people that Tibetan Buddhist teachers often have partners, marry and have children, unless they have taken final monastic vows, and are not necessarily vegetarian.

Second, psychologically we could say that we have an idealised and unrealistic image that we project onto the teacher. When we are young children we think our parents are perfect and don't realise that they are just human beings. Often we spend our life trying to recreate that in our relationships or with figures of authority, only to be disappointed. We expected our parents to be perfect, and we project that onto the teacher from the 'child' state within us and then accuse the teacher when he or she turns out to be less than our idealised version of perfection. It is our version though and may have nothing whatsoever to do with what is really happening. The Vajrayana path is one of transformation, not renunciation, like the Hinayana path, which is commonly found in Asian countries.

There is a traditional story that can be seen as a metaphor for how to work with our habitual patterns of mind, as well as describing the four different paths in Buddhism: Hinayana, Mahayana, Vajrayana and Dzogchen, which is regarded as the highest teachings within the Vajrayana path.

> **A group of people discover that a poisonous plant in their backyard. They begin to panic, as they recognize that this is very dangerous. So they try to cut down the plant ... Another group of people arrive ... [and] ...throw hot ash ... over the roots ... The next group of people ... are doctors ... and are not alarmed; on the contrary, they are very pleased, since they have been looking for this particular poison. They know how to transform the poison into medicine, rather than destroying it ... Finally a peacock lands, and dances with joy when it sees the poison. It immediately consumes the poisonous plant and turns it into beauty.**[2]

This peacock, of course, represents an advanced stage of meditation practice. It is not a literal recommendation that people eat poison but a description of directly using the substance that might kill you to become even more radiant, bypassing the need to transform.

Another viewpoint is that perfection is in the eye of the beholder and therefore the teacher becomes perfect when we have perfected our own mind. Also, we are often only viewing the teacher from our very limited, relative perspective and are used to judging only on outward appearance. We really do not know whether this teacher has an enlightened mind or not, which is why there are guidelines laid out on how to choose a teacher. A traditional illustration about perception uses the example of being ill with jaundice, but not knowing you have the disease. You see everything as yellow and think that is normal, not realising your perception is impaired because you are sick. Rinpoche contemporises the example, saying it's like looking at snow on a mountain top with yellow-tinted sunglasses on. You don't know you have the glasses on and insist the snow is yellow, not white. Even though many people tell you that the snow is white, you persist in trusting your senses. Until someone takes the lenses off your eyes or you realise and take them off yourself, you continue to be mistaken.

Harry also talks about his experience of Rinpoche never judging or seeing the imperfections in people and how that has helped him become less judgmental and negative with himself and others. This doesn't mean to say that Rinpoche is foolish or idealistic and doesn't see who people are. He probably knows more clearly what is going on than we ever will. However, he never judges like we tend to. The teacher is the vehicle through which the teachings come and devotion can be seen as a skilful means of developing pure perception. Often a teacher will purposely behave in a way that directly challenges how we think they should be, to help us become aware of our expectations and spiritual neuroses. If we have a childish notion that spiritual teachers wear pure white robes, and drift around preaching 'love and light' we will be sorely disappointed. Tibetan teachers are known for their practical nature, earthy sense of humour and down-to-earth commonsense. Perfection is more to do with pure perception, no self-interest and great compassion than some angelic qualities that we may project.

There is a story of a student talking to a teacher and outlining his side of a conflict with another student. The teacher appears to agree with the student, saying, 'Yes, yes I understand.' Then the other student outlines her side and again the teacher seems to agree. Another person watching asks the master, 'How could you agree with both of them when they have said completely opposite things?' The master laughs and says, 'But from their perceptions, they were both right. From my perception, I see no faults in anyone. From the ultimate point of view, none of it exists anyway, so why get upset?'

Part of the path is to see that we do have certain expectations of how our spiritual teachers are meant to behave and also what sort of setting and environment we are meant to receive teachings in. Again, culturally we assume that we will be in some sort of grand building, like a church or cathedral, synagogue, temple or mosque. Somehow we think we are going to learn more if we are meditating or receiving conventional teachings in a more 'formal' setting. What has become obvious to Harry is that in the Tibetan tradition a true teacher is teaching all the time, whether it is having a cup of tea with him, going to see a movie, helping with a project or in a centre. So having an opportunity to 'hang out' with a teacher who embodies the teachings, as well as receive teachings in a more formal setting can be just as useful.

One of Rinpoche's gifts is to take simple examples and transform them into Dharma teachings. Harry describes one of these about the dirt and the shirt. When we buy a new shirt, it is clean, rather like our intrinsic or Buddha nature. As we wear it, it becomes dirty and so we wash it and it is clean again. However, the point is that we don't tend to confuse the dirt with the shirt. We may say the shirt is dirty but we know the shirt is not the dirt. We often don't know that about ourselves, in that we don't recognise the fundamental and unchanging goodness in ourselves. Traditionally it is said that everything, no matter how bad we think it is, can be washed or purified. The meditation practices are like the washing machine.

Harry's story

I was born in Hong Kong and grew up in a Buddhist environment. That doesn't mean to say that I was interested in Buddhism, though. My mother and grandmother were always making offerings and would pray for prosperity, which is very common in the East. I really didn't like that and would eat all the offerings on the altar, which, of course, I wasn't meant to do. I thought it was just all superstition. Also I was young and didn't think it was very modern. I arrived in America at fourteen years old to attend a boarding school in Pennsylvania. I spent my holidays with an aunt where I started taking singing lessons. I remember I was taken to see an opera in the hills of North Carolina and became totally fascinated with the opera from then on. It was also an escape from being in a school that valued athletics. Of course, there were very few Asian opera singers at that time but I was still captivated.

During my university years, when I studied economics and literature, I kept singing and our singing group even toured in Europe. I think I have always loved singing, because, even though it is very ego-oriented to think this, it makes me somebody. I have needed to feel that I am somebody in my life. In America, I invented a new version of myself, where I could forget all my bad memories of Hong Kong. I then worked in New York in hotel management for seven years before returning to Hong Kong for a year in 1986. Even though I hated being back in Hong Kong, I became very sociable and always had my photograph in the social pages of the newspaper. I realised that I needed to leave, so invented a reason, telling my father I wanted to go to business school. I quickly discovered this was definitely the wrong thing for me to do and a friend suggested that I should sing. However, I didn't follow that idea up at the time and tried many different things. I returned to New York after business school in Boston. I still wasn't happy and entered into many different types of therapy to try to sort myself out.

Sorting myself out

Finally I contacted a singing teacher through a friend of mine. I always remember what happened when I first talked with her. She was extremely Germanic and she horrified and intimidated me. The first thing she said to me was, 'If you don't mean business, do not waste my time and do not waste your time.' So I was working and singing, and still being thoroughly miserable. Every week I wanted to move apartments, so my therapist suggested that perhaps I was wanting a change in my life. Of course, mental changes are not tangible and moving apartments is. Something wasn't working and I didn't know what it was.

A year after I started singing, my boss in the hotel sat me down and mapped out my career path for me. I thought to myself, 'If I did this, how happy would I be?' I came to the conclusion that I would be up to sixty per cent happy and forty per cent unhappy. I thought that was probably too much of being unhappy, so finally decided to change the direction of my life. I was very grateful to my boss for all his plans but I didn't want to follow through on them. So I reduced my hours, carried on with my singing lessons and eventually left in 1990.

I came to England in 1998. I always thought that England was the right country for me, and so far it has been. It fits me and is an antidote to my persistent nervousness. England helps me calm down and become relaxed.

On the track

Looking back, my singing teacher was the first positive influence in my life, even though she was terribly opinionated. Up to that point in my life, I felt I had been walking parallel to the train track of life. I wanted to get on that track but never knew how to. Somehow being with her put me on that track of being in life. After taking lessons with her for about a year, I finally summed up the courage to ask her if she thought I had the possibility of making a career out of singing. She quickly responded as she often did, telling me that I never listened to her. She said she had told me from the very beginning that I had possibilities. She then put me in touch with a very good

Jungian psychotherapist and instructed me to go and have my mind sorted out. She said, 'It all has to do with your mind, not your talent. It will make your life easier and it will certainly make mine smoother.'

Soon after that a friend of mine came to New York after just finishing a retreat with Dzongsar Khyentse Rinpoche. We were in a restaurant when I told her that perhaps I was now ready for Buddhism. She is a very colourful character and I remember she screamed aloud when I said that. She said that she had already been talking to Rinpoche about me, because he loves opera. I guess she was my connection into Rinpoche. She is one of the famous socialites from Hong Kong, is very beautiful and everyone knows her. I met her while I was working in a hotel and took her luggage. I thought that she was very strange because, in Asia, when you work for someone you are invisible. However, she talked to me and asked me lots of questions. She, in fact, told me about Rinpoche.

First impressions

How I actually met him was an interesting occurrence. I went to Thailand to visit a friend, who was talking with great affection about His Holiness Dilgo Khyentse Rinpoche. At the time I was still a little suspicious, because I thought maybe it was a cult. Of course it wasn't, but I didn't know that at the time. He asked me to deliver an airline ticket for Dzongsar Khyentse Rinpoche to the airport, which I did. Five days after that I met Rinpoche in person, in Hong Kong, when my friend took me to a teaching that was held in someone's house. Initially I thought all the people were quite strange and I felt apprehensive, uncomfortable and negative. However, the first opinion I had when I met Rinpoche was that he was a very kind person. As for the teachings, I think I had rather an arrogant attitude, thinking that what he was saying was quite obvious and just commonsense.

I saw Rinpoche again in London in early 1992. I was going skiing in Europe so I sort of dropped by before I was to leave. I thought the teaching was very boring and it was very uncomfortable sitting on the floor. Again I wasn't impressed with the people there. I was hanging on for a very bad reason — my ticket couldn't be changed and I was stuck there. I decided that because other people had meditation practices to do, I should have some too. I guess I was just being greedy and didn't want to be left out of anything. One day I asked Rinpoche if I could talk to him, determined to get some meditation practice from him. I talked non-stop about complete nonsense to prevent him from saying that I could not have the practice. He did give me a practice to do, however, and immediately after that I left.

One of the things Rinpoche said during those teachings made a deep impact on me and actually made me cry. He gave the example of 'the shirt and the dirt'. He said that a shirt gets dirty but the dirt can be washed away. The dirt does not belong to the shirt. The shirt is intrinsically clean. It was so touching to me. Then I remember we went with him to a pub and I was quite confused by him at this stage. I saw that he ate meat and drank alcohol and I could talk to him about sex. He asked me how I was and I gave him my usual reply that my neck and back hurt. He suggested that I get a massage. I don't know what happened in that moment, but I just fell in. I can't explain but I knew, 'I'm in it.' I just began to smile and I thought, 'I'm in.'

Two worlds

It seems to me as if there is the real world and a parallel world with Rinpoche in it. We bring exactly the same problems of our life to the parallel world or community. Our best and worst comes out and so we learn. The reason we do this in a rather controlled or artificial environment is that a lot of what we do is harmful, even though we may not realise it. In the ordinary world, this can cause big problems for ourselves and others. However, what we experience within the Sangha often prevents us from repeating our patterns and, even when we do, it does not create such a big mess. It can be transformed. In real life we usually have to pay for it dearly, but in this environment we don't. You learn and, chances are, you then don't repeat this in your life. It is a learning ground, but you are not going to 'fall down and be dead'.

Room for everyone

At the beginning, because I was insecure and somehow in my life felt that affection had passed me by, I used to compete for Rinpoche's attention. However, I realised very early on that Rinpoche is like an expandable sponge. He has room for everyone. He actually pays everyone the same attention and there is no need to compete. At the start I was just doing what other people did and spent my spare time with him. Actually I can now see the value of doing that, even though I was very judgmental in the beginning about all these people just hanging around Rinpoche.

I realised that part of 'hanging out' with Rinpoche is a lesson in itself, if you really open your eyes and see how he deals with other people and with certain situations. I have seen how he handles someone on the street or an unpleasant situation. I have benefited greatly by seeing for myself how he does things. Maybe I can't do it in the same way by myself but at least I have noticed how he deals with a particular situation in a certain manner, like averting an argument. It could be that someone says something particularly stupid, but he never insults them and just lets them speak. He is incredibly skilful. I have also learnt to be much more flexible. I used to be very annoyed that he didn't seem to have much of a schedule and sometimes was late. Yet, over time, I have seen how valuable this is. We are so caught up in linear time, we become rigid and inflexible in our expectations around time.

I find it hard to talk about Rinpoche, because as soon as I think I've figured out how he is, he changes. He's very hard to pinpoint. I really don't know what my relationship is with him. What I can say is that he saved my life. Also doing practice for all these years has changed me. I deal with situations, people and life very differently now compared to a few years ago. I mentioned that my singing teacher put me on the track of life. Rinpoche is like the oil that helps me go along smoothly.

Offering beauty

The similarity between singing and meditation practice is interesting. In terms of singing we are asked to concentrate on certain points of the body, like the forehead, the back of the throat and the heart chakra. These are also some of the points we concentrate on while meditating. They are focal points in singing so the sound has a centre. I was told that I should never be nervous when I sing, although of course with the adrenalin flowing, it is hard not to be. I believe that when you sing you are the closest to God. It is a very spiritual experience.

When I really lose myself in the music, I am a little less afraid on the stage. It's not about me, it's about offering beauty to the world. When you do that, you don't think about yourself. In the singing world, of course it's quite competitive and even cruel. People spend years studying and in one minute in an audition, someone's dream is shattered. I have also suffered disappointments but somehow Buddhism has helped me not to give up. I have thought of giving up many times and maybe it's my stubbornness that prevents me. I also realise that as every year passes I have to let go a little bit more.

When I hear really fabulous singers I'm not jealous. I am so happy that they possess such amazing qualities. You realise that the great singers are actually bodhisattvas. They are very special because they bring such joy and beauty to people. Sometimes I just stare at them because I want to see what incredible qualities they have. Their voice has such an incredible impact on millions of people. It is such a privilege to listen to someone sing or play the violin or piano.

Generosity of spirit

I have a feeling that all this has its parallel in Buddhism. It has a lot to do with generosity of spirit. People who are not mentally generous cannot offer such beauty to the world. We need to let go and let things filter through our body. For me, devotion is not giving up. It is having a belief that something is going to work and you stay with it through thick and thin. The difference between Rinpoche and everyone else I have ever met is that he never judges you. That is very special. He always has kind intention. Sometimes I have been confused about whether I should be devoted to Rinpoche or devoted to Dharma. Maybe they are not different. I know he is the conduit through which the teachings come. He is giving the knowledge. I think he would say it is the Dharma that is important, rather than him. He is saying, worship the person less and live the Dharma more. I remember once when people were asking him advice about teachers, he said, 'You see, some people go to certain gurus because of their charisma. Of course, it's very easy to like someone who has charisma. However, the moment the teacher doesn't start to behave according to your version or expectation, you turn against him. However, what he teaches will benefit you.' I have always been very moved by that, as again he is reflecting to us our lack of understanding, our expectations and the behaviour that follows from them.

I think Rinpoche is often trying to rip away our preconceived notions of what we think we should or should not be. He is trying to help us get a more focused vision. I have come to expect the most unexpected. For some reason, I don't expect Rinpoche to be perfect. The more I learn to accept my own imperfections the more tolerant I am of other people. Also Rinpoche loves us totally unconditionally. I have never experienced that from anyone before. Someone asked him once, 'Why do you never seem to see faults in us?' He didn't answer immediately, but then replied, 'If I see all this imperfection, then I am not a very good teacher.' Maybe he is not doing what we do to ourselves or to each other, which is judging everything we do or say. He doesn't judge. I think that meeting Rinpoche has turned me from being a very negative person to someone who at least attempts to go for the positive first.

The drama of life and death

One statement he made left a big impression on me. He said that in the end we are all truly alone. I think if we realised this, we would have a much better time dealing with life and relationships. In the end, we die alone and neither our spouse or friend or family can really help us. It made a profound impression on me in terms of letting go and not being so obsessed.

I think back to when my father died — he was lying in the hospital bed and I remember thinking that the whole thing was very strange. He was obviously the object of attention with lots of nurses and doctors rushing around and yet no one was looking at him. They were all glued to the heart monitor. Even in a situation where you would think a person would be the centre of attention, actually no one was really paying attention to him. I realised how stupid we are, that we make so much drama in life to be the centre of attention but, even in death, often we are not. My father certainly wasn't, even though in a few days he would just be ashes. So, in the end, nothing is that important. That experience went really deep in me. We create so much drama in life and want to be the centre of attention or want Rinpoche's attention and for what? In the end we all just turn into ashes.

This might be a good place to end. It may feel a little abrupt, but death is like that. Turning into ashes is where we all end up. Life is that abrupt, interrupted at the most unexpected time. Things happen and that's that. We always try to manipulate and change things the way we want them. We want everything to go our way. Actually, though, there is nothing we can really do and we spend our time in a state of anxiety, trying every day to make things how we want them. Buddhism is trying to point out to us, sometimes somewhat humorously, that we just have to let go. The best singing is when a singer has the training, the music in his mind, breathes and just lets it all come out spontaneously. That's also the best living and dying.

As a swan that glides upon the water without a ripple,
I try to settle and calm my mind.
I wish to sing praises of beauty to my precious teacher,
but wild and anxious thoughts prevail.
Teach and transform me and all those like me
who decide to accomplish freedom of mind,
So we may spontaneously liberate our fears and dwell
in the ocean of perfection.

13
ORDINARY MAGIC

POINTS OF VIEW

Once there was a group of monks who always disagreed with each other. The spirit of a famous teacher appeared to heal the rifts between them all and to create harmony in the community again. All the monks had seen the appearance of the guru and he had spoken one word only to them all. However, when questioned, it appeared that they all had heard something different.

> The one who wanted to die heard live.
> The one who wanted to live heard die.
> The one who wanted to take heard give.
> The one who wanted to give heard keep.
> The one who was always alert heard sleep.
> The one who was always asleep heard wake.
> The one who wanted to leave heard stay.
> The one who wanted to stay, depart.
> The one who never spoke heard preach.
> The one who always preached heard pray.
> Each one learned how he had been
> In someone else's way.[1]

Albert-Paravi Wongchirachai is a newspaper columnist and culture critic based in Bangkok, and he is fluent in four languages. Besides his column in *The Nation*, he contributes widely to regional publications such as the *Far Eastern Economic Review* and *Art Asia-Pacific*. His most recent work includes talks and commentaries for BBC radio, as well as for television programs on the Australian Broadcasting Corporation and Channel Four (UK). He is also a member of the Board of the Siam Society, a Thai heritage conservation society under the patronage of the King of Thailand, where he currently runs the Kamthieng House Museum project, an architectural restoration effort on the society grounds.

Albert-Paravi is the only contributor to the book who I have not met, yet I feel I know him through our numerous phone calls and emails. As I spoke to him at four o'clock in the morning from the transit lounge of Bangkok airport, I wondered at the coincidences of how we all connect together as part of the same community.

He has an intellectual knowledge of Buddhism as well as some personal experience;

ALBERT-PARAVI WONGCHIRACHAI

coupled with his talent for writing, his story encompasses a clear understanding of the nature of devotion and emptiness. He moves us through a journey from his grandmother dying, to an understanding of sacred outlook, to his first contact with Tibetan Buddhism.

Dzongsar Khyentse Rinpoche says that we should look for a teacher who improves the sacred outlook we have towards ourselves, as well as a teacher who shows us our imperfections. 'An authentic master gives you the good and the bad news. If you genuinely wish to follow the spiritual path, you must be willing to hear both.'

Albert-Paravi shares openly about his 'good and bad news', his emotional experiences and understandings of Buddhist theory. He describes in detail how depression can be seen as existing in almost a hell realm. It is said that one way to understand the realms described in Buddhist literature, such as the hell, hungry ghost, animal, human, demigod and god realm, is not as actual places, but as states of mind that we experience. Rinpoche says that the spiritual path cannot be reduced to a therapy, and this is true. Yet Buddhism can work together with therapy, while realising they are not the same. Therapy can help people stabilise themselves so that they can begin to receive the benefits of the meditation practice. Both can also help people identify and work through long-held existing habits. Rinpoche identifies expectations as one of the main ways that we make ourselves unhappy.

In regard to the student–teacher relationship, he says, 'The less expectation you have the better. Whenever students are emotionally disturbed and insecure, they expect their guru to perform miracles — healing all their problems with one touch of the head, for example. Yet, when they want to make merry and have fun, or introduce friends who are not spiritually inclined to their teacher, they expect him to act as a human being. Expectations as extreme as these are clearly inappropriate.'[2]

There is no escape when we have an outer guru, as he will reflect our expectations back to us. In fact, there is no escape from our mind, even though we may try to find a solution to that problem in drugs, entertainment, sex or holidays. Sogyal Rinpoche says that, if we wish to have a teacher who simply smiles at us and does not work in a real way with our ego, then we should have a picture of a smiling teacher on our shrine.

There are times when our teacher's wisdom-mind or spacious quality awakens our natural devotion and touches our hearts. Even though we were not there and maybe have never met him, it is as though we are invited, through Albert-Paravi's experience, into a relationship with Dilgo Khyentse Rinpoche. Albert-Paravi talks about emptiness and the guru–student relationship in a way that makes it easy to comprehend, and introduces us to a world of childlike magic and wonder. We begin to experience the vastness of mind and sense of limitless love and great presence that a wisdom master emanates, even after the death of his physical body. Dilgo Khyentse Rinpoche says, 'An authentic spiritual teacher is like the sail that enables a boat to cross the ocean swiftly. If you trust his words, you will find your way out of samsara easily; that is why the teacher is considered so precious. Enlightenment is not something that can be accomplished just by following your own ideas....'

Dzongsar Khyentse Rinpoche has given a whole series of teachings on 'referencelessness' and Albert-Paravi essentialises the feeling of having no reference point to hang on to, from the first time he met Rinpoche. We somehow always fool ourselves that everything is concrete and solid, that it will last. Dzongsar Khyentse says that we create ideas that we then accept, take for granted, assume and then expect to be real. We hang on to the ground beneath our feet, so to speak, even as it is slipping and sliding away from us. We don't want to see the reality of life as it is, and continue to believe in having fixed points of reference, in our belief systems, our concepts, habits and fixations. Rinpoche says that, in Buddhism there are no references whatsoever. Ultimately there is not even an ego to overcome or be abused. Yet there is so much talk of ego; like the Zen koan, it is mysterious, frustrating and utterly engaging, until you find the key that fits the lock, you open the door and are free. Or are you? On the ultimate level, there is no such concept as freedom anyway. Life is as a dream, a magic show, a mere illusion.

Albert-Paravi extends this theme by taking the example of viewing life as if it were a film or a play. If we knew this, we wouldn't take things nearly so seriously. We wouldn't get so caught up in the drama or the plot, and would feel as if we had more choices to change the script. Instead of being emotional, frightened or angry, we would have more distance from it and know that it was just drama, as Albert-Paravi says.

Albert's story

A Grandmother's legacy

If I had to draw a family Buddhist lineage, I'd have to go back to my old Manchu grandmother, who died calmly, calling the name of Amitabha Buddha, Lord of the Sukhavati Pure Land Paradise. The morning of her death, aware of her impending passing, she called the children round, gave them her last advice, and bid them farewell. Though my mother inherited the legacy of that morning, she did not make use of it until late in her life, when illness and family turmoil reminded her of it.

The household I grew up in, in Thailand, was spiritually eclectic. My family were Shanghai emigres, part of the Chinese diaspora after the Communist takeover in 1949. In the fashion of most progressive liberals of those turbulent times, my grandfather and great-grandfather were both Christian converts, having rejected the native religions as feudal relics. My father, caught between colonial onslaught and revolutionary sentiments, became a sort of paradoxical Christian, half gnostic and half armchair Maoist–Marxist. Pride of influence, however, must go to the household staff, shamanistic Buddhists from north-eastern Thailand, who inhabited a world of magic monks and animistic rituals, and my British kindergarten, where we read *Winnie the Pooh*, and sang 'All Things Bright and Beautiful'. All in all, it was a pretty good muddle of everything.

Oddly enough, my interest in Buddhist meditation started with a teenage fascination for Hong Kong swordsman television epics, the ones where they jump four storeys at a leap by virtue of inner yogic power. As a somewhat troubled teenager, I escaped into a world of sci-fi and psychic fantasy, consuming all kinds of books on the power of the mind, anything from ESP to concentration trances and yoga.

Fortunately, in my meanderings, I also came across some Dharma books, especially one by the late Thai Buddhist master, Buddhadasa, on *anapanasati*, mindfulness of breathing, which was his specialty. I started to try that by myself, which, looking back, was a bit of a mistake, as I probably needed some guidance. The practice yielded some blissful tranquility states but I didn't know how to use them properly for analysis and contemplation, relishing them rather as something between a mental jacuzzi and a quick-fix escape.

Somehow, I didn't manage to meet Buddhadasa until much later, in the last year of his life, so there was no particular teacher in the Theravada tradition I had strong devotion for. My first teachers, in fact, were two lay women practitioners of Vipassana mindfulness practice, in the lineage of the Burmese meditation master, Venerable Mahasi Sayadaw. Khun Mae (Mother) Charoensri and Khun Mae Siri had both practised under the Thai meditation teacher, Chao Khun Dhepsiddhimuni of Wat Mahathat Temple, himself a direct disciple of the late Mahasi Sayadaw. Nonetheless, it was there, in the foundation of mindfulness and awareness, that I was to find my way to the devotional experience.

Sacred outlook

On the ground level, like Camus's protagonist in *The Stranger*, devotion is faith in the daily round, in small reassurances — that the sun comes up, that in-breath follows out-breath, that the world remains round, and that I'm coping, more or less, with myriad anxieties of existence, or non-existence, for that matter.

This is to me what Tibetan Buddhists call 'sacred outlook', which, despite its mystical wording, is just the training of relating to things as they are. Sacred outlook is a profound acceptance — transcending resignation and rejection — that sits squarely in the experience, letting things be what they must. It is this basic acceptance that somehow makes every moment of our lives sacred and, eventually in the process, a devotional experience. If I were to see a painful experience as somehow sacred, I would immediately have a different relationship to it, wouldn't I? Keeping this sense of the sacred, as a commitment in daily life, is my definition of devotion.

In Vajrayana Buddhism, this training, this relating, this path, is also seen as the goal, because sacred outlook starts from the basis of things as they really are, not just through the filter of our neuroses. Sacred outlook training starts with me saying to myself, 'Hey, things are not necessarily as I perceive them.' So I decide to take the sacredness of things as the true basis, the actual reality. The commitment to that view becomes the devotion. At first, it's a bit artificial of course; it's a skilful means. But, eventually, devotion becomes the most excellent way to relate to reality.

In this sense, devotion is about awareness, about being precisely in the moment. The two are inextricable. I don't think you can really have the one without the other, though the link isn't really obvious at first, or even most of the time. Devotion need not manifest as an earth-shattering enlightenment experience; neither visions in the sky, nor voices from on high are required. But devotion is often awakened by a teacher.

Presence of mind

When we meet the right teacher, devotion is a spontaneous event. And I don't mean some sort of mushy, flower-power self-hypnosis. It is, rather, a moment of great simplicity, an opening of the mind to the presence and space of awareness.

I had my first real sense of devotion during a retreat with Chögyal Namkhai Norbu, the Tibetan scholar and Dzogchen master, at the end of a short session of Guru Yoga with him. Guru Yoga is the practice of mixing our mind with the guru's and, though I didn't really comprehend its full meaning at the time, I knew I had caught a glimpse of a possibility. Something clicked and fell into place. I can't quite express it, except as an instant of openness. My first thought when we finished the session was, 'Can it be so simple?'

I had come to Norbu Rinpoche through a small text of pith-instructions he had written, called *The Mirror: Advice on the Presence of Awareness*. As I was coming from a background of Vipassana mindfulness training, I could relate to Rinpoche's advice on awareness. This is the heart of the Buddha's teaching, and here I was rediscovering it in the Tibetan tradition, amid all the ornate and fascinating visualisations of mandalas and multi-armed deities. Vajrayana Buddhism had always fascinated me, but I could not connect with it until then. In another book, *Crystal and the Way of Light*, Norbu Rinpoche traces the complex technology of Vajrayana Buddhism, through Sutra, Tantra, Mahamudra and Dzogchen, all from the basis of awareness. Anything can be used to foster that practice.

So you might say my encounter with Norbu Rinpoche appeased both my heart and my intellect, clearing a path. From that moment on, I felt a natural devotion for Norbu Rinpoche. That's the odd thing, no one needs to tell us to generate devotion. It's just there, spontaneously, when we open up our minds.

Depression and intellect

My encounter with Chögyal Namkhai Norbu was all the more significant for the fact that I had had a history of chronic depression. Devotion, as either path or process, was certainly the furthest choice in my mind, as a means of relating to my life, though it was the devotional process in the end that slowly coaxed me out of my inferno.

Some time in the mid-1980s I went into deep depression. Each morning as I awoke to do my daily sitting practice I experienced a terrible abyss, an unending pain — both enveloping and real — that continued sometimes for days, sometimes for weeks or even longer. I wasn't particularly spiritual then, except in the yuppie self-help notion that meditation would make for a stronger mind. I had read a few books on meditation and was continuing to muddle through by myself.

I had also begun to do individual psychotherapy once a week with a wonderful therapist called Levana Marshall. I discovered years later that she was a student of His Holiness Dudjom Rinpoche and Thich Nhat Hanh, and had the habit of doing one-month Zen retreats every year. She didn't tell me at the time, so we used to have heated discussions about meditation and where therapy was taking me.

In a Buddhist sense, depression is indeed a 'realm', a karmic space and time where habitual visions overwhelm us. The all-pervading bleakness, so endless in its suffering and impoverishment, is akin to abandonment in a forest of terrifying appearances, with no help in sight, and the last light of day fast fading. Anything and everything is felt to be a threat. It's a bit like the episode of the Buddha subduing Mara [ego] forces that hinder spiritual enlightenment, taken upside down. In the Buddha's case, the arrows of Mara turned into a cascade of fragrant blossoms. In my realm, even the blossoms turned into arrows. The smallest concern was experienced as reproach, an assault on my vulnerabilities.

It is a fearsome realm that allows no sustenance. Everything arrives with the fire of molten lava, the numbness of ignorance, and the unreachability of a world cut off from warmth and compassion. And it is the irony of such realms that salvation is sought through more fear, protection and control.

I had no teacher I really trusted before I met Norbu Rinpoche. Or rather I did not trust my own instinctive judgment of anyone. So I created a tremendous system of intellectual hoops people had to jump through before I would trust them. This went for friends, colleagues, lovers or teachers; everyone in fact. Like all depressions, there was a quest for some solid ground. I was looking for some indisputable, invincible intellectual cosmos, which I needed desperately at the time to mediate the world. I was so emotionally vulnerable. But that's the irony of intellect. It doesn't hold up to the light. It's just a mirage.

Alice Miller, in many books on psychology, has written eloquently about the counterpoint of depression and grandiosity. And it was here that I had to start, amid this need for an intellectual cosmology, or a divine drama perhaps, that I could believe in. My Vipassana practice was shredding my vision to threads, and I had nowhere and no one to turn to. It was, perhaps, a bit of what Buddhist teachers call the 'wisdom of no escape', manifesting in my life. The depression was both a curse and a blessing. And if it was the source of confusion, it also became the source of some clarity, eventually leading me to His Holiness Dilgo Khyentse.

Oceanic feeling

The quality I remember most about His Holiness Dilgo Khyentse was his presence. He was so large he just loomed above you, like a huge banyan tree. It wasn't just his physical size, though he was considered tall even for a Khampa [eastern Tibetan]. It was rather the size of his presence, an all-pervading quality, as if he were everywhere. And yet, when you looked up into his face, there he was, totally present, gentle and oozing affection, looking like Marlon Brando, a Navaho chief and your grandmother all rolled into one. There was a strange enveloping feeling when you sat there with him, as if you were held somehow, and yet you knew there was nothing whatsoever holding you. Yet there you were, held, cradled like a child. The feeling was distinctive — I can recall it even now — but ungraspable.

It's probably what Freud chose to call the 'oceanic feeling' — in his attempt to understand French poet Romain Rolland's fascination with the Hindu mystics, Ramakrishna and Vivekananda — though I don't necessarily attribute it with his connotations of a regressed, infantilised state. The presence was as vastly tangible as it was unfathomable and ungraspable, like the ocean waves.

You could usually sense his presence as soon as you got to the outer hall entrance of his first-floor sitting room at Shechen Monastery in Baudanath. The presence was tangible, but subtle. I could always sense it when I relaxed, settled down and let go a bit. Then the presence worked its magic, slowly dissolving thoughts and anxieties, to the point that I would invariably end up just doing some sitting practice in his presence and forget all the usually very long lists of questions I had prepared to ask him. Then I'd leave to go about my business, and an hour or so back in my habitual muddle I'd look at the questions and get in a frenzy again about their importance. 'Why didn't I ask them when I had the chance?' I'd lament. Of course, they really weren't terribly important in terms of practice.

So Rinpoche had this oceanic quality, provided you were open to it. It's what the Tibetans call 'blessings', I guess. The Taoists would call it a 'ch'i-chang', an energy field. We could still feel it after he died, oddly enough, at all the places he'd spent time in Bhutan.

Starting the journey

My story with His Holiness Dilgo Khyentse Rinpoche actually began with a summer retreat in Dordogne in 1990. Dzongsar Khyentse Rinpoche — a young lama who later became my main teacher — had told me that His Holiness was giving teachings and empowerments from all eight main lineages of Tibetan Buddhism, especially for people going into three-year retreat. It sounded wonderfully medieval and grand, acolytes gathering to the master. I was somewhat bitten by the 'exotic bug', having grown up on, among other things, a mish-mash of Tolkien, Lobsang Rampa and Alexandra David-Neel's *Magic and Mystery in Tibet*. So off I went on this journey.

I had just finished a second degree at the School of Oriental and African Studies, University of London, focusing loosely on Hindu-Buddhist art of South-east Asia, and had been doing some pre-doctoral courses at the Oriental Institute at Oxford. My main interest at the time was to undertake some fieldwork on contemplative traditions in Thailand. However, I found myself more and more drawn by the Tibetan context, because the complexity was well documented, in detail, and in keeping with a tradition handed down meticulously from the great Buddhist universities of Northern India in the eighth century.

The daily teachings in Dordogne were held in a large tent that sloped to one side, getting progressively more crooked each day. I saw His Holiness at a distance except for two occasions, when we went for short interviews. I still remember the scene. His Holiness sat like an unshakable mountain, composing a letter on his lap, surrounded by six or seven people receiving sadhana [advanced practice] instructions and divinations, to plain old life advice. He seemed unperturbed by the commotion around him, and flowed from one thing to the next, all in a continuous stream. He responded to whatever arose in the moment and, when there was a lull, he continued writing his letter. It was the way he taught too. Once he started, he just continued without stopping, the words flowing spontaneously out of him. He never paused to compose a thought and, of course, never used any notes.

The words of my perfect teacher

One morning Dzongsar Khyentse took me to see His Holiness. Dzongsar Khyentse Rinpoche had repeatedly invited me to do so over two or three days and, wondering at the significance of his insistence, I took up his offer.

It wasn't easy to see His Holiness that summer, as his health was rather frail. He spent most of the time quietly in La Sonnerie, the main house. The afternoon teachings and empowerments were soon moved to the garden surrounding his room, because he was a bit frail to be moved about much. It was late morning when we went in to see him, and there was another twenty minutes left to his morning silent retreat. His Holiness looked at me, held up his mala [prayer beads] to signify his silence, and nodded with a smile.

It was a magical morning. Golden light streamed in from the window and His Holiness looked majestic and glorious, like a magnificent child basking in the warmth of morning sunshine. The room felt warm and complete; so full of the voluptuousness of wisdom and kindness, with love so thick you could chew it.

'I remember you. I've seen you twice before. So are you a Buddhist?' His Holiness grinned and started our conversation. And what happened next was so bizarre. For the next ten minutes I could not think.

As Dzongsar Khyentse Rinpoche translated each question, I found my mind suspended in space, as if it weren't quite functioning. I was fully cognisant and aware, but my mind had emptied out. I answered each question with the first thought that arose, and it always seemed a bit ridiculous. But I had no choice. It was the only response I could give at that instant, and no other. So the answers didn't make much sense, but they were spontaneous and genuine.

To this day, I'm not sure what happened, except that it was a teaching and a blessing, without words. There was an appearance of a conversation, but that was not what went on. You might say that nothing was happening, and at the same time, everything was happening. It was indescribable. As I looked into his face, beaming and radiant, I just spaced out and lost all reference point. All sense of fixation was dissolved, yet there was definitely a focal point. I can't quite describe it. It was as if he were everywhere around me, within and without, with no sense of boundary. Boundary was not the point, or the issue. It was irrelevant. It was beyond boundary. It was just open, spacious and present. It just was.

We were separate entities, I was conscious of that notion. But then again we were not. I didn't feel we were separate. Yet it wasn't as if there was a great merging into 'oneness' with thunder, lightning and a celestial chorus. It was just an extremely simple moment. Yet so grand and vast and immeasurable at the same time.

I felt like a child looking up with wonder and awe at this giant presence. Wonderment because it was so gentle, kind and loving. It was incredibly simple; a moment of basic openness and love. I hesitate to use this word, because everyone thinks of the Beatles and the Maharishi, with orange caftans and flowers in your hair — psychedelic love. But it wasn't like that. It was much more subtle, not at all flashy, or maudlin. Just gentle, nurturing and substantial.

In wonderland

My definition of devotion has a lot to do with that morning, and it may explain why I prefer to describe it as the experience of 'ordinary magic'. It's a child's twist on 'sacred outlook'. We all need some magic in our lives, don't we?

Sacred outlook looks at devotion from the student's perspective, from the point of view of the training we each undertake. Ordinary magic sees it from the perspective of a child in a lollipop store, or at a fun fair, or watching a movie. There's not much to do. We just have to surrender. It's not a matter of choice any more. It's a bit like Alice in Wonderland. Once we wander in, the magic is there, and we have no choice but to believe. It's drama. We know Gwyneth Paltrow as Juliet doesn't really stab herself to death on sight of a dead Romeo, but we still cringe when she thrusts in the dagger. We may even weep.

Devotion is really about relationship to our world as reflected by our teacher. We have a hard time relating to ourselves, don't we? But we have an easier time relating to our issues through movies, fiction, theatre. Because there's some distance to the process. We're left some space to rediscover our thoughts and feelings and we're not crushed by the onslaught of life itself. We can say to ourselves, 'Oh, this is just make-believe.'

Ordinary magic is a bit like that. We collude with the guru to create a drama. Through that drama we relate to ourselves and the world, to both outer guru and inner guru. Initially at least, there can't really be devotion without an object of devotion. So at the very start, ordinary magic is about a relationship, initially with the teacher, and later with ourselves, our life, our path.

When I once remarked how His Holiness Dilgo Khyentse Rinpoche never seemed to need to reproach any of his students to keep them in line, Dzongsar Khyentse Rinpoche responded, 'Don't worry, he has a way of coming round to play your games with you.'

The flaming sword of wisdom

I feel I owe Dzongsar Khyentse Rinpoche my link to His Holiness Dilgo Khyentse Rinpoche, though to this day Khyentse Rinpoche would always say, 'You think I brought you to him. But maybe it was he who brought you to me.' He may have a point. Perhaps the drama — the ordinary magic — had already begun then, only I didn't know it.

I must confess I felt extremely uncomfortable with Dzongsar Khyentse Rinpoche the first time I met him in the summer of 1988, at the London home of one of his Bhutanese cousins. I didn't quite dislike him, but I was tremendously irked and bothered by him.

Rinpoche was sitting in an armchair, going through his daily prayers. As I knelt down to offer the traditional Thai prostrations to a member of the Sangha, he busily gestured me to stop. I was a little confused, coming from a Theravadin monastic tradition. Rinpoche was in robes, but neither a monk nor a layman. Thai Theravada has many great lay teachers, of course, but it recognises no incarnate lamas, and its primary ideal remains monastic.

Rinpoche made me uneasy and generally at a loss for something to hang on to. He seemed to give no reference points, or rather they kept shifting, like sand dunes. Significant and graspable for an instant, then elusive and dissolving. It was, and can still be, extremely disorienting.

The instant Rinpoche shut his prayer book, he managed to provoke every precious belief I held in thirty seconds flat, which was no mean feat. It's not what he said, probably; it's how he said it. Or maybe even why he said it. He was pushing all my buttons. It's a bit like having someone take out a knife and cut the bullets out of your wounds. You can't quite forget the experience, though you hate it all the way.

He has this uncanny ability of getting under your skin, second-guessing your thoughts, taking words out of your mouth, and even a way of telling you something to your face, while ostensibly saying nothing at all. The comment might simply be, 'I just love oranges!' and it would be extremely significant for you, at that moment. However, no one else would have heard it the same way. Any attempt to tell anyone else otherwise would be treated as sheer projection and the result of a too-avid imagination.

Rinpoche left a strange impression in my mind and for weeks I couldn't quite get him out of my head. He was always there, somehow, as a reflection of my anguish, jealousy and wishful self-images. If he was not graspable in person, he certainly became a reference point in his absence. He became a sort of sacrificial object onto which I projected my anger and frustrations, a sort of mental scapegoat. An effigy of the parts of me I wanted but could not have, or had but did not want. He became the mirror, which sounds trite, because that's what they tell you in books, but I'm not quite sure how else to describe it.

Rinpoche is altogether there for me, and still altogether not there. So I generally give up explaining him at all. Sometimes I think of him as a friend, because that's how he frames the dialogue. And yet, in poignant moments, he is the total boss, tyrant and teacher. Paul Breiter once called Ajahn Chah, the famous Thai Buddhist meditation master, 'the most compassionate sadist in the world'.[3] We sometimes call Dzongsar Khyentse 'the wisdom-torturer'.

No exit

With an outer guru, we are not allowed to be complacent. That is what the relationship is about. It's all encompassing and there is no escape. He pushes us to the limits, tortures our repressed, dormant, slothful habits, so they rear up in annoyance. And when they do, they can finally be dealt with. They are finally seen, known, recognised. And just that power of awareness can unlock so much. In the Theravada Vipassana tradition, this groundwork of awareness is laid in the practice of 'bare attention'. It keeps us precisely in the here and now.

In the end, it's a bit of a trust game, isn't it? That's why it's called devotion. To use our earlier simile, it's like suspending disbelief as we walk into a play. We do retain a free will to walk the walk, talk the talk, to disbelieve, or even leave. It's just that, in the magic of the plot action, we tend to forget. And therein lies its power.

People tend to think of devotion as a total surrender of one's judgment and as an abdication of responsibility for oneself. This is a complete misconception. We surrender in the way we surrender to a good story, a play or a game. As a collaborative act, the devotional relationship is a two-way thing. The magician conjures the magic, but it's up to the audience to respond to that illusion as it will. There is tremendous choice, space and freedom. It's also inevitable that the student paces the relationship as well.

Somehow, even when we do look up close and see the sleight of hand and illusion, we are still fascinated by the vision. It still amazes us like the power of the storyteller. Aladdin isn't really there with his genie, but we can just about feel ourselves rubbing an old worn lamp, wishing, wishing. The fact that there is no one there doesn't diminish the magic. If anything, it adds to it. In Buddhist terms we would say that it's empty, yet it appears. It's nothing, yet it's all there, in its ability to frighten, attract, dominate, persuade and enlighten. So this relationship we have to the guru, this drama we enact with the guru becomes, on close scrutiny, the very metaphor of life itself. Fragile, pervasive, magical yet empty.

Devotion evolves from attraction to the story to suspension of disbelief, to emotional involvement, then to surrender and the ending of the drama. It continues to the examination of the nature of the drama, to an understanding of the illusion and to a wonderment at the power of the story. All along, devotion increases, as a commitment to the artistry of this ordinary magic.

Zen koans

When I met Dzongsar Khyentse Rinpoche I didn't quite know how to use what was happening, because I didn't know anything about devotion or sacred outlook. If no one ever tells you what to do with the grime on your face when you look in the mirror and see a mess, what can you do? Someone has to equip you with soap at least. The guru may be a mirror, but that's no use if you don't know what to do with what you see. My first reaction was to get upset.

To some extent, devotion is as much a technique to be learnt as anything else. It's like the story about the meeting between two Buddhist masters from different traditions, one was the Korean Zen master Seung Sahn Sunim, the other the Tibetan high lama Kalu Rinpoche.[4] The two Buddhist masters sat down on their cushions facing each other. Kalu Rinpoche was chanting the mantra of compassion quietly on his mala when Seung Sahn Sunim took an orange from his sleeve and launched into a Zen invective. 'What's this?' he asked Rinpoche, 'What's this?' After a few fierce repetitions, Kalu Rinpoche stirred from his seat and whispered to the translator, 'What's wrong with him? Doesn't he have oranges where he comes from?' Apparently, the conversation ended right there.

So, in the same way as a Zen koan, devotion requires some training. In its function, it is surprisingly like the koan. Devotion pushes you back on yourself. You own back your projections completely. Like the koan, it requires an initial faith in its efficacy, an initial commitment of faith. This then pushes your thoughts and projections back to yourself, sometimes to breaking point, sometimes to silence. The two, ultimately, are the same. With a living teacher, of course, the initial leap of faith often happens from the inspirational qualities of the guru himself.

If you take inspiration in the archaic meaning of the word, as in 'giving life and breath', then Dzongsar Khyentse gave life to my shadow.

Cosmic bully

Ordinary magic is in fact both medium and message. As the metaphor through which we navigate our path, it has tremendous power to transform our lives. In time, it becomes both the means and very manifestation of the devotional relationship itself.

Dzongsar Khyentse once depicted devotion as 'taking the guru as path', which I like to believe is somewhat the same as taking the path as guru — seeing the teacher in every precious moment and aspect of one's life.

The most consistent guru we encounter, inevitably, is life itself. Through all the vicissitudes that life puts us through, it is one big bully we would rather forget. Day in, day out, we connive and contrive to vanquish our emotional and habitual conditionings. It's a kind of bullying so specific to us, no one else around really notices. In its relentless pursuit of our naked self, life is a bit like the muscled bully kicking sand in our face. It calls us a wimp, which we hate and, more importantly, which we are. So we have two choices: either we go out and prove otherwise, which is the standard Charles Atlas tactic; or we start to examine the foundation of that insult.

Either way, we're forced to face our infinite constructions of self — from self-love to self-loathing — phantom self-images we carry with us through countless lifetimes.

Ignorant of true devotion, I struggle each day amid the endless births and deaths of habits. Ignorant of the guru, I flounder between one arising and the next, thrown among endless waves of emotion. With ruthless insecurity as my companion, I can only train in knowing precisely where I am.

The gentle rain of kindness trickles into my mind,
yet depression and pain cramps and confines me.
My teacher and I are beyond meeting and parting,
yet still I cling to his physical form.
Teach and transform me and all those like me
who suffer from unceasing fabrication,
So we may live the meaning of the profound teachings
and take them to heart.

ONE CONTINUOUS MISTAKE* 14

Oh Guru Rinpoche, Precious One,
You are the embodiment of the compassion and blessings
  of all the Buddhas,
The only protector of beings,
My body, my possessions, my heart and soul,
Without hesitation I surrender to you.
From now until I attain enlightenment,
In happiness or sorrow, in circumstances good or bad,
In situations high or low,
I rely on you completely, oh lotus born, you who know me.
Think of me, inspire me, guide me, make me one with you.[1]

When I first met Ian Maxwell, many years ago, from the moment I laid eyes on him I considered him as one of my teachers. I have no idea why. It was even more strange because, back then, I was very particular that my teacher, if I was to have one, would have to be Tibetan — certainly not English. Anyway, interestingly enough, Ian is now one of three Westerners who Sogyal Rinpoche has empowered to teach. I requested an interview at Lerab Ling in 1997 and was delighted and touched when he agreed, because I knew he was immensely busy, tirelessly working to help all beings and the Dharma. He has a vast scope of responsibility that includes assisting Rinpoche and travelling around the world visiting and instructing at Rigpa Centres. He is also part of the International Coordinating Board, which organises and oversees numerous projects for the Rigpa Fellowship, and supervises the one-year retreatants at Dzogchen Beara retreat centre in the west of Ireland. He is also helping to set up a Rigpa study college in France.

In fact, it wasn't until Ian came to Australia in early 1999 to teach at the Myall Lakes retreat, that he managed to find time for us to meet. The most fascinating thing about the whole experience was how unexpected it all was. From beginning to end, and beyond, there was so much to be learnt. It displayed that we can learn from every situation whether in a formal setting or not. Ian really is a demonstration of transformation in action and an

---

*   **A famous definition of the spiritual path from the Zen tradition.**

IAN MAXWELL

inspiration to many of us. Speaking with him revealed so many surprising aspects about him, and about myself.

I had spent quite a lot of time observing my hope and fear about whether there was time for our talk to take place or not, walking a fine line between trust and mistrust. We talked over lunch sitting by the lake and it was actually very beautiful. The sky was very clear and spacious and there were children playing in the lake and laughing. People were wandering back and forth and it was a very calm, beautiful setting. As Ian talked about being in beautiful places in nature, yet having a racing mind, I knew completely what he was describing, as I was certainly experiencing it in that moment. We sat there on the grass, with all the ants and mosquitos biting. I very happily brought out my insect repellant. As he went to put it on, it flashed through my head to tell him that it tasted revolting, but I didn't. The next minute he was spitting out his lunch, because the repellant on his hands had got on his food. I kept thinking that I should not only buy a natural rather than a chemical insect repellant, but that the whole experience was a perfect example of how we keep smearing ourselves with the poisons of aggression, ignorance and desire. When these three poisons, which are at the root of samsara, dissolve we become more and more pure.

So we began, although it was difficult to choose where to direct his attention because his knowledge and experience is so vast. His personal story seemed important, as he is someone from our time and culture who has become a senior instructor, but then doubt arose. It wasn't until later, on reflection, that I realised I had done what he described. He talked about thinking on railway tracks and having certain expectations and concepts, rather than being open in all directions in a totally spontaneous way. It wasn't until close to the end, when asked to choose a title for his chapter, that a whole new aspect emerged about how much he identified with continuously making mistakes on the spiritual path. It was a topic close to my heart.

Students often talk about the obstacles that arise on the spiritual path. Ian says that the obstacles are the path. It is working with our difficulties, blockages and mistakes that can really show us how to develop compassion and wisdom. We usually don't need to develop more love, patience and generosity towards our friends when our lives are going well. It is when there are problems, or when we deal with an angry or difficult person, or we feel we have failed, that we really get to know whether we are putting into practice what we have learnt about spaciousness and love. Ian always emphasises that having openness, trust and confidence in a teacher is the context in which we can actually begin to have openness, trust and confidence in our own nature. The relationship we have with the teacher is a reflection of the relationship we have to ourselves and to others. The teacher is the context.

Ian's story

Initially I wasn't looking for a spiritual path or a teacher. I was very interested in travelling and took a year off after school and went to Africa. I come from an English working-class, left-wing political background and was brought up, if anything, anti-religious and rather a snob. When I was young everybody was going off to India and finding gurus. I didn't want to do that at all. I wanted to go to Africa and look at animals.

I liked travelling in anonymity, going to a place where no one knew me so I could just be myself. It was extraordinarily liberating for me to go travelling and realise I could try anything. None of the people I met had any model of who I was supposed to be, so I could be anybody. I grew up in a very specific cultural background and being exposed to totally different cultures made me realise that much of what I thought was reality was actually just cultural norms I had been given or assumed. I went to a fairly traditional English public school and had lived in an environment where you were not allowed to touch each other at all. Touch, other than playing rugby, was a deeply suspicious activity! When I travelled, I came across cultures where people actually liked being close.

Anyway, I happened to see an advertisement in London that a lama would be teaching music and meditation. I never really felt any particular affinity with Tibet, though I had read one book about Zen and was intrigued in a theoretical way by shamanism. I had just read a serious book about American Indian philosophy and I found that very impressive and beautiful, particularly because of the sense of connection with the natural world.

One of the things that drew me initially when I began to attend Rinpoche's teachings was the affinity with nature and similarity to shamanic traditions. I went along with a friend of mine to this talk on music and meditation. We arrived late and it was completely dark and they were playing some music, Tibetan trumpets. These days I find it very special music, quite thrilling and inspiring, but at the time I thought it sounded like cats being strangled. We came into this completely dark room with this kind of 'Anheehhhehh' sound being played extremely loudly. Suddenly the lights came on and there was Sogyal Rinpoche, wearing a teaching robe. Even in the dark he had noticed people arrive and made sure they had a place, throwing cushions around the room and laughing, saying, 'This is called giving up territory.'

He talked about relationships — why they worked and why they didn't. I just found the whole experience intriguing, very unexpected, and a lot of what he said made deep common sense. I had thought of many of these things myself but I wouldn't have been able to express them in such a fresh way. Afterwards we went to the pub. A bit later Rinpoche and three or four of his older students also came into the pub. Rinpoche was dressed in completely ordinary clothes and sat and had a beer. Again that didn't fit in to whatever sort of strange unformed model I had of what a spiritual person would be like. I went back the next week to a talk and then a couple of weeks later a small group of maybe fifteen students got together. In retrospect it was a very special time. I think Rinpoche also felt that something was going to happen in London. Several of us who are now thought of as older students appeared around that time in 1977.

Is this religion?

Rinpoche hadn't yet become well known or started travelling extensively. His teaching was very, very intensive and I was struggling with the whole experience. On the one hand, it made amazing common sense and, although I couldn't understand a lot of it, some of it connected in a way that nothing else ever had. It took me a while, but suddenly I began to realise that something I had thought of as very far away, perhaps contained in a shamanic tradition, could actually be happening in a house in Kilburn. This seemed an incredible idea at the time. However, on the other hand, I would go into, 'But this is religion. I don't want to get into religion.' I was really shocked the first time I saw people prostrating. I thought they were just religious fanatics. I was sure that they were never going to catch me doing that.

After a month or so, though, I could sort of get my head around meditating as a kind of mental hygiene, like brushing your teeth every day, a basic way of cleaning up. Rinpoche was then giving extraordinary teachings, many of which I can still remember. I was coming in and out a lot and I would sort of flip-flop. I would come for a few weeks and feel so stirred up, touched by what was happening, and then I would again think, 'Oh this is religion and I'm not into this.'

No model

Looking back, it seems that, quite quickly really for several of us, we developed a feeling that if you missed an evening you really missed out and that there was something happening that you couldn't afford to skip. The way Rinpoche was teaching was so strong, and then he would suddenly be outside of that teaching context and be totally ordinary.

It was very, very confusing but also quite marvellous in retrospect, because you couldn't possibly put him on a pedestal. There was something extraordinarily lofty about his teachings and, at the same time, he had this incredibly earthy presence. Rinpoche definitely completely intrigued me, because I couldn't put together in my head the kind of earthiness he had with my ideas of what it meant to be spiritual. Also, I knew that something very, very powerful was happening. I could feel it. Sometimes an evening talk would feel like open-heart surgery. At the beginning I was also intimidated by Sogyal Rinpoche and found it very difficult to talk with him. I felt like he knew me already, even though he had hardly spoken to me. In a way, I found that really scary.

I thought he was ferociously practical as well. I just didn't know what to make of him, I couldn't place him at all. This, of course, is one of the extraordinary things about the relationship with a lama. You try to project all your models about a relationship onto them. You try to make them fit into your particular set of models and they just keep not fitting. Eventually you realise you have no model to accommodate this being.

Losing territory

About six months after meeting Rinpoche, he invited His Holiness Sakya Trinzin, who is a childhood friend of his, to come and stay at the centre. I had an opportunity to have an interview with him. By that time, the practice and the teachings were really kind of biting. I went to see His Holiness and I think I meant to say something polite and meaningless like, 'How are you and isn't the weather nice?' Instead I suddenly found myself sitting in front of him, telling him I felt I was in the middle of a hurricane. It reminded me of a silent movie, either Buster Keaton or Charlie Chaplin, where he is trying to hold a door closed against an enormous wind. He doesn't realise that the whole of his house has actually blown away and there's just the door that's left. It is only there because he is holding it up. That's exactly how I felt. His Holiness is extraordinarily calm, quiet and stable. He just sat there very, very quietly doing mantras, while I told him this story. At the end, he just said, 'Oh very good,' and that was the end of the interview. This made me furious. I went away muttering to myself about the fact that these Tibetans couldn't possibly understand what I was going through.

Now I can see that I had a very strong quality of self-indulgence, of being quite self-absorbed, just concentrating on me and what I was going through. At this stage there was very much a feeling of losing territory. I had a strange sense of losing my ground and yet, at the same time, I was being introduced to something else. I couldn't call it ground but it was much, much fresher and somehow sort of real.

When I started to practise meditation, I found it very difficult because my mind was churning with so many thoughts and emotions. I didn't realise it at the time but it actually threw me back to a time when I was going across the Sahara Desert. I was sleeping one night in a sand dune, after accidentally coming across a Berber wedding. It had been a most extraordinary evening and I was in the most beautiful place with millions of stars. It was so peaceful, with an extraordinary quality of space and silence. In the middle of all this peace and solitude, my mind was just churning and racing. It was so frustrating that, even in this amazing environment, my head was caught up in all kinds of bullshit so that I couldn't really be there. I can't remember what I thought about it at the time, except 'This is wrong, I don't want to be like this.'

When I started to do sitting meditation, I found looking at a photo of Jamyang Khyentse Chokyi Lödro's face incredibly reassuring and stabilising. I used to sit looking at his amazing face and looking at my mind, churning in the past and the future, all my hopes and fears. Gradually I started to see that meditation was actually helping and shifting something.

Experiencing ceremony

Another time Rinpoche invited His Holiness Karmapa. That also affected me a lot. I went along to a 'black hat' ceremony at Chelsea Town Hall. I suppose there were about 2000 people there. That was the first time I saw him. He came into the room smiling and the room actually got brighter. I thought at the time, 'Oh, that's a clever trick isn't it? They wait until he comes in and smiles and they just flick the lights up a little bit.' Of course they hadn't; the room actually did get brighter. He just had this extraordinary smile and charisma. Then he sat down and did this ceremony and I didn't have any idea of what was going on. Just before meeting Rinpoche, I had started a T'ai Chi class and had begun to experience the energy just below the navel called the 'hara'. In the middle of the ceremony, my hara started churning up and I thought,

'This is really weird. This guy can sit at the other end of a room of 2000 people and not do anything. He's just sitting with a hat on his head and he can churn up my hara more than I can myself.'

Rinpoche never used to do ceremonies, but when I started to meet other more traditional masters, I was very struck by the sense, when the ceremony started, that there was something really powerful happening, a ritual that meant something. At the same time everybody was really relaxed with it. The monks would casually walk around with these weird tormas [ritual objects], but the lamas weren't in some sort of ecstatic, intense spiritual state. They were just sitting there 'hanging out', very relaxed, very at ease, and at the same time there was a tremendous sense of something authentic happening. So again it didn't fit in with my model of what a 'tantric ceremony' would be like. I found that very interesting.

From loneliness to aloneness

About a year after I met Rinpoche I ended up, through an odd set of circumstances, being given a cottage that I could stay in, at a very cheap rent, in the west of Ireland. So I did an informal retreat for about eleven months, mainly doing sitting meditation practice and prostrations. Being in retreat was one of the happiest times of my life. In many ways it was a very important period for me when a lot of things, like painful childhood memories, were stirred up, but also a basic confidence began to come that everything was workable. Things began to make sense to me and I felt that now I had some tools to understand more about other people. I had never understood why people behave like we do. I also realised that our parents do love us, but they still can't make us happy; only we can. I moved from a sense of loneliness to a sense of aloneness during that time. After the retreat, I think I was a bit different with people. I had always wanted to please people and used to be quite a clown when I was a kid to fit in. That had actually functioned as a pressure on me. I started to realise some of these patterns during the retreat.

Then a letter arrived from England saying that His Holiness Dudjom Rinpoche was going to visit, so I went back to London. I had worked a bit as a bartender and a waiter, so it was thought I might be helpful in serving meals to Dudjom Rinpoche and his family. In fact, my experience proved to be completely useless because I had worked in quite a formal restaurant and it was very, very clear after the first meal that they weren't at all interested in formality. They just wanted to be in a family situation.

Nevertheless, I was very fortunate to be allowed to stay in the house and generally help to make things happen. Although I can't now remember much of the teachings that His Holiness gave, I do remember being in the house with him and his family and what that was like. Dudjom Rinpoche, most of the time, was just completely ordinary, but he had exquisite manners. Most of the time he would be sitting there very softly and quietly doing his prayers or writing or giving some dictation to his secretary. He was kind of changing all the time. Sometimes he would really look like a woman and then sometimes he would look very much like a man. Then he even didn't look like either. He wouldn't be paying any attention to me at all. I'd just be pottering around, bringing some tea. He had an extraordinary kindness, and when he looked at me it was completely impersonal and, at the same time, it was as if he saw right through me. I felt incredibly naked but also incredibly known, and it was deeply reassuring. I couldn't say why it was reassuring because really there was nothing at all reassuring about it.

Just occasionally I'd get a little flash of something else. Sogyal Rinpoche said once that Dudjom Rinpoche was like a very, very old tiger who has been everywhere and done everything and has got absolutely nothing to prove. Completely for his own reasons he has accepted temporarily to come and live with you and be your pet and sit on a rug in front of your fireplace and purr. But just once in a while he would get out one claw and you would just see this flash of something that would make you realise why he was considered one of the great yogis of this century. He very much reminded me of a great American Indian chief.

Dealing with the unpredictable

Mind you, I don't have any idea, and still don't, of what a great yogi would be like. Maybe he would be completely spontaneous and unpredictable, which is both extraordinarily refreshing and also quite intimidating at times. This is because you can't develop any kind of strategy that will carry you through the situation, because you have no idea what the situation is going to be. About the best you can do is try to 'surf'. That can be very interesting because occasionally I could see myself start to get the hang of surfing. For a couple of tiny seconds I would be surfing a bit, but then I wouldn't quite be able to work out how I had done that.

I remember well the first day that Dudjom Rinpoche arrived. The house had a very steep, narrow staircase and Dudjom Rinpoche had a problem with asthma and was tired and jetlagged. Sogyal Rinpoche was quite anxious about him walking up the stairs. We decided that we would put him in a chair and carry him to his bedroom. He sat down and we all grabbed one leg of the chair and started up the staircase, which was so narrow it was very difficult to be two abreast. We were all really nervous, trying to be 'together' and coordinated but I, for one, was tense and quite tight about it. I remember him looking at the four of us (Sogyal Rinpoche, Dudjom Rinpoche's son, Patrick Gaffney and myself) in this incredibly playful, knowing way. You could see he knew exactly what was going on.

About half-way up the stairs he started to laugh. He had a quiet but incredibly infectious sort of laugh, with so much humour you would find yourself joining in. The four of us completely got the giggles. We were doubled over laughing, desperately trying to hold onto the chair, which was lurching all over the place because we were all laughing so much. Of course, the more you have the giggles, the more you try to control yourself, and the more you try to control yourself, the more the giggles get uncontrollable. In the middle of it all, I suddenly realised that he was completely physically relaxed. I felt unbearably tense, laughing semi-hysterically; his chair was diving all over the place yet he was completely relaxed. I had never been that close to somebody who was that relaxed.

Later I met Dilgo Khyentse Rinpoche, in 1982. He was so different. Dudjom Rinpoche had become my model of what a great master was like. Dilgo Khyentse Rinpoche was physically enormous, massive, while Dudjom Rinpoche was so tiny and fine and delicate, like porcelain. Dilgo Khyentse was like a mountain, a lump of granite that had been pounded by an ocean for 2000 years. He was also extremely majestic. At first, you'd think he hadn't noticed you at all. Most of the time you'd think he wasn't taking the slightest interest in what was going on around him or knew anything about you. Gradually I realised he was taking in everything that was going on. If somebody had different earrings or shoes on, he would always notice.

Getting stretched

After His Holiness Dudjom Rinpoche's visit, I started working much more closely with Sogyal Rinpoche. He had started to travel a bit more because he was functioning as His Holiness's translator. I started having a really interesting training, packing and unpacking Rinpoche's suitcase. I seemed unable ever to get it right. He was very precise about where things were and what he had. I remember, on one occasion, he had returned from a trip and he started handing me a complete assortment of things — texts, pieces of paper, phone numbers, reminders to do things, clothes, pictures and messages to give to people. I made different piles of everything while he emptied his suitcase. About three-quarters of the way through he said, 'Oh, give me that thing back.' I couldn't remember where it was or even which pile it was in any more. He said, 'It's about fifth down from the bottom on that pile there — you put it there.' He had actually worked out the whole filing system that I was making up in my head, which I couldn't even remember myself.

I got stretched a lot, which was very uncomfortable and also really exhilarating. I had never come across anything before, even in slightly dangerous situations, that gave me that feeling. I began to see who Rinpoche was much more, because I could observe him operating on an everyday basis. I realised that I had only been seeing the strange projections of who I thought he was. I really had no idea about his kindness or how extraordinarily 'on the ball' he was. It can be quite confronting and exhausting when you are with somebody like that when you're not. He was just amazingly present and extremely flexible the whole time. The way I was thinking was more like on railway tracks. Even though he wasn't making any special effort to show me that I was thinking on rails, just the fact that I was with someone who thought laterally — in all kinds of directions all the time and had several different attitudes to a situation simultaneously — showed me how my mind was. It was like there was an incredibly graceful bullfighter moving around me, not trying to kill me but, just through his grace, showing me how clumsy I was, all the time. Rinpoche actually often talks about feeling awkward around a master, so it's probably a common experience.

The relationship with a Dzogchen master is very special because there is a tradition of informality, which also cuts directly to the heart of things. Even before the students are aware that they're ready, the teacher is being very direct with them. There isn't some kind of formal courtship where you sign a contract saying, 'OK boss, now I'm ready.' You just turn up and they are extremely direct with you. It's very demanding and inspiring to work with yourself in that way, again and again. Quite early on, even when I had lots of misconceptions and projections about Rinpoche, I felt incredibly fortunate when I met other students who were just wandering from teacher to teacher without ever making a real connection to them.

A working context

Rinpoche often says that the teacher is actually a working context for the student. I was so lucky to meet just exactly the teacher that I needed to work on me. The process has got deeper and deeper over the years. Rinpoche often uses an image of an onion. We have to peel, layers and layers of confusion. Unless we are exceptional students, we don't just pop open, we have to peel. As the layers come off and we get some insights into ourselves, almost simultaneously with that sense of liberation, comes the next layer that needs to be worked on. Usually you're the last person to be conscious of what that is. It's about learning to be somewhat comfortable and at ease with that process as it is revealed and trying to resist it less and less. It actually took me a long time to relate to Rinpoche as my teacher, even though he was. When I finally formulated it in my mind, long after the relationship was actually happening, I found it a very strange idea.

Banging your nose

I have been relatively fortunate that Rinpoche has sometimes given me a specific role. That's quite unusual, because normally you try out different things and can look for your strengths and what you have to offer. The lama is also actually looking for what your particular gift is, in a very informal, friendly sort of way. Eventually, especially if you get to the point of aspiring to be useful, rather than just thinking you are 'hanging out', then you start to find ways to be of use.

It gives you incredible opportunities to see your patterns and the ways that you limit yourself and how you relate. It gives you fantastic feedback. Rinpoche is a great believer in situational learning and gives you lots of space to make your own mistakes. He doesn't necessarily pick you up immediately when you fall into a particular pattern. He may say or do something, that when you reflect, gives you clues, but you have to work it out yourself. He also gives tremendous amounts of support and is fantastically loyal.

There's a Tibetan saying, 'The more you bang your nose, the more you learn.' Rinpoche gives you lots and lots of space to bang your nose and sometimes you think, 'Why didn't he tell me?' However, there is a much deeper learning happening. Once you start to get the hang of it, it's extremely empowering because you are doing it all yourself, rather than someone doing it for you. You're not in a passive relationship. It took me a long time, though, to realise all this and to learn and apply, probably because I lacked confidence in myself.

I was tremendously grateful to Patrick Gaffney because, although he is someone who would very rarely say anything to anyone else about their behaviour, once or twice he gave me a couple of pointers that were very important. Just watching him work with Rinpoche was tremendously helpful. That was really my first sense of what sangha could be.

Shortcuts

The point is that when you are on the spiritual path, it creates a whole new pattern, which includes remembering that you are a buddha. On the other hand, I think that the spiritual path is one continuous mistake. I don't mean, of course, that the path itself is a mistake, but that I identify with encountering 'my envelope of limitations', my difficulties and struggles. That's what I have to work with, that's what my practice is about.

One of the most powerful tools of working with the process of refining our understanding, appreciation and our perception, is within the context of the teacher–student relationship. If we are interested in getting enlightened quickly, there are two shortcuts: compassion and devotion. This is because they just cut straight through our normal, conceptualised, rigid patterns of thinking. They 'bust our boxes' and take us outside ourselves into another dimension, which is the nature of mind. We really have no model in the Western context, to talk about this relationship.

There are actually some very old prophecies that describe the symptoms that occur in the kind of age we live in. They state that there will be a lot of spiritual misunderstanding, spiritual 'supermarket mentality' and misuse, and people who just want to be a guru who don't have the training or wisdom to deal with that kind of responsibility. The responsibility of a teacher is awesome.

It's important to be aware of that and also to be clear about the meaning of devotion. We are not talking about making someone else very high and ourselves very low, or someone else very pure and ourselves impure. Devotion does not mean that we don't have the right to think, or that we lose our critical faculties and become a brainless zombie. We are also not talking about giving up responsiblity for our own lives and handing it over to someone else. This is our life and we have to work with it. The Buddha said, 'I can show you the path, but you have to walk down it yourself.'

Rinpoche often says that we are highly accomplished practitioners of confusion. However, we have this active, dynamic, vivid quality of our own truth, our inner teacher, which is constantly trying to wake us up. For most of us, that inner teacher has to function through situations and circumstances in a generalised way, through perhaps listening to some inspiring music or being in a beautiful landscape or being in love. Momentarily, we completely step outside ourselves and our normal narrow concerns, and something vast opens up. Suffering and terrible situations can also do this, by embarrassing and shocking you by revealing your manipulations and strategies. Normally we indulge in the wonderful situations and try to freeze them and make them permanent. So we have all kinds of expectations, attachments, hopes and fears, which immediately poison even the most wonderful situation. Then when it changes, because everything is changing, there is tremendous suffering because we feel we have lost something, been let down again. These situations are powerful messages from our inner teacher, but it can be rather haphazard as to whether we learn or not.

Sometimes, for some of us, in a way that seems accidental, the inner teacher finds an outer spokesman, a mirror, an outer expression that crystallises in the form of a teacher who shows you the truth of your own nature, a catalyst that sparks off a reconnection with your buddha nature. He cuts through the relative façade. When the teacher touches your heart and there seems to be some kind of truth in the teaching, it's *your* truth that's resonating. In the mirror of the teaching we discover our own face. The teacher is the living expression of the teaching.

As the eagle soars high, I leap beyond normal mind,
but thoughts race from the past to the future.
Deeper and deeper into boundless space,
I struggle with confusion and craving.
Teach and transform me and all those like me
to stabilise our minds and receive the blessings,
So we may recognise the unchanging essence and
become a source of inspiration to others.

CONCLUSION

There really is no conclusion to these stories. These people will continue their lives and their spiritual journeys. Some may become teachers in their own right, others will quietly work 'behind the scenes', helping whoever and wherever they can. They will not proclaim themselves — their training has been too thorough for that and their humility is genuine. Their teachers will often not recognise them openly; this is not a tradition of putting people on pedestals.

Those who say they are the guru, often aren't. Those who declare their own enlightenment, often have had glimpses and think it's the real thing, hardly surprising in this age of hamburgers and fizzy drinks. Those who have a lengthy lineage, long years of genuine training and whose teachers empower them to teach, most likely have a lot to offer. Only if you watch and listen carefully for some time, will you begin to see and appreciate the ongoing dedication, relentless hard work and utter devotion of some of these people. They themselves will always underplay their contribution or make light of it.

Most people were unwilling participants in this book, with no wish to promote themselves and only agreed to be involved because they hoped it may help others to connect with a spiritual path. None said that Buddhism was 'the way' for everyone; just that it had been useful for them. There was no sense of wanting to convert people or to preach. All, without exception, just wished that anyone reading this would find whatever they needed to make their lives more meaningful for them. However, it is clear from the example of who they are, that Tibetan Buddhism is a genuine and authentic path that has lasted thousands of years. It is said that the teacher should not be judged by the students. However, in this case, it is clear that the students are a credit to their teachers, the teachings and themselves.

The alchemical fire

There is a strength of character, courage and willingness needed to open ourselves continuously so that we may be able to be of service to others. We often enter the spiritual path wanting things, but the true awakening and joy is when we stop thinking so much of ourselves and rejoice in the happiness and try to remove the suffering of others. We move from being self-absorbed and self-indulgent to giving up our territory and acting in the interest of others. It is always much easier to do well when things are going our way. It is when obstacles and difficulties arise, in whatever form, like jealousy, feeling unloved and unwanted, losing our partner, health, job, house or money, that the truth of who we really are emerges. To be authentic and genuine, compassionate, graceful and caring while under immense pressure only comes from 'sitting in the alchemical fire' for a long time.

It is also true that some students who have been in close contact with their teachers leave. A few even speak publicly against their teachers, to whom they originally proclaimed great devotion. Often this is done in sincerity and with good intention, to try to protect people. It is perhaps better to make no judgment, as many of us know how easy it is to turn against someone we have once loved. It does reflect, though, some of the difficulties and misunderstandings that we still have about this great tradition and how easy it is to misinterpret what devotion means. Tibetan Buddhism always emphasises the importance of logic and reason, critical thinking, and actively encourages the asking of questions and discourages having 'blind faith'. The Gyalwang Drukpa says:

> **If Westerners are disillusioned with masters now, it is their fault. They are so hungry for a spiritual touch that as soon as a 'master' comes, they take to him or her and don't check first. Some simply fall in love. People are so hungry, firstly for spiritual guidance, and secondly for emotional support ... You develop devotion once you have taken many years of your life, and considerable trouble, to check that person who claims to be a master, is indeed an authentic master.**[1]

The inner practice

As a culture, we externalise everything, continually projecting outwards and accustomed to only giving validation to action. To sit with ourselves and spend time with our own inner world seems rather difficult. Often we only trust, believe or give credit to our internal experiences or believe in their reality when we see them outside ourselves. Maybe a friend has had a similar dream or we read or see it in a film. Yet true confidence and belief in ourselves cannot be given from the outside. It is like building a house on shifting foundations. As soon as a little storm comes along, everything falls down in a heap.

Buddhism has sometimes been accused of not being so actively involved with helping people, as some other traditions do through such things as running soup kitchens. It is true that it is the motivation or intention that is paramount, but it is a misunderstanding to think that action is not part of the path. Limitless and endless dynamic action coming from pure motivation is the crystallisation and result of meditation. Sogyal Rinpoche always emphasises and encourages what he calls 'dynamic mindfulness'. He says that this means entering into a situation and, at a glance, seeing the bigger picture as well as all the minute details and knowing immediately what needs to be done and doing it. Eventually inner and outer become completely congruent in a never-ending dance of reflections, mirroring the wisdom mind through prayer, meditation and action.

We can also often fool or convince ourselves that we are really quite devoted and think that no one really recognises who we are. We become inflated and deluded, thinking that we should be a teacher. The flip side of this, which is the same, is that we want to hide ourselves away and never feel good enough to help anyone. If, somehow, we can get through these testing times without turning against people and holding on to anger, hurt and bitterness, then this is the beginning of the real learning.

Students often talk about the obstacles that arise on the spiritual path. Actually, the obstacles are the path. It is working with our difficulties, doubts, blockages, mistakes and failures that can really show us how to develop compassion and wisdom. All the things that we may think are obstacles are turned upside down in this tradition and used as the basic material for transformation. This is the battleground of the spiritual warrior, where the enemy is transformed into the friend, where universes of flowers are sent to the one who has hurt you the deepest, where failure can be the greatest teacher and true love, compassion and forgiveness can blossom. In the heat of the difficulties, the outer practices that we do every day, of meditation, chanting, praying and visualising, have the opportunity to transform us and deepen into a true inner practice.

It is said, 'If you want to go faster, go deeper.' Going deeper and deeper, we 'peel ourselves like an onion', layer by layer, to reveal the true heart of wisdom and compassion. As the layers of confusion come off, we obtain insights about ourselves and then, with that sense of freedom, we have to be ready to work with the next level. In the end, it's our attitude that counts, and every thought, word and action becomes deeply imbued with pure motivation, spaciousness and dedication that whatever we do may benefit all beings. It is the cauldron in which the metal is fired and honed to the burnished gold.

We may aspire to be sent into the most difficult situations. This is because it is where we are needed the most. When life is easy and comfortable, we have a tendency to fall asleep again. We need to learn how to have the stamina, consistency, spaciousness of mind and skilful means so that we do not make more of a mess, but can be of genuine help to those in difficult situations. It is wise to have great aspiration and intention and yet recognise our present limitations. We need to learn and grow rather than rush straight in, thinking we can solve everything when, in fact, we are just adding to the confusion. Otherwise, we just end up either contributing to the problems or burning out.

The examples and stories of these students and great masters inspire and help us to understand that every one of us, no matter what background we come from can begin to take the first step to discovering who we really are. Common themes emerge, such as the love and gratitude that students feel, how they tried to project all their models about relationships onto their teachers to realise finally there is no model, how ordinary the teachers seem in everyday life and then how totally extraordinary they become when they teach. Many comment on how confusing, confronting and unfamiliar their experiences have been, but also marvellous and intriguing, how kind the teachers are and yet so spontaneous and unpredictable, how personal they can be, yet also impersonal and intimidating. Some have said that they were not at all interested in religion, yet most describe meetings with the great masters as powerful, surprising and exhilarating. Waking up, creating new patterns, learning together, remembering that we and everyone else are buddhas and discovering the truth of the vast and unobscured nature of mind encourages us all to devote ourselves to realising the essence of being alive. Following the master is the ultimate skilful means of following our own true nature and wisdom.

The Buddha said, 'I can show you the path, but you have to walk down it yourself'. So, if we pay attention at certain times in our lives, and don't allow our personality, history and habitual patterns to get in the way, key questions begin to emerge. What's the point of being alive? Is there any meaning or purpose in life?

Can we find lasting and inner freedom? What does that mean and why would we even be interested in finding out? Sometimes we make half-hearted attempts to answer them, but feel it is too difficult, or our familiar lives pull us back into what we know, and we deaden ourselves again and let them drift away. They never fully disappear, and sometimes gnaw away in the background, manifesting as occasional depression, disappointment or disillusionment.

Sometimes we begin to explore them, but they can open a particular 'can of worms' or sore spots, and we decide it is too painful to continue. Occasionally, if we are lucky enough to be encouraged to explore these unknown areas, we begin to see them as opportunities. They begin to call us into the unknown, the unfamiliar, the 'nagual'. When these possibilities present themselves and we dare to enter, we can begin to live our highest dreaming and become the best of who we can be. These are questions that are worthy of setting out on a journey to answer. Sometimes the answers are so simple that we just miss them. They stare us in the face every day, yet we cannot see them.

Transplanting a tradition

It is still early days in transplanting this tradition to the West, and will be so for some decades to come. The cultural and gender differences that we presently feel are so important will perhaps prove to be less of a problem than some imagine. If we have a true, deeply embodied experiential understanding of what is being offered, we will realise that the heart is beyond gender and culture.

The beauty of this tradition is that it is transmitted on so many different levels it can suit everyone, no matter what their capability. So, no matter what level we find ourselves on, it can help and have meaning for us. Maybe, in the end, there will only be a few of us who have the limitless capacity to continue the lineage forward into the new millennium. Maybe there are only a few who will truly realise the essence, the pith instructions. Yet it doesn't really matter, because all of us can realise our buddha nature, all of us can become more aware, all of us can contribute in helping others. The lesson of Vajrayana Buddhism, in the end, is that everything depends on our perception. This wonderful poem from Chandrakirti essentialises this view:

> Like a flickering star, a mirage, or a flame,
> Like a magical illusion, a dewdrop, or a bubble on a stream,
> Like a dream, a flash of lightning, or a cloud —
> See all compounded things as being like these.[2]

Again the Gyalwang Drukpa points out where and how we face problems with devotion. He says:

> Westerners don't really know what true devotion is and they don't want to know. Culturally they have a tendency to have free and open relationships with everybody. Then they feel that it is difficult to deal with devotion, because when they get close to the guru, or the reality

of the teachings, they feel they are now a close friend. They may be very attracted by the guru, his or her way of teaching or how he walks and smiles. Therefore attachment is spontaneously there because the culture is so free.

True devotion though is the belief in the ultimate truth, beyond the relative world and phenomena. If you don't have any idea of the ultimate truth, then you get stuck in the relative world and go up and down, even with your guru. You can't see your guru as Buddha and regard him as your friend. We might not say that, but it is how we feel. Then a friendship is a friendship and one year it works and the next year it doesn't. It's full of attachment and hope and fear, which is not supposed to be there. So true devotion is simply the belief in the ultimate.[3]

Sogyal Rinpoche emphasises that devotion is the supreme short-cut. He recently told a story of a student who asked Nyoshul Khen Rinpoche what the main point is. The reply was 'Open your heart to me.' Sogyal Rinpoche continued:

So, opening our heart to the teacher is opening our heart to the teachings. That's what devotion is. It allows our heart and mind to open to allow us to hear the acoustic of the truth and allow the truth to enter in. Devotion is a path, a supreme tool of training the mind to see in a pure way. The teacher is the teachings brought alive and where we can confront our difficulties. When you really become the teachings, then you are the teacher.[4]

Our minds are so complicated and confused that simple happiness escapes us. It's like travelling around the world, over and over, searching and looking for something, when what we are searching for is inside us all the time. Yet if we don't do the journey, we will never realise what we had at home. This is a path where we can learn to come home to ourselves, become who we truly are and manifest our buddha nature. It can take lifetimes or can happen in an instant. It's up to us. Why else are we here anyway?

Postscript

I hope these stories have helped a little to shine some light on what it means to be truly engaged with an ancient tradition as it settles its roots in the Western world. Whatever mistakes, misunderstandings or incorrect assumptions might be contained here belong solely to me and my limited knowledge, so please forgive me. I hope that it has given some small benefit to you or, at least, some momentary happiness in reading it. For more lasting happiness, which is beyond me at present, I would humbly recommend and sincerely wish that you have the great good fortune to meet a teacher, in whatever shape or form you need, and devote yourself to the realisation of enlightenment. I pray this book may sow a seed that blossoms and grows into spaciousness and limitless happiness for you all.

Only searching for happiness prevents us from seeing it,

It's like a vivid rainbow which you pursue without ever catching,

Or a dog chasing its own tail.

Although peace and happiness do not exist as an actual thing or place,

It is always available and accompanies you every instant. [5]

Lama Gendun Rinpoche

GLOSSARY[1]

absolute nature . . . . . The realisation of the ultimate truth of emptiness.

alchemy. . . . . The alchemical process transforms base metals into gold and base matter into spirit. The alchemists sought 'the secret of God'.

anapanasati . . . . Mindfulness of breathing.

bhakti yoga . . . . The path of devotion and surrender to God through the yoga of prayer, ritual and ceremony.

bodhichitta . . . . The heart of enlightened mind, the wish to obtain enlightenment in order to benefit others.

bodhisattva . . . . A practitioner on the path to Buddhahood, who has vowed to attain enlightenment for the sake of all beings, thereby dedicating his or her whole life to benefitting and helping all beings.

Buddha . . . . Literally, one who is awake. One who has completely awakened from ignorance and has opened to his/her vast potential of wisdom.

Buddha nature. . . . . . The potential of every sentient being to realise Buddhahood.

compassion . . . . The wish for all sentient beings to be free from suffering.

dakini day . . . . A celebration and feast day representing the feminine principle associated with wisdom. A dakini is also known as a sky goer, a female being who bestows a quick means of attaining Buddhahood.

Dalai Lama . . . . The temporal and spiritual leader of Tibet, recognised as the human embodiment of the Buddha of compassion.

Dewachen . . . . The pure field, world or dimension of the Buddha of Limitless Light, where beings progress swiftly to enlightenment.

Dharma . . . . The teachings of Buddha Shakyamuni and other enlightened beings, which show the way to enlightenment.

Dilgo Khyentse Rinpoche
(1910–1991). . . . . One of Tibet's foremost poets, scholars, philosophers and meditation masters of Vajrayana Buddhism.

Dudjom Rinpoche
(1904–1987)......... One of Tibet's foremost yogis, scholars and meditation masters. Considered a living representative of Padmasambhava, he was a prolific author and Terton.

Dzogchen .... The Great Perfection or Great Completion. One of the highest forms of meditation, which aims at a direct realisation of the ultimate nature of reality.

empowerment ...... Transmission and initiation received from a Tantric teacher giving permission to a disciple to engage in the practices of a particular meditational deity.

enlightenment ...... Full awakening, having reached Buddhahood. All limitations have been removed from the mind and one's positive potential has been realised.

Gelugpa .... One of the four schools of Tibetan Buddhism.

gompa .... Temple or monastery.

guru .... A Sanskrit term, meaning 'heavy' with good qualities. A spiritual guide or teacher who shows the student the path to liberation.

Guru Rinpoche ..... A title given to Padmasambhava, meaning 'the lotus born', the Precious Guru. He introduced Buddhism to Tibet in the eighth century.

Guru Yoga .... The meditational practice of mixing one's mind with the teacher's mind.

hara .... An energy centre on the body located just below the navel.

Hinayana .... Often called the 'root', or fundamental, vehicle, it is the path based on the aspiration for individual liberation.

His Holiness Gyalwa Karmapa
(1923–1981)......... A great master and the head of the Kagyu school, one of the four main schools of Tibetan Buddhism.

His Holiness Sakya Trizin
(1945–present)...... A great master and the head of the Sakya school, one of the four main schools of Tibetan Buddhism.

hospice .... A caretaking facility for the terminally ill, offering home care and family support.

Jamyang Khyentse Chökyi Lodro
(1896–1959). . . . . Authority on all traditions and holder of all lineages, the most outstanding Tibetan master of this century.

karma . . . . Literally 'action', or the result produced by past actions.

karma yoga . . . . The yoga of selfless action and service.

khatta . . . . White silk scarf traditionally offered to the teacher, representing purity of motivation and mind.

koan . . . . A riddle or puzzling philosophical problem used as a topic in Zen meditation.

lama . . . . Spiritual teacher or guru who is the manifestation of all the activities of all the Buddhas in the past, present and future.

mahamudra. . . . . Literally 'great seal', a teaching or meditation practice aimed at the direct realisation of emptiness.

Mahayana . . . . Literally 'great vehicle', the path to attain enlightenment for the sake of all sentient beings.

mala . . . . A string of beads, usually 108, for counting mantra recitations.

Mani prayer. . . . . 'Om mani padme hum', the mantra of compassion.

mantra. . . . . That which protects the mind; the recitation of words or syllables associated with deities that represent the manifestation of supreme enlightenment in the form of sound.

Marpa (1012–1096) . . Founder of the Kagyu tradition, renowned Tantric master and translator, disciple of Naropa and guru of Milarepa.

Milarepa (1040–1123) A great Tibetan yogi and poet and supreme disciple of Marpa. His biography and spiritual songs are renowned among Tibetan Buddhists.

nagual . . . . The unknown or unfamiliar.

Naropa (1016–1100). . Indian scholar and siddha, disciple of Tilopa and guru of Marpa.

nature of mind . . . . . The innermost essence of our mind, pure awareness that is intelligent, cognisant, radiant and always awake, the knowledge of knowledge itself.

ngakpa . . . . A lay advanced practitioner.

Ngondro . . . . A preliminary or foundation practice to train the mind for the visualisation and meditation practises of Vajrayana.

Nine Yanas (the) . . . . Within the Nyingma tradition, a system of practice that brings together all the approaches of the Buddha's teaching into a single comprehensive path to enlightenment.

Nyingma . . . . 'The ancient ones', the first school of Tibetan Buddhism, following the traditions introduced by Guru Rinpoche and handed down by masters such as Longchenpa, Jigme Lingpa and Jamyang Khyentse Wangpo.

Nyoshul Khen Rinpoche
(1926–present) . . . . . . A great Dzogchen master and renowned for his mastery of the works of Longchenpa.

Padmasambhava
(eighth century) . . . . . Guru Rinpoche, incomparable master who embodies the compassion and wisdom of all the Buddhas. He is venerated as the Second Buddha and as the founder of Vajrayana teachings in Tibet.

prima materia . . . . . . Part of the alchemical process of transforming base metals into gold.

Process-oriented Psychology or
Process work . . . . Developed by Dr Arnold Mindell (a Jungian analyst) in the or 1970s, is a comprehensive therapeutic system that combines psychotherapy, bodywork, relationships, altered states and large group dynamics to bring awareness to individual and collective change.

protectors . . . . Beings who have pledged to protect and uphold the Dharma.

refuge . . . . The foundation of all the Buddhist paths; to seek protection from the dangers of samsaric existence; entrusting oneself to the three jewels of Buddha, Dharma and Sangha.

Rinpoche . . . . Literally 'precious one', a title given to incarnate lamas and greatly respected teachers in Tibet.

samsara . . . . Literally 'perpetual wandering', the wheel of suffering or cycle of conditioned existence in which one is endlessly propelled by the force of one's actions and negative emotions from death to rebirth.

Sangha . . . . Spiritual community; historically the community of ordained monks and nuns, but now generally accepted as a community of lay spiritual practitioners as well.

Shantideva (690–740) Famous Indian master and author of numerous works, including the Bodicharyavatara, which outlines the path of being a bodhisattva

spiritual warrior . . . . . One who seeks a genuine and fearless existence as a human being.

Sutra . . . . A discourse taught by the Buddha.

Tantra . . . . Literally 'thread or continuity', the root texts of the Vajrayana teachings based on the original purity of the nature of mind.

Tao . . . . A forcefield permeating the universe, the eternal flow of all things.

tangka . . . . A Tibetan scroll painting.

Terton . . . . A great master who reveals the hidden visionary teachings of Padmasambhava.

Theravada . . . . The form of Buddhism widely practised in South-east Asia and Sri Lanka. It is the last remaining school of the eighteen schools of early Indian Minayana.

Thich Nhat Hanh . . . World-renowned contemporary Vietnamese Zen Buddhist master and author.

Three Poisons (the) . . The three negative emotions of attachment, aversion and ignorance.

Tonglen . . . . Literally 'giving and receiving', a practice for developing compassion.

torma . . . . A ritual object or cake used in practices and rituals, often made of flour and butter.

Trisong Detsen
(790–844) . . . . The thirty-eighth King of Tibet, who helped establish Buddhism in Tibet.

Vajrayana . . . . Literally 'diamond vehicle'; aims for the path of enlightenment for all beings more rapidly by using the techniques of the tantras.

Vipassana . . . . Insight meditation.

yana . . . . Literally 'vehicle', a means of evolution or spiritual development.

Yeshe Tsogyal. . . . . . . Padmasambhava's mystic consort and greatest disciple. She had perfect faith in him and helped to spread his teachings, concealing spiritual treasures to be discovered later for future disciples.

yogi . . . . A male spiritual practitioner who practises uniting insight and abiding tranquility, a tantric adept.

BIOGRAPHIES

Dzongsar Jamyang Khyentse Rinpoche

Dzongsar Jamyang Khyentse Rinpoche, born in 1961, was recognised at the age of seven as the incarnation of Jamyang Khyentse Wangpo (1820–1892), the great nineteenth-century saint who played a pivotal role in the preservation of Buddhism in Tibet. Dzongsar Khyentse, also known as Khyentse Norbu, is one of the most important incarnate lamas in the Tibetan Buddhist tradition today and is viewed as an emanation of Manjushri, the Buddha of Wisdom.

He is the grandson of the late His Holiness Dudjom Rinpoche — one of the most revered Buddhist visionaries of the twentieth century — and the son of Thinley Norbu Rinpoche. He has among his root-teachers, all throne-holders of the four main lineages of Tibetan Buddhism, His Holiness the fourteenth Dalai Lama (Gelugpa sect), His Holiness Dilgo Khyentse Rinpoche (Nyingmapa sect), His Holiness the sixteenth Gyalwa Karmapa (Kagyupa sect), and His Holiness Sakya Trizin (Sakyapa sect). He is the living heir to the Rimé Movement and the Khyentse lineage, has undergone a rigorous training in the Buddhist classical tradition and exemplifies the non-sectarian spirit.

He has also received transmissions and empowerments of all the major Tantras from the most illustrious lineage gurus of the last half-century and has completed several solitary retreats of profound Buddhist practices. He is also deeply interested in filmmaking and, as the first serious filmmaker in Bhutanese history, Dzongsar Khyentse Rinpoche has made the first Tibetan-language feature film ever, called *The Cup*.

He is the throne-holder of the Dzongsar Monastery in eastern Tibet, and spiritual director of two advanced meditation centres, one in east Bhutan and the other in Sikkim. Khyentse Norbu's two Buddhist colleges, the Dzongsar Institute in Bir, India, and Chökyi Gyamtsho Institute in Dewathang, east Bhutan are known for their non-sectarian commitment and offer a nine-year graduate program in classical Buddhist philosophy and practice. He has also founded Yasodhara Publications, a non-profit publishing house, to conserve rare Tibetan texts in computerised digital format. In recent years, Dzongsar Khyentse Rinpoche has set up several Buddhist centres around the world, including Sea-to-Sky Retreat Centre in Canada, Vajradhara Gompa in Australia, and numerous practice communities in South-east Asia and Europe. He bridges old and new, East and West and continues to be a source of inspiration to all those who come into contact with him.

His Holiness the twelfth Gyalwang Drukpa

His Holiness the twelfth Gyalwang Drukpa, or Drukchen Rinpoche (the Great Dragon), is the twelfth incarnate head of the Drukpa Kagyu lineage. He is considered an emanation of both Chenrezig, Buddha of Compassion, and the King of Shambhala. He is also the reincarnation of the great masters, Naropa and Gampopa.

The Drukpa Kagyu lineage originated in the eleventh century AD, descending from Gampopa, principle disciple of the renowned yogi Milarepa, who embodied the Vajrayana principle that spiritual realisation can be accomplished in one lifetime.

His Holiness the Gyalwang Drukpa was born in 1963 in northern India at Tso Pema, sacred lake of Guru Rinpoche. His Holiness's father is the Nyingma master, Bairo Tulku Rinpoche, the incarnation of the renowned translator Vairochana, and his mother Mayumla is a supreme practitioner of Dzogchen and the daughter of a yogi. Upon the day of his birth, His Holiness was immediately recognised by His Holiness Dudjom Rinpoche and then officially recognised by His Holiness the fourteenth Dalai Lama and His Holiness the sixteenth Karmapa. He was enthroned in Darjeeling in 1967. He studied under the guidance of his principal guru, Kyabje Thuksey Rinpoche, as well as receiving many teachings and initiations from His Holiness the Dalai Lama and many other exalted masters.

There are numerous Drukpa Kagyu monasteries, located in Darjeeling, Ladakh, Tibet, Bhutan, Nepal, Sikkim and India, as well as centres which have been opened in the Far East and in the West. He is also the founder of the Ladakh school project, which aims to provide a comprehensive modern education combined with traditional culture and value systems for the new generation of Ladakhi children. The Gyalwang Drukpa teaches widely in England, America, Europe, Australia and Asia.

Sogyal Rinpoche

Sogyal Rinpoche was born in 1949 in Tibet and raised as a son by one of the most revered spiritual teachers of this century, Jamyang Khyentse Chökyi Lodro. After Jamyang Khyentse passed away in 1959, Rinpoche continued his spiritual education with Dudjom Rinpoche, Dilgo Khyentse Rinpoche and many other great masters. He studied at university in Delhi and in Cambridge (UK), and began to teach in the West in 1974. Rinpoche is a master of the Dzogchen tradition, and the founder and spiritual director of Rigpa, an international network of centres and groups that follow the teachings of the Buddha under his guidance.

Having lived and taught in the West for more than twenty-five years, Rinpoche has developed a profound insight into the Western mind. His rare gift for communication cuts through cultural, religious and psychological barriers, to reveal the essential truth of the Buddha's teaching. Both the ease and humour with which he teaches, and his very presence, open the hearts and minds of his audience to an intensely personal experience of their own true nature. All this, as well as the remarkable success of *The Tibetan Book of Living and Dying*, have made Rinpoche one of the most celebrated interpreters of Tibetan Buddhism in the modern world.

Rinpoche teaches widely in Europe, America, Australia and Asia and participates in a broad range of interdisciplinary conferences. He has become among the most important Buddhist masters teaching today, considered by many senior Tibetan masters as having a special role to play in the future of Buddhism, in both the West and the East.

BIBLIOGRAPHY

Batchelor, Stephen, ed, *The Jewel in the Lotus: A Guide to the Buddhist Traditions of Tibet*, Wisdom Publications, London, 1987

Breiter, Paul, *Venerable Father: A Life with Ajahn Chah*, Buddhadhamma Foundation, Bangkok, 1994

Conze, Edward, trans, *Buddhist Scriptures*, Penguin Books, London, 1959

Dao, Deng Ming, *The Wandering Taoist*, Harper and Row, San Francisco, 1983

Das, Lama Surya, *The Biography and History of the Drukpa Kargyud Lineage*, Dzogchen Foundation, Massachusetts, 1992

Das, Lama Surya, *Eight Steps to Enlightenment: Awakening the Buddha Within — Tibetan Wisdom for the Western World*, Bantam, New York, 1997

Das, Surya, *The Snow Lion's Turquoise Mane: Wisdom Tales from Tibet*, HarperCollins, San Francisco, 1992

David-Neel, Alexandra, *Magic and Mystery in Tibet*, Dover Publications, London, 1971

Epstein, Mark, *Thoughts Without a Thinker: Psychotherapy from a Buddhist Perspective*, Duckworth, London, 1996

Feldman, Christina, and Kornfield, Jack, eds, *Stories of the Spirit, Stories of the Heart: Parables of the Spiritual Path from Around the World*, HarperCollins, San Francisco, 1991

French, R. M., trans, *The Way of a Pilgrim*, Harper, San Francisco, 1965

Harvey, Andrew, *A Journey in Ladakh*, Houghton Mifflin Co., Boston, 1983

Henderson, Julie, *The Lover Within: Opening to Energy in Sexual Practice*, first published by The Tiger Flower Alliance, Sydney, 1987; Station Hill Press, New York, 1988

Loden, Geshe Acharya Thubten, *Path to Enlightenment*, Tushita Publications, Melbourne, 1997

Longaker, Christine, *Facing Death and Finding Hope: A Guide to the Emotional and Spiritual Care of the Dying*, Century, London, 1997

Norbu, Chögyal Namkhai, *Crystal and the Way of Light: Sutra, Tantra and Dzogchen*, Viking Press, London, 1995

Norbu, Chögyal Namkhai, *The Mirror: Advice on the Presence of Awareness*, 1996

Norbu, Thinley, *Magic Dance: The Display of the Self-Nature of the Five Wisdom Dakinis*, Jewel Publishing, New York, 1985

Ricard, Matthieu, *Journey to Enlightenment: The Life and World of Khyentse Rinpoche, Spiritual Teacher from Tibet*, Aperture Foundation, New York, 1996

Rinpoche, Patrul, *The Words of My Perfect Teacher*, HarperCollins, San Francisco, 1994

Rinpoche, Sogyal, *Dzogchen and Padmasambhava*, Rigpa Fellowship, Berkeley, 1989

Rinpoche, Sogyal, *The Tibetan Book of Living and Dying*, HarperCollins, San Francisco, 1992

Shah, Idries, *Tales of the Dervishes*, E. P. Dutton and Co., New York, 1970

Shah, Idries, *The Way of the Sufi*, Penguin, London, 1974

Suzuki, D., *Essays in Zen Buddhism*, Ch'eng Wen Publishers, Taiwain, 1971

Suzuki, D., *Zen Doctrine of No Mind*, Rider & Co, London, 1949

Thomas, E. J., introduction to *Buddhist Scriptures*, London, 1913

Trungpa, Chögyam, *Cutting Through Spiritual Materialism*, Shambhala, Boston and London, 1973

Trungpa, Chögyam, and Freemantle, Francesca, trans, *The Tibetan Book of the Dead*, Shambhala, Boston, 1975

View, international magazine of the Rigpa Fellowship, published by Dharma Kosha, London

Yeshe, Lama, *Introduction to Tantra: A Vision of Totality*, Wisdom Publications, Boston, 1987

Yogananda, P., *Autobiography of a Yogi*, Rider, London, 1969

BUDDHIST ORGANISATIONS

If you would like any information on meditation classes and activities of the following groups in Australia, please contact:

SOGYAL RINPOCHE

RIGPA OFFICES
Rigpa Sydney
PO Box K56, Haymarket
Sydney NSW 1204
Tel: 02 9211 5304

Rigpa Newcastle
10 Swan St
Cooks Hill NSW 2300
Tel: 02 4929 4436

Rigpa Canberra
PO Box 4067
Kingston ACT 2604
Tel: 02 6230 5093

Rigpa Melbourne
PO Box 1153
South Melbourne VIC 3205
Tel: 03 9388 0952

Rigpa Adelaide
22A Willunga St
Eden Hills SA 5050
Tel: 08 8223 2456

Rigpa Western Australia
4 Wentworth Way
Padbury, WA 6025
Tel: 08 9401 4262

DZONGSAR KHYENTSE RINPOCHE

Siddhartha's Intent
PO Box 1114
Strawberry Hills NSW 2012
Tel: 02 9398 6048

Vajradhara Gompa
PO Box 345
Kyogle NSW 2474
Tel: 02 6633 1382

HIS HOLINESS THE GYALWANG DRUKPA

Bairo Ling Inc.
PO Box 499
Queanbeyean ACT 2620

GESHE LODEN

Tibetan Buddhist Society
175 Dennison Road
Dulwich Hill NSW 2203
Tel: 02 9569 0918

FOOTNOTES

Foreword
1   Thank you to Tulku Pema Wangyal for translation

Introduction
1   Lama Yeshe, *Introduction to Tantra: A Vision of Totality*, Wisdom Publications, Boston, 1987, p. 27
2   Patrul Rinpoche, *The Words of My Perfect Teacher*, HarperCollins, San Francisco, 1994, p. xciv
3   Sogyal Rinpoche, teaching at Konocti Habour, USA, 3 December 1998
4   'The Song of Milarepa', in Stephen Batchelor, ed, *The Jewel in the Lotus: A Guide to the Buddhist Traditions of Tibet*, Wisdom Publications, London, 1987, p. 103
5   Sogyal Rinpoche, *The Tibetan Book of Living and Dying*, HarperCollins, San Francisco, 1992 p. 138
6   Ibid, p. 136
7   Deng Ming Dao, *The Wandering Taoist*, Harper and Row, San Francisco, 1983, p. 107
8   Sogyal Rinpoche, *The Tibetan Book of Living and Dying*
9   Andrew Harvey, *A Journey in Ladakh*, Houghton Mifflin Co., Boston, 1983, p. 161

Chapter 1
1   Adapted from 'Early Buddhist Tale', in Christina Feldman and Jack Kornfield, eds, *Stories of the Spirit, Stories of the Heart: Parables of the Spiritual Path from Around the World*, HarperCollins, San Francisco, 1991, p. 302
2   Adapted from the Jataka Tale in 'Being on Top of Things', *View*, no. 2, 1994, p. 4
3   Patrul Rinpoche, *The Words of My Perfect Teacher*, HarperCollins, San Francisco, 1994, p. 254
4   Gurdjieff (1866–1949), author and teacher of esoteric philosophy

Chapter 2
1   'Rumi', translated by John Moyne and Coleman Barks, *Say I Am You*, Maypop, Georgia, 1994
2   Christine Longacker, *Facing Death and Finding Hope: A Guide to the Emotional and Spiritual Care of the Dying*, Century, London, 1997, p. 11
3   Ibid, pp. 25 and 26
4   Iguen Chariton of Valamo, *The Art of Prayer; An Orthodox Anthology*, translated by E Kadlovbovsley and EM Palmer, London, 1966, p. 63

Chapter 3
1. Adapted from 'The Watermelon Hunter', in Idries Shah, *The Way of the Sufi*, Penguin, London, 1974, p. 227

Chapter 4
1. Adapted from 'The Tale of the Sands', in Idries Shah, *Tales of the Dervishes*, E. P. Dutton and Co., New York, 1970, p. 23

Chapter 5
1. Adapted from 'A Singing Yogi Achieves Flight', in Surya Das, *The Snow Lion's Turquoise Mane: Wisdom Tales from Tibet*, HarperCollins, San Francisco, 1992, p. 237
2. Ch. 6, Verse 10, *Engaging in the Bodhisattva Deeds*, Shantideva, Stephen Batchelor, trans, Library of Tibetan Works and Archives, New Delhi, 1979

Chapter 6
1. Adapted from 'Ben of Kongpo', in Patrul Rinpoche, *The Words of My Perfect Teacher*, Harper Collins, New Delhi, 1997, p. 174
2. Sogyal Rinpoche, *The Tibetan Book of Living and Dying*, Harper Collins, San Francisco, 1992 pp. 134 and 144

Chapter 7
1. Adapted from 'Fatima the Spinner and the Tent', in Idries Shah, *Tales of the Dervishes*, E. P. Dutton and Co., New York, 1970, p. 72

Chapter 8
1. Adapted from 'The Man Who Looked Only at the Obvious', in Idries Shah, *Tales of the Dervishes*, E. P. Dutton and Co., New York, 1970, p. 198
2. Sogyal Rinpoche, *The Tibetan Book of Living and Dying*, HarperCollins, San Francisco, 1992, p. 189

Chapter 9
1. Adapted from 'The Evil Eye', in Surya Das, *The Snow Lion's Turquoise Mane: Wisdom Tales from Tibet*, HarperCollins, San Francisco, 1992, p. 86
2. The twelfth Gyalwang Drukpa, 'My Crazy Tale', in Lama Surya Das, *The Biography and History of the Drukpa Kargyud Lineage*, Dzogchen Foundation, Massachusetts, 1992, p. 29

Chapter 10
1. Adapted from 'Chassid Tale of the Monastery', in Christina Feldman and Jack Kornfield, eds, *Stories of the Spirit, Stories of the Heart: Parables of the Spiritual Path from Around the World*, HarperCollins, San Francisco, 1991, p. 30
2. Sogyal Rinpoche, *The Tibetan Book of Living and Dying*, HarperCollins, San Francisco, 1992, p. 137

Chapter 11
1 Adapted from 'The Story of Geshe Chekawa', in Patrul Rinpoche, *The Words of My Perfect Teacher*, HarperCollins, New Delhi, 1997, p. 227
2 Patrul Rinpoche, *The Words of My Perfect Teacher*, HarperCollins, New Delhi, 1997, p. 152

Chapter 12
1 Adapted from Lama Surya Das, *Eight Steps to Enlightenment: Awakening the Buddha Within — Tibetan Wisdom for the Western World*, Bantam, New York, 1997, p. 387
2 Taken from Sogyal Rinpoche, *Dzogchen and Padmasambhava*, Rigpa Fellowship, Berkeley, 1989, p. 80

Chapter 13
1 Adapted from a poem by Pierre Delattre, in Christina Feldman and Jack Kornfield, eds, *Stories of the Spirit, Stories of the Heart: Parables of the Spiritual Path from Around the World*, HarperCollins, San Francisco, 1991, p. 283
2 *View*, Issue 1, 1994, p. 30
3 Paul Breiter, *Venerable Father: A Life with Ajahn Chah*, Buddhadhamma Foundation, Bangkok, 1994
4 Mark Epstein, *Thoughts Without a Thinker: Psychotherapy from a Buddhist Perspective*, Duckworth, London, 1996, pp. 13–14

Chapter 14
1 Sogyal Rinpoche, *The Tibetan Book of Living and Dying*, HarperCollins, San Francisco, 1992 p. 145

Conclusion
1 The Gyalwang Drukpa, 'The Guru Question', *View*, no. 9, 1997, p. 13
2 Matthieu Ricard, *Journey to Enlightenment: The Life and World of Khyentse Rinpoche, Spiritual Teacher from Tibet*, Aperture Foundation, New York, 1996, p. 19
3 Interview with the author, Brittany, France, 1993
4 Sogyal Rinpoche, London, March 1999
5 Lama Surya Das, *Eight Steps to Enlightenment: Awakening the Buddha Within — Tibetan Wisdom for the Western World*, Bantam, New York, 1997, p. 430

Glossary
1 Compiled from the following:
Stephen Batchelor, ed, *The Jewel in the Lotus: A Guide to Buddhist Traditions of Tibet*, Wisdom Publications, London, 1987
Patrul Rinpoche, *The Words of My Perfect Teacher*, HarperCollins, New Delhi, 1997
Lama Yeshe, *Introduction to Tantra: A Vision of Totality*, Wisdom Publications, Boston, 1987

CREDITS

Grateful acknowledgment is made to the following for permission to adapt copyrighted material. The publishers have made every effort to contact the holders of copyright material included in Sherry Marshall's *Devotion*. They would be pleased to hear from anyone who has not been duly acknowledged.

Text: Chapter 1 'The Travellers' adapted from 'Early Buddhist Tale' in *Stories of the Spirit, Stories of the Heart* by Christina Feldman. Copyright © 1991 by Christina Feldman and Jack Kornfield. Reprinted by permission of HarperCollins Publishers, Inc.; Chapter 2 'Rumi', translated by John Moyne and Coleman Barks, *Say I Am You*, Maypop, Georgia, 1994; Chapter 3 'The Man and the Melon' adapted from 'The Watermelon Hunter' in Idries Shah, *The Way of the Sufi*, Penguin, London, 1974; Chapter 4 'The Stream and the Desert' adapted from 'The Tale of the Sands' in Idries Shah, *Tales of the Dervishes*, E.P. Dutton and Co., New York, 1970; Chapter 5 'Shabkar, the Singing Yogi' adapted from 'A Singing Yogi Achieves Flight' in *The Snow Lion's Turquoise Mane: Tantric Tales from Tibet* by Surya Das. Copyright © 1992 by Jeffrey Miller. Reprinted by permission of HarperCollins Publishers, Inc.; Chapter 6 'Ben of Kongpo' adapted from *The Words of My Perfect Teacher*, 2nd edition copyright 1998, published by AltaMira Press: Walnut Creek, CA; Chapter 7 'The Tent Maker' adapted from 'Fatima, the Spinner and the Tent' in Idries Shah, *Tales of the Dervishes*, E.P. Dutton and Co., New York, 1970; Chapter 8 'Seeing the Obvious' adapted from 'The Man Who Looked Only at the Obvious' in Idries Shah, *Tales of the Dervishes*, E.P. Dutton and Co., New York, 1970; Chapter 9 'The Non-existing Demons' adapted from 'The Evil Eye' in *The Snow Lion's Turquoise Mane: Tantric Tales from Tibet* by Surya Das. Copyright © 1992 by Jeffrey Miller. Reprinted by permission of HarperCollins Publishers, Inc.; Chapter 10 'The Messiah in Us All' adapted from 'Chassid Tale of the Monastery' in *Stories of the Spirit, Stories of the Heart* by Christina Feldman. Copyright © 1991 by Christina Feldman and Jack Kornfield. Reprinted by permission of HarperCollins Publishers, Inc.; Chapter 11 'The Leper's Gift' adapted from Patrul Rinpoche, *The Words of My Perfect Teacher*, 2nd edition copyright 1998, published by AltaMira Press: Walnut Creek, CA; Chapter 12 'Attention' adapted from *Awakening the Buddha Within* by Lama Surya Das. Copyright © 1997 by Lama Surya Das. Used by permission of Broadway Books, a division of Random House, Inc.; Chapter 13 'Points of View' adapted from a poem by Pierre Delattre in Christina Feldman and Jack Kornfield, eds, *Stories of the Spirit, Stories of the Heart: Parables of the Spiritual Path from Around the World*, HarperCollins, San Francisco, 1991; Chapter 14 Prayer from Sogyal Rinpoche, *The Tibetan Book of Living and Dying*, HarperCollins, San Francisco, 1992.

Photographs: 1. Photograph by Julian Englesman; courtesy of the Rigpa Fellowship. 2. Photograph by Graeme Horner. 3. Photograph courtesy of the Rigpa Fellowship. 4. Photograph courtesy of the Rigpa Fellowship. 5. Photograph by Michael Kern. 6. Photograph by Kim Yeshi Tushita; courtesy of the Tibet Image Bank. 7. Photograph by Michael Kern. 8. Photograph by Phillippe Lelluch; courtesy of the Rigpa Fellowship. 9. Photograph by Cliff Venner; courtesy of the Rigpa Fellowship. 10. Photograph courtesy of the Rigpa Fellowship. 11. Photograph by Sherry Marshall. 12. Photograph by Michael Kern.